Bankrupting Nature

This powerful book shows us that we are in deep denial about the magnitude of the global environmental challenges and resource constraints facing the world. Despite growing scientific consensus on major environmental threats as well as resource depletion, societies are largely continuing with business as usual, at best attempting to tinker at the margins of the problems. The authors argue that regardless of whether governments respond to the economic crisis through additional stimulus packages or reduced government spending, environmental and resource constraints will remain. The crisis will be exacerbated by the combination of climate change, ecosystem decline and resource scarcity, in particular crude oil. The concept of Planetary Boundaries is introduced as a powerful explanation of the limits of the biosphere to sustain continued conventional growth. The book breaks the long silence on population, criticizing donor countries for not doing enough to support education of girls and reproductive health services. It is shown that an economy built on the continuous expansion of material consumption is not sustainable. De-growth, however, is no solution either. The growth dilemma can only be addressed through a transformation of the economic system. A strong plea is made for abandoning GDP growth as the key objective for development. The focus should instead be on a limited number of welfare indicators. The trickle-down concept is seriously questioned, to be replaced by one of sufficiency. Rich countries are called upon to hold back their material growth to leave room for a rising living standard among the poor. Alternative business models are presented, such as moving from products to services or towards a circular economy based on re-use, reconditioning and recycling – all with the aim of facilitating sustainable development.

Anders Wijkman is senior advisor at the Stockholm Environment Institute, Sweden, and Vice President, Club of Rome. He has been a Member of the Swedish Parliament and the European Parliament, as well as Secretary General of the Swedish Red Cross, Director General of the Swedish Agency for Research Co-operation with Developing Countries and Assistant Secretary General of the UN and Policy Director of the United Nations Development Programme. Wijkman is a member of the Swedish Royal Academy of Sciences and the World Academy of Art and Science.

Johan Rockström is a Professor of Natural Resource Management at Stockholm University, and Executive Director of the Stockholm Resilience Centre. He is an internationally recognized scientist working on global sustainability issues; for example, leading the recent development of the new Planetary Boundaries framework for human development in the current era of rapid global change. Rockström also co-chairs Future Earth, an international research initiative on global sustainability.

"The world is headed for a major transition and unless we recognize and deal with that, it could very well be a major disaster for humanity. Wijkman and Rockström have provided the clear evidence and practical policy ideas to allow us to seize this moment as an opportunity to make the transition to a much better, more sustainable and desirable world. We cannot afford to miss this opportunity." – *Robert Constanza, Visiting Fellow, Crawford School of Public Policy, Australian National University*

"Growth has pushed the physical scale of the economy beyond planetary boundaries and has thereby become uneconomic growth – growth that now increases environmental and social costs faster than production benefits, making us poorer, not richer. This book will help citizens, and maybe even politicians and economists, understand what is happening." – *Herman E. Daly, Professor Emeritus, School of Public Policy, University of Maryland, USA*

"*Bankrupting Nature* summarizes succinctly our human challenges, correctly focusing on re-designing today's global financial casino. Ignored in most textbooks, finance is now a flywheel of social and environmental destruction while economists are still suffering 'theory-induced blindness'. The authors demonstrate conclusively that it is high time for humanity to grasp scientific realities and re-integrate our knowledge systemically – Important, constructive advice for politicians, scientists, NGOs and all who work toward cleaner, greener, equitable, sustainable human futures." – *Hazel Henderson, author, President Ethical Markets Media (USA & Brazil) producers of the Green Transition Scoreboard®, Transforming Finance Based on Ethics and Life's Principles, co-creators of the Calvert-Henderson Quality of Life Indicators.*

"... this contribution by Wijkman and Rockstrom is so important. It does not leave us with the problem alone. It takes us to the blueprint for a true-green economy. It is about the way that we can reinvent growth for all, which is affordable, equitable and sustainable." – *Sunita Narain, Director-General, Centre for Science and Environment, New Delhi*

"Wijkman and Rockström convincingly show the strength and necessity of an integrated systems perspective of world development, that combines an understanding of how climate change interacts with ecosystem changes across the world, and how social and ecological factors interplay and ultimately determine our ability to provide welfare and wellbeing for a rapidly growing world population. Their book is a timely wake-up call for all politicians, businessmen and citizens of Earth." – *Pavan Sukhdev, Founder-CEO of GIST (Green Indian States Trust) Advisory and Study Leader of TEEB.*

"The public discussion on climate change and the environment has lost its momentum. The focus is on other issues, like finance and the economy. Wijkman and Rockström show convincingly why this must change. Wealth generation based on carbon can not continue much longer. We are borrowing resources belonging to future generations, and in the process imperiling their right to livelihood. Today´s great denial will be revealed. The combination of solid science, vast experience from politics and public affairs and profound compassion makes this book extraordinarily useful." – *Anders Wejryd, Archbishop of Sweden*

Bankrupting Nature

Denying our planetary boundaries

Anders Wijkman and Johan Rockström

First edition published 2011
by Medströms Bokförlag, Stockholm, Sweden

This revised edition published 2012
by Routledge
2 Park Square, Milton Park, Abingdon, Oxon, OX14 4RN

Simultaneously published in the USA and Canada
by Routledge
711 Third Avenue, New York, NY 10017

Routledge is an imprint of the Taylor & Francis Group, an informa business

This edition is an authorized translation of *Den stora förnekelsen*,
published in Swedish by Medströms Bokförlag, Stockholm.
ISBN: 978-91-7329-042-5

British Library Cataloguing in Publication Data
A catalogue record for this book is available from the British Library

Library of Congress Cataloging-in-Publication Data
Wijkman, Anders, 1944-
[Den stora fornekelsen. English.]
Bankrupting nature : denying our planetary boundaries / Anders
Wijkman and Johan Rockström.
p. cm.
"First edition published 2011 by Medströms Bokförlag,
Stockholm, Sweden."
Includes bibliographical references and index.
1. Global environmental change. 2. Environmental policy.
3. Environmental protection. I. Rockström, Johan. II. Title.
GE149.W5513 2012
304.2'8–dc23
2012019197

ISBN13: 978-0-415-53969-2 (hbk)
ISBN13: 978-0-203-10798-0 (ebk)

Typeset in Baskerville by
Saxon Graphics Ltd, Derby

Contents

Illustrations

Foreword by Sunita Narain

This is not a book about climate change, say the authors. This, I believe, says it all. The fact is that climate change is only a symptom of what is so terribly wrong with the way the world is running its affairs. It is a sign of the things that have come, because we refuse to repair our relationship with Planet Earth.

The fact is that we have been taught, and have practised what has been preached, that we can consume our way to growth and then consume our way out of any slow-down period. 'Don't worry, just consume' is the mantra. If we cannot 'afford' to consume, then, too, we should not worry. The financial systems will ensure that we get cheap loans to buy homes, cars, washing machines, or anything else we may not need but desire. After all, it is only if we consume that growth indicators will look rosy again and the world will remain happy.

The problem with this model is that we do little to ensure we can bring the cost of the product down so that it is affordable. In other words, we do not plan, design, manufacture and sell products and services that meet the purchasing abilities of people. We don't demand that technology should work for affordability. We also don't share wealth so that more can afford this growth – afford the house or the car – without the loans that will make the banks boom and then go bust.

Over time, this simple logic of enabling people only to consume got lost in a labyrinth of economic and fiscal instruments designed to subsidize and advance credit, in order to keep the consumption-related stimulus going. Thus, as costs of production increased in the first world because of increased costs of labour or environmental protection, industry moved to the second, third and even fourth world to get a cheaper deal. This also helped to unite the entire world in the frenzy of buy cheap, buy disposable. This model drove banks over the moon, over into the dark side.

This economic system has another dark side: growth is threatening to destroy life as we know it. Today, climate change is stepping up its pace. Each year, with seemingly increased intensity and ferocity, different regions of the globe are lashed by natural disasters and freak and extreme weather conditions. It is clear that these extreme weather events are devastating large parts of the world and are combining to make the poor even poorer and even more vulnerable. This is the beginning of the impact of climate change, which science has so surely predicted will occur in exactly this manner. It is just that we refuse to read the writing that is so clearly on the wall.

We refuse to accept that the challenge is two-fold: first, the world has to reinvent the growth paradigm because in its present form it is costing the world growth itself. Second, the world has to reinvent growth because it is costing the Earth. That is why this contribution by Wijkman and Rockström is so important. It does not simply leave us with the problem. It takes us to the blueprint for a truly green economy. It is about the way that we can reinvent growth for all that is affordable, equitable and sustainable. It is only when we have learnt these lessons that we can secure our present and our future. It is only then that we can exhale.

Sunita Narain
Director-General, Centre for Science and Environment, New Delhi

Foreword by Pavan Sukhdev

We live in the *Anthropocene*: an era in which humans are the largest geological force on Earth. It is a staggering thought that the consequences of seven billion of us and our consumption patterns have an impact on the Earth as a whole that is *stronger* than natural biophysical and geological processes. But why are we surprised? Human biomass exceeds that of all other 'megafauna' put together by around two orders of magnitude, and our impacts by several more. We are powered by ancient sunlight as we continue to depend on fossil fuels, our ecological footprint today is one and a half times what the earth produces, and in doing so we risk the future survival of innumerable species including our own. In other words, we are consuming the past, present, and future of this biosphere, our only home, in an unthinking rush for profits and GDP that we call 'progress', belying our species name *homo sapiens*.

Exploring this conundrum in depth in their book, Anders Wijkman and Johan Rockström bring us a combination of knowledge of political economy and environmental science that is indeed powerful. They methodically expose the vacuity of climate naysayers, the fundamental failure of international politics and institutions to address global problems, and the deep denial by society of the size of the environmental crises facing the world.

This book is also particularly poignant and timely, following close on the heels of the failure of the Rio+20 Conference, in June this year, to deliver any significant outcomes. Much of the "The Future We Want" was a statement of the obvious, and did not commit governments to timely or significant action that would reflect the reality that we are fast approaching, or have already breached, several crucial planetary boundaries. Governments remained fixated with stale rhetoric and hackneyed north-south arguments such as "who will fund sustainable development?'. By now, it should be self-evident that *every* nation must fund as well as benefit from sustainable development, bearing common but differentiated responsibilities to follow national "green economy" paths towards an elusive "sustainability space" where per-capita ecological footprint is below per-capita planetary bio-capacity, and where human development are above minimum levels. That is the sustainable future that we all want.

However, this future will certainly not happen with the wrong economic model (free-market capitalism) pursuing the wrong tasks (optimizing production, rather than optimizing wealth) through the wrong economic agents (today's corporations, targeting short-term financial profit for shareholders whilst causing long-term natural capital loss for stakeholders).

Wijkman and Rockström argue that "more of the same" will simply not do. Traditional stimulus packages only aggravate the situation. What is urgently needed is a new economic policy framework that takes nature into account and – at the same time – effectively adresses a host of social challenges, including growing inequities and unemployment.

A strong plea is made for abandoning GDP growth as the key indicator for development. The focus should instead be on a set of true welfare indicators. Rich countries are called upon to hold back their material growth to leave room for rising living standards among the poor. Alternative business models are presented, such as moving from selling products to services or towards a circular economy based on activities such as re-use and recycling, with the aim of facilitating sustainable development.

The economic invisibility of nature and its consequences for human well-being in general and poor nature-dependent communities in particular (an issue dear to me and the 'TEEB' community) is very well captured by the authors, who argue convincingly that we must value what nature delivers to human society and reflect such valuation in national policies, national accounts and economic plans. Perhaps there were reasons in the past (eg: complexity, uncertainty, and the lack of data) for not attempting such reflection. However, the work pulled together by 'The Economics of Ecosystem services and Biodiversity' (TEEB) in recent years, and the doubtful ethics of inaction, strongly support the view of the authors that *all* societies must take nature into account by valuing ecosystem services, in their own appropriate ways. Valuation is a human institution, and missing institutions are problems - either already happening, or waiting to happen, but in any event, problems not to be ignored.

Wijkman and Rockström convincingly show the strength and necessity of an integrated systems perspective of world development, that combines an understanding of how climate change interacts with ecosystem changes across the world, and how social and ecological factors interplay and ultimately determine our ability to provide welfare and wellbeing for a rapidly growing world population. Their book is a timely wake-up call for all politicians, businessmen and citizens of Earth.

Pavan Sukhdev
Founder-Director, Corporation 2020, and Study Leader, TEEB

This publication is a Report to the Club of Rome

Bankrupting Nature is a 'Report to the Club of Rome', signifying that it is peer reviewed by the Club of Rome and its expert members to ensure it is scientifically rigorous, innovative and contributes a new, important element to the debate about humanity's predicaments. Since *The Limits to Growth*, the first 'Report to the Club of Rome' in 1972, 32 publications have received this *imprimatur*.

The Club of Rome was founded in 1968 as an association of leading independent thinkers from politics, business and science. It now has 1500 individual members, an international centre in Winterthur, Switzerland and National Associations in 30 countries. An important element of National Associations' work is to shape national agendas.

A unifying strand among members is a concern for the future of humanity and the planet, and addressing the root causes of the systemic crisis: the need for a different set of values, to change economic theory and practice and safeguard resources; to create a more equal society, which generates full employment; and the need for governance systems that put people at their centre. This holistic approach is needed more now than ever.

The Club pursues its objectives through scientific analysis, communication, networking and advocacy and cooperation with a wide range of partners. Its main products are books, discussion papers, policy briefs, conferences, webinars, lectures, high-level meetings and events. Key findings are used to challenge policy makers in the public and private sectors to help shift to new ways of thinking and to new forms of action.

Acknowledgements

We would like to extend special thanks to Jim Wine for his invaluable advice as regards the content of this book and, in particular, for its translation into English.

1 The environmental space is limited

> We are looking ahead, as is one of the first mandates given us as chiefs, to make sure and to make every decision that we make relate to the welfare and wellbeing of the seventh generation to come.
>
> Oren Lyons, Faithkeeper, Onondaga Nation

This is not a book about climate change, even if we do devote several chapters to the issue. Our ambition is to go beyond that and critically examine the relationship between human beings and nature and the threats we pose to the complex natural systems on Earth that are the preconditions for all life.

We want our book to change the perspective from the conventional view that sees societal development and the environment as isolated, often contradictory phenomena, towards a vision that perceives the living biosphere and natural resources as the prerequisites for prosperity and development in the future. Such a perspective is obvious to most natural scientists. But for many other disciplines, the perspective has been different and more limited. The economists' models, for example, focus foremost on the relationship between producers and consumers. Access to energy and raw materials – not to mention ecosystem functions – have more or less been taken for granted.

We want to communicate that humanity is facing a critical reality. An abundance of scientific reports clearly point out that we are very close to a saturation point, where the biosphere cannot handle additional stress. We are already witnessing the hard impact that global environmental change has on both regional and local economies.

Our focus is on cultural and lifestyle issues and the way we have organized our economy, because these are the areas where the key changes must occur in order to address the serious threats to the biosphere. Every day our production and consumption systems result in a growing impact on the environment, through pollution, by displacing and eradicating countless species and ecosystems, and by disrupting the climate balance. This endangers the very basis of humanity's future development and prosperity.

The media is full of reports about the financial crisis. But the loans and the debts extend far beyond the monetary economy. The degradation of important ecosystems, the loss of biodiversity and an increasingly unstable climate are at least as serious a mortgage on the future as financial debt. But in the debate so far about the crisis in the economy, few commentators bring up this dimension. Rather than recognizing the close links between the monetary economy and the economy of nature, all the attention is directed to the financial system.

The flaws we see in the relationship between humanity and the natural environment lead us to question how the economic system, together with the research and educational systems, have been organized. We further question whether today's political system is at all prepared to take on the long-term challenges posed by globalization, population growth, climate change and the over-consumption of both finite and renewable resources.

The Earth lacks a balance sheet

We need a balance sheet for the planet. In recent years, all signs reveal that our lifestyles and consumption patterns are on a violent collision course with nature. Russia suffered record heat in 2010, resulting in terrible fires. Floods in Pakistan put 20 per cent of the country under water, turning already precarious conditions of life into a nightmare for millions of people. Icebergs the size of Manhattan broke free from calving glaciers. Seven years of drought in Australia were followed by serious flooding. Both droughts and floods hit record levels in the US during 2011 and 2012.

Extreme weather events such as these come as no surprise to those who have followed the work of the UN climate panel, IPCC, over the years. The events of 2010, 2011 and 2012 are a premonition of what may become commonplace in the future.

The threats to ecosystems and biodiversity are equally serious. Deforestation of tropical forests has declined slightly in recent years, but annually an estimated 13 million hectares still disappear. Overfishing in many marine areas continues relentlessly. Lack of fresh water is becoming more prevalent in regions around the world. In total, two-thirds of the most important global ecosystems are overexploited, according to the United Nations global evaluation, Millennium Ecosystem Assessment (MEA), 2005.

The UN Conference on Biological Diversity in Nagoya in October 2010 was a step in the right direction. It was decided to increase the protection of unique ecosystems both on land and at sea. The question is how far such a decision goes to meet the mounting pressure both from population growth and rapidly expanding economies.

When individual households live beyond their financial means, the resulting equation is easy to grasp. Assets and liabilities simply do not add up and after a time credit lines are cut off and the next step is bankruptcy. Imbalances in nature are more difficult to apprehend. One reason is that most people do not see and experience nature's deterioration with their own eyes. The majority of the world's population lives in cities. Most people get their food from the supermarket, rarely reflecting on how or where it is produced or how ecosystems are faring as a result.

Another reason is the inadequacy of our method of accounting. When tropical forests are depleted or oceans are vacuum-cleaned of fish, the results are posted as a positive item in the GDP statistics. The fact that natural capital in the form of fish stocks and trees has suffered a loss of value –one it may never recover from – is nowhere to be found on any balance sheet. Nor are degraded ecosystems that are likely to 'tip over thresholds' with disastrous consequences reflected in national accounts. Examples of possible tipping points include the risk that inland seas (such as the Baltic Sea) will die, that the Amazon rainforest will dry up, and that the paths and seasons of tropical monsoon systems will shift.

The fact is that we do not have a proper balance sheet for the planet. National accounts are primarily geared to reporting the aggregate production of a country in terms of GDP. This report is supplemented by the NDP, the net domestic product, which attempts to take into account the wear and tear that occurs in the physical capital – mainly machines and buildings; this is then subtracted from GDP. There is no corresponding accounting of the deterioration of natural capital such as farmland, tropical forests, freshwater resources, fish stocks and biological diversity. Our knowledge of, and control over, the availability of finite resources such as oil, phosphorus and certain metals are also limited.

We have cheap oil to thank for the outstanding increases in the standard of living experienced by parts of the world during the 1900s. Most governments and companies seem set on the notion that oil will continue to flow. Yet we see more and more evidence that the era of cheap oil is over. A series of analyses indicate that the extraction of crude oil will soon level off and then fall. When this happens, most countries will be poorly prepared. The price of oil might go through the roof. Many poor countries, which already have a hard time paying for their oil imports, will be forced into rationing. Today, the cost to Africa of energy imports exceeds the total development funding it receives. Certain sectors where there are no substitutes, such as transport and agriculture, will be hit even harder. Taken together, these pose a substantial risk of a profound crisis in the global economy.

Why is today different?

Throughout history humanity has been faced with problems due to scarce resources. With varying degrees of success the problems have been solved through technology and innovation, such as the step from using wood as an energy source to fossil fuels, or through large-scale migrations. But history is also full of examples of how societies and cultures succumbed as a consequence of natural changes in climate or the over-exploitation of water and land resources. Prominent examples are the first high culture in Mesopotamia in 2300 BC and Easter Island in the seventeenth and eighteenth centuries. What sets the current situation apart is that over-exploitation of both the atmosphere and our global commons occurs on such a large scale and that processes are set in motion that may be impossible to stop or reverse. Greenhouse gases that remain in the atmosphere for hundreds of years, glaciers that begin to melt, tundra that starts to thaw, fresh water reserves that are depleted, land areas that become desert, are all examples of processes that are very difficult, if not impossible, to stop and that are far beyond the control of any local community.

The difference between per capita resource usage in developed countries and developing countries is still very large. In Jared Diamond's book *Collapse* (2005) it was estimated that more than one billion people living in developed countries have on average a per capita resource usage 32 times larger than the 5.5 billion people who live in what we call developing countries. But a broad middle class is currently emerging in many developing countries, especially in China and India, and its resource usage is rapidly moving towards the level we have in the West. If China's per capita consumption, which is now less than a tenth of the US level, were instead the same as in America, it would mean a doubling of demand for natural resources in the world. Consumption of petroleum, paper and the most important metals would double; the demand for grain would go up by 70 per cent, and so on. If the Chinese had the same car density as the United States today, there would be 1.1 billion vehicles in China alone.

China and other developing countries have every right to development and modernization. But it cannot happen in the same way as it has in industrial countries because the rapidly increasing pressure on the natural resource base and the atmosphere would be devastating. Industrialized countries have introduced habits of consumption that cannot be sustained for their own people, let alone the whole world. Therein lies an enormous challenge.

The myth of endless material growth

Our society has long been built on the myth of endless growth. Nature's cupboard is perceived as infinitely large. Nature is also accorded an almost infinite capacity to take care of various wastes and pollutants and render them harmless. Having participated actively in the environmental and climate change debate for more than twenty years, we understand that this myth is powerful and very difficult to dislodge.

Humanity is living far beyond its means. No previous generation has borrowed so freely from the future. The short-term bill came due with the financial crisis that erupted in 2008. The long-term bill will come sooner or later in the form of catastrophic climate change and environmental impacts. Just as unsound loans in the banking and financial world almost caused the collapse of the entire financial sector, our manner of using nature's capital risks bringing our life support system to the brink of collapse. As the economy is structured today, it is only a matter of time.

The economic crisis struck suddenly and hit hard. The climate change and ecosystem crises will do the same, albeit with some delay. The consequences of climate change and the over-exploitation of natural systems such as forests, farmland, fisheries and fresh water will look different in different parts of the world. Some regions will suffer more than others, but in the long run no part of the world can protect itself and avoid the negative consequences. Ultimately it is the supplies of energy, water and food that are in danger.

There were warnings before the financial crisis, but few took them seriously. There have been many similar warnings about climate change and environmental degradation. But even here, too few are listening. Many hear what they want to hear, and adjust their rhetoric to accommodate descriptions of the problem. But at heart their attitudes are those of denial. Decision makers are, unfortunately, no exception.

Why isn't more being done?

Why, then, haven't the numerous and powerful warnings about the dangers we face by neglecting the many threats to the natural systems received a better hearing? The environment is in much worse shape today than fifty years ago, despite the adoption of a large number of laws and regulations. Many calls have been made in support of a thorough policy review in favour of radically changing production and consumption systems. Serious perspectives and studies have piled up, from Rachel Carson's *Silent Spring* (1964), via the Club of Rome's *Limits to Growth* (1972) and the UN's *Brundtland Report* (1987), to the UN climate panel's IPCC report (2007), the *Millennium Ecosystem Assessment* (MEA 2005) and the OECD *Environment Outlook 2050* (2012). Added to these is the ongoing work to develop 'Planetary Boundaries'. In an article in the British journal *Nature* (September 2009) a group of more than thirty researchers, led by Johan Rockström, one of the authors of this book, describe a total of nine different biophysical processes on the planet that are vital to humanity's future on Earth (Rockström *et al.* 2009a). In the current growth model we are rapidly eroding the living ecosystems and the natural resources that ultimately form the basis for future human welfare. We find ourselves on a collision course with nature. Environmental issues may regularly end up high on the lists of important issues in opinion polls, but real action is still a long way off.

What 'is the reason for this passivity? We can only speculate about the causes. In preparing this book we have taken note of a large number of research papers, books and articles, among them *Macroshift* (UNESCO, 2001), written by philosopher Ervin Laszlo.

Laszlo differentiates between knowledge and awareness. He believes that many people are familiar with – know about – problems like climate change, but are still not aware of the problem on a deeper level. Climate change can thus be seen as 'abstract', which keeps people from acting in real life.

We think that Laszlo is on to something important on the road to understanding. Awareness of how everything is connected – and how our own actions affect the whole – emerges as a vitally central issue in the change processes that lie ahead. Here behavioural scientists should have significant insights, but during many years of working with these issues we have seldom encountered, let alone sought, the advice of behavioural scientists.

A variant of Laszlo's reasoning can be found in recent discoveries in brain research, which assert that most people do not change their stance on an issue merely by being presented with new facts – especially if these facts do not fit their picture of the future. The cognitive base is of great importance, according to the American professor of cognitive linguistics George Lakoff: '

> Facts that do not fit into our world view are regarded as irrelevant or even crazy.' 'This is the reason why conservatives and liberals in the US see each other as idiots. They do not understand each other because their brains are organized differently.'

You might call that cognitive dissonance.

Research from the US shows that people who have developed an individualistic approach to life – and a strong belief in free enterprise and as little government regulation as possible – often have a negative attitude toward environmental and climate research reports because they believe that such reports will inevitably lead to government interventions in the economy, something perceived as a 'threat to freedom' (Kahan *et al.* 2010).

Without doubt, both values and 'awareness at a deeper level' are important factors when trying to explain the slow progress in moving society in a more sustainable direction. But there are other factors as well:

- the lack of adequate education about the indispensable role that ecosystems and biodiversity play in the provision of welfare and well-being;
- unwillingness among most people to change habits and lifestyles;
- shortcomings in the ways by which welfare and progress are reported and accounted for an increase in GDP is not the same as an increase in welfare;
- powerful business interests that strongly defend business as usual and investments already made;
- the conception in several of the major religions that man is above nature and has the right to exploit nature for his own purposes;
- the lack of a holistic approach in science: reductionism has been pushed too far, the number of specialists is forever increasing but there are few researchers working on systemic issues in an attempt to understand the whole picture of our reality;

- the research community's inability – and often unwillingness – to communicate vigorously the threats we face;
- the tension that has developed between environmental groups on the one hand and the business community on the other: most environmental organizations don't understand the world of business and most companies lack real understanding of the serious challenges posed by climate change, ecosystem decline and resource constraints; as a result these two communities most often talk past each other and most importantly
- our economic system is built upon the myth of endless material growth, a notion that guides decision-making around the world, at both government and corporate level, along the same route that is gradually eroding the foundation – the living ecosystems and natural resources – upon which we all ultimately depend; no environmental legislation in the world can rein in an economic system that has endless material growth as its starting point.

The planet is limited

We must come to the realization that the capacity for biological life on Earth is limited. This applies to all species, humans included. Unlike other species, however, we are equipped with consciousness and an ability to choose between different options. Therefore we have a great responsibility both to reflect and to act. But for a long time now most of us have behaved in ways that will severely limit the prospects of future generations. Blind faith in our conventional type of growth will undoubtedly jeopardize the very basis of progress towards providing welfare and wellbeing over the long term.

Few people during the development of the industrial society thought that growth could have negative consequences. World population was much smaller, as was the scale of the world's economies. Today the situation is radically different.

Even if the problems we face are huge, there are ample opportunities for changing course. We have obtained a lot of knowledge in recent years about the risks posed by our unsustainable production and consumption systems. If we use this knowledge wisely, by seeing human evolution so far as a learning process, we should be able to draw the right conclusions and adopt strategies in favour of a more sustainable development. What is needed is a radical rethinking of the human condition, above all a realization that humans are inextricably linked with nature. It should then be possible to develop a better model, a model where there is harmony between humans and nature. For this to be possible, at least three things are required:

- a relative consensus on the problems we face;
- a well-articulated vision of what kind of society we want to see in the long term;

- a strategy for the transition itself, to guide society from the position in which we find ourselves today to that place evoked by the vision.

The purpose of this book is to try to make a constructive contribution to such a development. No one today can know, much less guarantee, that we can change the course of development in time. Humanity faces a host of problems, not least our ingrained habitual patterns, our narrow economic interests and – both in terms of climate and ecosystems – the fact that we do not yet thoroughly comprehend what is at stake. But we owe it to each other and our children to make a serious effort.

2 'Politics in crisis' by Anders Wijkman

> Why do we experience such difficulty even imagining a different sort of society? Why is it beyond us to conceive of a different set of arrangements to our common advantage? Are we doomed indefinitely to lurch between a dysfunctional 'free market' and the much-advertised horrors of 'socialism'?
>
> Tony Judt, 2010

I have politics to thank for much in my life. Work as a member of a parliament is rich and diverse. In no other setting have I encountered so many committed individuals. Eight years in the Swedish parliament in the 1970s and then ten years as a member of the European Parliament (MEP) from 1999 to 2009 have given me unique insights into how political parties think and work.

In spite of my positive experience, I am very concerned about the current state of politics, particularly the development of political parties. Society's increased complexity ought to be addressed through a broadening of perspectives, increased learning, new institutions, greater emphasis of the principle of global solidarity and justice, and a more long-term approach in decision-making. But we see little of this. Instead, political decisions continue to be dominated by tunnel vision and shortsightedness.

Seen from my perspective, the current political system is poorly equipped to deal with many of the complex problems faced by our societies. An economic model that worked well during the post-war period does not automatically provide the right framework for today's increasingly globalized and complex world. The tension between capital and labour – the main division in politics during the 1900s – is still very relevant. But a great number of new issues have surfaced, to which political parties have offered appallingly few solutions. Above all, there are serious shortcomings in the approach to globalization. The world is tightly knit. Dependence on other countries deepens. Yet in most countries the political debate gives priority to narrow national perspectives. It is increasingly obvious that the nation-state is an inadequate decision-making framework for a growing number of issues.

European co-operation has of course added an important dimension to politics, but mostly in the formal sense. Although Sweden has been a member for more than seventeen years, the European Union (EU) perspective is rarely present in the political discourse. Apart from the benefits of the common market, a long-term vision for the EU is not on the agenda. One often cited reason for this lack of interest is that the EU is too technocratic and that co-operation suffers from a 'democratic deficit'. But these very deficiencies ought to be the starting point for a broad discussion by political parties on how EU co-operation can be developed and deepened. However, as is often said, 'We don't win votes discussing the EU', and therefore we have no debate. Where did leadership go?

Lack of interest in European issues pales in comparison with the lack of interest in the global level. 'We cannot have a global economy without a global society,' stated George Soros at the end of the 1990s. Yet the problem of lack of global governance is as great, if not greater, today as it was then. In the absence of international agreements concerning everything from financial markets to climate change and the protection of vital ecosystems, the risks are building up on many fronts and may soon become unmanageable.

Where did the vision go?

It's not just the narrow geographical perspective that is worrying. The vision has gone. Politics, in my view, should be dominated by long-term vision. This was the ambition during most of the twentieth century. But in recent decades, vision has increasingly given way to pragmatism and claims to power. I have witnessed politics becoming increasingly symbolic, while its content has been watered down. The media's obsession with people rather than ideas contributes strongly to this dilution. Personality, ways of expression, and timing have become far more important than the message itself. When the scope for decisions is also decidedly short-term, the responsibility for many critical issues ends up compromised. Shortly before he died Vaclav Havel wrote:

> 'Never before has politics been so dependent on the moment, the public's volatile moods, or the media. Never before have politicians been so compelled to engage in the short-lived and shortsighted. It seems often as if many politicians run from the evening news on TV to the polls the next morning and to his own image on TV in the evening.'

Why has it come to this? Many different factors are involved; here are some of the most important. First, the societal goals from the early 1900s – to eliminate poverty and develop a common welfare state – have essentially been achieved in most developed countries. Few political parties, if any, have managed to formulate a coherent vision for the future. Interest in party politics in society is also declining fast. Young people do not lack interest in political issues but they have little interest in joining political parties. One reason is the aforementioned lack of vision; another has more to do with the ways parties work. Being a member of a party is pretty much the same today as it was fifty years ago; this doesn't attract young people and so the membership base erodes. An elite gladly takes over, to the detriment of internal party democracy and the place of politics in society, a development that is precarious for a democracy.

Financial market deregulation in the 1980s sharply reduced government control over the economy. The structure of the financial sector today suffers serious deficiencies when it comes to how new credit is created and the ability – read inability! – to take social and environmental risks into account. Such risks are instead passed on to society. You only have to study the events surrounding the financial crisis of 2008 and, most recently, the Euro crisis to recognize the situation.

A further factor is the myth of continuous material growth and thus the unwillingness to recognize that we need to re-think both the goals of the economy and how we organize it. Political parties usually have only one approach to development: growth in material terms. They do not want to accept that for reasons of climate change, environment and natural resources, we cannot continue to live as we have. Continued material growth is not sustainable from an environmental and climate perspective. But, in the words of Professor Tim Jackson, 'de-growth is no solution either for economic and social reasons'. So we face a dilemma, which very few political parties want to acknowledge or discuss. No one today expects a solution to this dilemma, but that practically no politician even dares to take up the debate reveals how stagnant political parties have become.

The growing commercialization of the media is another important factor in the loss of political vision. Newspapers try to offset declining sales (due to most of the content being available online) with content that is oriented to the superficial and sensational. News coverage becomes shallower and deteriorates. Political issues are squeezed out; entertainment becomes much more important than in-depth analysis and discussions on vital issues for society. All of this changes the conditions both for politics and recruitment to it. It can be argued that shortcomings in the media are balanced by the rich opportunities for seeking information online, but to do this you need to know where to look. For the average person, this increasing deterioration of news media coverage weakens their basis for forming opinions.

Energy and thermodynamics

I was elected to the Swedish Parliament for the Conservative Party in 1970, when I was 26 years old. In hindsight, this was far too early. I was barely out of university, my experience was limited and my values were still evolving. This gradually led to frequent conflicts between what the party stood for and what I thought was right and eventually these tensions led me to leave the Conservative Party.

Energy policy-making took up a significant part of my time as a legislator. The oil crisis in 1973, when OPEC countries reduced production, revealed the vulnerability of our heavy dependence on imported oil. Security of energy supply quickly became a mainstream political issue and my responsibility was to closely monitor this issue for the party. The energy situation in Sweden was very special. As early as the 1960s Sweden began to develop its own nuclear programme. Rapid nuclear expansion was seen by many, especially industry, as a solution to our extensive dependence on oil. At the beginning, this was not a very controversial issue, but when the Centre Party decided to make the storage of radioactive waste a main issue for the election in 1976, the energy issue became political dynamite.

During those years, Staffan Delin, a Swedish natural scientist, had a strong influence on my views on both energy demand and economic development in general. Delin had a broad academic background and had, among other things, been delving deeply into issues around the principles of thermodynamics. The basic premise of thermodynamics is that energy is indestructible and can only be converted from a higher quality level to a lower one. The sun is the only force that constantly provides us with an injection of high quality energy and thus helps to both build up new resources through photosynthesis and, in the process, convert waste and residue materials into new resources.

Delin made me aware of how industrial society over time risks jeopardizing the very conditions for life on Earth by its rapid increase in the exploitation of natural resources and the waste and pollution that this creates. We extract increasing volumes of substances from the Earth's crust, leading to increasing concentrations in the biosphere – something that is often harmful to both humans and nature. At the same time the 'green base' is undermined when natural areas are converted to monocultural agriculture and forestry, lost through erosion, or paved over as large areas are used to build cities and roads; the 'green base' is also undermined by the depletion of biodiversity. When green areas are reduced, the capacity to build up new resources through photosynthesis, and to take care of and detoxify residue materials, is also diminished.

Delin explained that it was relatively easy to calculate when human society had gone from being in balance with nature to being a drain on it. Similarly, it was possible to calculate, as the Club of Rome (at this time a highly regarded group of businessmen and academics) tried to do in 1972 in its landmark report *Limits to Growth*, how long it would take before conventional growth would create such severe disruption that the life support systems would gradually be destroyed, with dire results.

Growing doubts

The report by the Club of Rome, coupled with Delin's lectures, made me doubt not only Conservative Party policies but party politics in general – based as they were on the greatest possible stimulation of material growth, which resulted in increasing withdrawal of energy resources and raw materials. Just to count the quantity, in terms of GDP growth, and not care about the content and quality seemed to me both simplistic and dangerous. My doubts were strengthened by a lecture in Stockholm in the mid-1970s by Dutch economist Jan Tinbergen, one of the first to receive the Swedish Central Bank's Prize in Economic Science in Memory of Alfred Nobel. Tinbergen was an early critic of the conventional concept of growth, not least the mistake governments make in equating an increase in GDP with a rise in human welfare.

I tried to discuss these issues with the leadership of my party. but to no avail. Criticism of the Club of Rome report by leading economists (Tinbergen was an exception) had made a strong impression on the Conservatives. The main argument was that the Club of Rome had ignored the role technology and innovation would play in tackling imminent environmental and resource problems. My own party leader (Gösta Bohman) brushed aside my objections. Instead of digging deeper into the substance of the issue, he advised me to reconsider my membership of the party – which I eventually did. A little more than a year after our discussion, I left parliament. I was asked to become the secretary-general of the Swedish Red Cross, which I gladly accepted. I felt that I needed to get some perspective on politics.

To the European Parliament

More than twenty years after leaving the Swedish Parliament, and after exciting and meaningful work with the Red Cross, the Swedish Society for Nature Conservation, the Swedish Agency for Research Co-operation with Developing Countries (SAREC) and the UN Development Programme (UNDP), I was asked in 1998 to stand for the European Parliament as a Swedish Christian Democrat (Kd) candidate. It was not an easy decision. I had not been politically active for more than twenty years and my knowledge of Kd's politics was limited. However, time and again while working with organizations like the Red Cross and the UN, I ran up against problems that required changes in key policy frameworks, both at national and international level. I had come to realize that if I truly wanted to get things moving – whether it was mobilizing resources for the prevention of various types of disasters, also to getting more stringent legislation to regulate pollution and waste and provide greater protection for the world's forests and fish stocks, or trying new approaches to poverty reduction – it would only come about through politics.

Having agreed to stand, I developed a platform for my work. My primary goal was to raise awareness of the dilemmas of conventional growth and the need to develop a more sustainable economic model. To me this should not be a partisan issue. The message from science was very clear: space for biological life on the planet is limited for all species, including humans. Negotiating these conditions on conventional political terms was fundamentally wrong and I was therefore determined to help the centre-right parties take a more proactive stance on these issues. I had limited success. When it came to influencing legislation in the EU, I was quite satisfied with my efforts on both climate and energy. My impact on the Christian Democrats' policies in general, however, both nationally and in Europe, fared less well. Deeply disappointed, I left politics in 2009.

Political brakes

Working as a member of the European Parliament (EP) was rewarding in many ways. The EP is undoubtedly the most dynamic and open international institution I have ever worked in. But I always had the feeling, that my forehead was bleeding from banging it against the brick wall that was the Group of Christian Democrats, whenever I proposed changes in their approach to environmental and climate issues. In a group of about 250 members it was a long uphill climb that forced me again and again to recognize how difficult it is to change party politics. Parties who should take the lead often act as a brake instead.

On some issues the opposition was solid, as the following examples show.

Fisheries policy

Throughout my years in the EP the Christian Democrats group was strongly opposed to reforming the EU's fisheries policy. Regardless of the consensus of scientific opinion that repeatedly warned of the risk of overfishing, the European People's Party (EPP) voted – along with many members of the other political groups – for increased or preserved fish quotas. Support for expanding the fishing fleet in the EU continued unabated. Yet any sober analysis would have realized long ago that it was not the shortage of fishing boats that was the problem, but the lack of fish.

Trade policy

It was the same with trade policy. For a long time there was broad support for dumping food onto the world market, which undercut local food production in poor countries. In parallel, the EU's free trade policy strongly discriminated against imports of value-added goods. Commodities were exempt from customs duties, but restrictions applied to anything processed. Both the Christian Democrats and the Liberals – as well as major parts of the Socialist Group – supported this policy most of the time. The result was a policy where the EU gave with one hand through aid, but took with the other through trade policy.

Chemicals policy

The REACH chemicals policy is another example. When the EU Commission introduced the new legislation it was already a compromise arrived at after tough negotiations with the chemical industry. The purpose of the policy was to remove from the market those chemicals that posed a danger to health and the environment. Based on my positive experience of Swedish legislation, which for quite a few years had imposed far stricter regulation of chemicals, I thought that the new policy would have a positive reception. I couldn't have been more wrong. The opposition was massive, especially from the German chemical companies. The perceived threat was that Europe's chemical industry would die. The issue became the subject of years of protracted negotiations between the Parliament, the Member States in the Council and the European Commission. On many points the Christian Democratic Group acted almost as a defence lawyer for the chemical industry.

I had a very positive attitude towards the bill and worked, for example, to strengthen protection against the so-called endocrine disruptors. These efforts were met with disapproval by the Christian Democratic leadership and I was repeatedly asked to close ranks and toe the line. I refused and managed in the end to rally some 40 Christian Democratic members behind certain important votes. As a result the final compromise was significantly better than the position of the Christian Democrats.

My struggle with this issue left a bad aftertaste. It was beyond my comprehension that narrow industrial interests were allowed to outweigh serious risks to human health, especially as the transition periods in the proposed REACH legislation were generous. Compared to the rapid and unregulated changes that constantly take place in sectors such as the electronics industry, the chemical companies should have seen REACH as feasible to manage.

Emissions trading

Another example of where short-termism and concern for industry were pushed very far was the proposal in 2008 for a revised directive on emissions trading. The perceived costs to energy-intensive industries were blown out of proportion. The threat of 'carbon leakage' – that businesses would relocate outside Europe – was used as a general argument against emissions trading. Yet various studies showed that only a very minor part of the European industry was likely to consider relocation. In the end, when the negotiation process crossed the finishing line, the most essential points of the directive had been substantially watered down. Electric utilities would be subject to more stringent regulation (including the auctioning of allowances) from 2013, but other industries were given unreasonably long periods of transition. As a result, the directive in its original form comes into full effect only in 2027! Again, it was a majority of the Christian Democrats – along with substantial factions among the Socialists and Liberals – who provided the toughest opposition and led efforts to soften the directive.

The willingness and openness of political parties to rethink major issues is thus severely limited. Short-term considerations and concerns take over.

One advantage in Sweden and Europe, compared to the US, is of course that money does not play as large a role in politics. Political parties are freer from various economic interests. At the same time, we should not underestimate the significance of the deregulation of the financial markets. Compared to the past, politics nowadays has only limited room to manoeuvre. How the world's stock markets will react to a particular political decision is vastly more important than the commentaries of editorial writers or the public in general.

The idol of growth

Politics, of both the right and the left, seem to assume that the type of growth economy that has dominated development since World War II will continue for ever. Everyone talks about increasing growth, but rarely asks how long this growth is possible.

The reason is simple. Our entire societal model is built on the premise that the economy will continue to expand. The type of growth we have is dependent on a rapidly increasing flow of high quality energy and raw materials – from finite resources as well as from ecosystems. Here lies the problem. The pressure on many ecosystems, such as tropical forests, arable land, fresh water and fish stocks, is already too high. Meanwhile, there are more frequent reports of risks to the supply of crude oil. Not that oil will run out, but it will be increasingly difficult to meet a rapidly rising demand from countries such as China, India and Brazil at affordable prices.

Questioning conventional growth is not popular. But we face a serious dilemma. To quote Tim Jackson again: 'While growth may be unsustainable, de-growth is unstable.' Today's economic model cannot continue indefinitely. We live on a small planet. The population and the economy are growing, but the planet is not growing. A model that worked well for a few billion people in the past is not automatically viable in the future. World population has tripled since World War II. The world economy is more than ten times larger, and if it continues to grow at such a pace will be close to a hundred times larger by 2100! Does anyone think this is possible?

According to most economists, strong growth in the economy is a prerequisite for spreading prosperity to the poor of the world. 'A rising tide lifts all ships,' as Margaret Thatcher expressed it. Prosperity will trickle down to the poor. But development over the last twenty years does not suggest that the 'trickle down' theory works overly well. With the exception of China, the statistics in most countries today show a mixed picture, with many examples of an opposite effect, a kind of 'trickle up', where the rich get richer, the middle class is shrinking and the poor are left behind. Moreover, if both the environment and resource space are shrinking, we simply have to rethink how the economy is organized. The prerequisites for 'more of the same' are simply not there.

Two crises, one root

Many people saw an opportunity for change during the financial crisis of 2008. The financial and environmental crises have the same roots: non-sustainable use of resources in the money economy as well as in the natural world. Now, since attempts were being made to tighten up the financial system, the same should be done for the climate and the environment.

There have been attempts in the right direction. More than 15 per cent of the US stimulus package in 2009 was earmarked for investments in the 'green' economy, such as renewable energy and energy efficiency. Other countries such as China and South Korea have made similar priorities. But the greatest anxiety of the vast majority of governments was to recreate the situation that prevailed before the financial crisis as fast as possible. Most importantly, the stimulus packages around the world – totalling several thousand billion dollars – were spent on general stimulation of consumption and not on investments in a more resource-efficient and fossil-free world.

The deepening economic crisis affecting the US and Europe during the second half of 2011 led to somewhat different reactions. Instead of broad stimulus packages, the recipe suggested was austerity – at a time when unemployment was rapidly growing in many countries, especially among young people. How such an approach was expected to manage social tensions is a mystery! Worse, the crisis discussions continue to focus only on the money economy. Few decision-makers seem to care that we are eating into the future by degrading natural capital and ecosystem services and destabilizing the climate system. From this perspective, the crisis we face is as much about finance and economy as it is about climate, resources and the environment. The unwillingness to rethink and broaden perspectives could have disastrous consequences. Talk about denial!

Listen to the natural scientists

Perpetual growth in the throughput of energy and raw materials on a limited planet is impossible. That many economists cherish the idea does not make it right. In the long run we cannot continue to deny very basic natural laws, but many policy-makers still stick their heads in the sand. It is a mystery to me that we are not listening more to the natural scientists, many of them Nobel laureates, who have repeatedly warned against this predicament – as manifested at the Nobel Symposium on Global Sustainability in Stockholm in May 2011. Instead, we let economists of the conventional school dominate decision-making. I have studied economics and know how little attention is still paid in an economics education to an understanding of how nature works.

The current organization of the economy leads us astray and will end in disaster unless we quickly change course. But neither the political parties on the centre-right, nor on the centre-left, demonstrate the necessary innovation and leadership. The Green parties have indeed questioned the current model, but their policy proposals seldom have a sufficient systems-view and they are therefore perceived mostly as nay-sayers.

The challenge in the short term is to give greatly increased emphasis to the content and quality of growth and to develop strategies for the necessary transition to a future system that is sustainable. There is much in society that needs to grow and develop, such as culture, education and research, investment in environmentally friendly technologies and infrastructure, health and social care for children and the elderly. But it must be done within a framework where the throughput of energy and materials in the economy is not constantly increasing. If the economy could develop in this direction, it would mean an inevitable end to the throwaway mentality and wasteful practices that dominate consumption patterns and business models today. The transition will not be easy. But there should be no doubt whatsoever that it ought to be possible to organize the flows of energy and materials in a different and more sustainable way. We have talked at length about closing the loops. It is high time to let such principles dominate politics.

The vast majority of political parties are stuck in the logic of the industrial society. I have personally experienced how difficult it is to change a political party from the inside. The frankest advice I can give political parties is this: Revise your policies. Today's political platforms lack sufficient relevance to the globalized world in which we now live and the types of problems we are challenged to solve. Take a break. Make a broad analysis of the world we live in and develop new policy platforms. Otherwise, new political parties will sooner or later emerge and step by step force today's intransigent parties out into the cold.

3 Science's role and responsibility by Johan Rockström

"History is a race between education and catastrophe".

H G Wells

World governments have signed over 500 international environmental agreements in order to reverse negative and often dangerous environmental trends and point them into a sustainable direction. Nevertheless, we have so far failed in all but possibly one case, namely the Montreal Protocol that aims to ban substances that destroy the ozone layer. The Montreal Protocol is interesting because it is a negotiated international agreement that is based entirely on science. No one had seen or felt the effects of the ozone hole. But through the pioneering research of Sherwood Rowland, Mario Molina and Paul Cruzen (later to be awarded the Nobel Prize) science was able to prove that CFCs deplete the ozone layer and that this could have disastrous consequences for all land-based life on Earth.

But the Montreal Protocol is an exception. In all negotiations on the future of life on Earth there is a party absent from the negotiating table, namely the Earth. However, through science the planet does have a voice. Therefore it is incredibly important that science has a strong voice in global environmental negotiations and that science itself manages this voice with integrity, objectivity and great respect. On both these points (science's influence and its responsibility) there are gaps'. To address these gaps has become the rationale for my own commitment to conducting and leading interdisciplinary research on sustainable development and, not least, to communicating research on the state of the planet and the challenges facing humanity.

Climate change is a serious example of our constant compromise with the planet, that is, with science. For instance, there is no conclusive scientific evidence that a concentration of greenhouse gases at 450 parts per million (ppm) (CO_2 equivalents) would be enough to avoid 'dangerous' climate change. Yet it is this level of concentration of greenhouse gases (compared to 280 ppm before the Industrial Revolution) that stands as a 'safe' limit in the political climate negotiations.

Also based on political compromise rather than scientific evidence, the threshold for 'dangerous' climate change has been set at 2°C, i.e., that the global average temperatures increase should not exceed 2°C. Thus the assumption is that 450 ppm is equal to a warming of no more than 2 °C (i.e., to 450 ppm ≤ 2 °C). Is this correct? The answer is no. There is no scientific evidence that limiting greenhouse gas concentrations to 450 ppm would guarantee that the warming caused by human activity would keep the increase in global average temperature below 2 degrees. In fact, to make matters even more frustrating, there is also no scientific evidence at all that 2 degrees would be a 'safe' limit (more on this later in the book).

But suppose for a moment that this was actually the case, that 450 ppm = below 2 degrees = OK. What would it take to reach this target? There is, of course, a great scientific uncertainty on this issue, because we do not yet understand exactly how the complex and self-regulating planetary system works, and thus how it will respond to our 'interference' when we inject an energy imbalance through our emissions of greenhouse gases. But in the political arena it is often asserted that there is a clear answer. A halving of carbon emissions by 2050 has been portrayed by leaders around the world, including the Swedish government and the EU leadership, as the 'required target' to meet the 2 degrees limit. (On the Swedish side, this was asserted despite findings to the contrary by the scientific climate committee appointed by the government in 2007.) If that was not enough, this kind of political goal-setting is often quickly followed by comments like 'because the science says so', or 'we rely on the science'.

Unfortunately such reasoning is not correct and it constitutes a serious erosion of the credibility of science and its role in society. What generally happens with regard to environmental issues, and with climate change in particular, is that society compromises the knowledge presented by science and thus distorts its message. Science is being used to justify trade-offs with environmental policy. When this occurs in a situation where scientists generally tend to stay away from the broader public debate, and where the media are unable to convey difficult scientific issues and moreover often make the mistake of giving well-established scientific findings the same space as extreme and thus marginal opinions (as from climate deniers), there will be serious consequences. The result is that politics often ends up formulating the so-called 'truths' in the name of science. This also means that the level of ambition with regard to mitigation is lowered to what for the moment is considered 'possible' to achieve.

A recent example was the risk that California, which as a region has one of the most ambitious climate policies in the world, would be forced to back down from its plan to reduce emissions by 30 per cent by 2020 (compared to 1990), because of political pressure 'to invest in jobs' during an economic downturn. The notion was put forward that jobs would be lost if the old fossil-based economic engine was subject to regulation. Governor Arnold Schwarzenegger struck back, especially since the campaign against his policy was being funded by the fossil industry.

This deep ravine between what science indicates to be necessary and what society translates as possible is an important root of my insistent engagement' to communicate, as effectively as I can and often with a fool's stubbornness, the current state of scientific knowledge on the environmental hazards to which we are exposed. Sometimes this is portrayed, as indeed am I, as a kind of doomsday prophecy. I see it in exactly the opposite way, ie as extremely positive that – thanks to the advancement of science – we are aware of the many possible threats to future welfare created by our way of organizing the economy. We thus have the knowledge to navigate away from the most dangerous reefs. Until recently we were like a blind Columbus in an infinite ocean, assuming a short, straight path to gold and infinite growth. Now we know that the planet is a complex archipelago where advanced navigation is necessary to avoid sinking the ship.

In all honesty, I have not always had a real sense of the risks we face and the critical need to act on several fronts simultaneously (climate, air, water, biodiversity, ozone, etc.). I remember as an enthusiastic PhD student in the mid 1990s doing field trials in the arid West African savannah, where the main goal was to improve water-use in local small-scale agriculture. I concluded then that climate change was not a priority in promoting sustainable development in Africa. There were more pressing issues, among them land degradation, water shortages, corruption, lack of markets and infrastructure and acute shortage of electricity. Climate change was assumed to be a creeping change that would play out over a century; the real variations in precipitation extremes that local peasants lived with every day – from deep drought to major flooding – far exceeded the (relatively) small alterations that climate change appeared to cause. So I just didn't think that climate change was a main priority, and was thus, during this period, 'Lomborgian' in my thinking. Bjorn Lomborg's attitude, manifested in his so-called 'Copenhagen Consensus', has long been that even if humans are causing climate change, it is not worth investing money to solve that problem because humanity is facing more pressing problems (such as food shortages, HIV Aids, and infectious diseases). I must admit that this error of judgement marked my early work with development issues in Africa and is difficult to defend, given that already back in the mid 1990s the IPCC' had its first report on the table, Jim Hansen had given his strong testimony before the US Congress (1988), and Charney had long since provided his scientific conclusions about the risks of a doubling of the concentration of greenhouse gases (1979). There was no excuse then, and there is even less excuse today when we have begun to see the adverse effects of interacting global environmental problems upon people around the world.

Highlighting the dangers of the recurring compromises between scientific knowledge and societal engagement is a strong driver of my own work. Of course I am not naïve. I do realise that compromise is the lifeblood of politics and often of leadership. But then we must all be clear about the risks we are taking when we compromise scientific insights.

Yes, yes, you may say, but science is never in full agreement, you never know what to 'believe' in (as if it were a matter of 'faith'). It is true that science has not and will never give crystal-clear and definitive answers to complex questions such as how sensitive the planet is to an increase in the amount of greenhouse gas emissions. It's the very nature of science that there are uncertainties, and that scientific research is constantly seeking new knowledge and refining insights. But this is the way it always is, in everything we do. We can never know with certainty what will happen around the next corner, or how markets, human behaviour, or industrial innovations will respond and be received in a reality that is constantly changing. But science provides an increasingly clear picture of the panorama of risks we are facing. Through global scientific assessments, such as the UN Panel on Climate Change and the Millennium Ecosystem Assessment, we have reached a point where, as citizens of the planet, we have clear and scientifically anchored insights that support us in our actions. Nobody should be able to dispute this, yet up to now we have not been willing to do what is necessary to radically reduce the risks; rather, we have fallen prey to the short-term allure of compromise.

I continue to face this dilemma in my dialogues with politicians, business leaders, media and the public. In the spring of 2009, I tried several tactics to communicate the lack of sufficient scientific evidence that a halving of carbon emissions by 2050 would give us a 'secure' future with a warming below 2 degrees. I based my action on the fact that even the IPCC's Fourth Assessment Report shows that a halving of emissions would lead to a 50 per cent risk that warming would exceed 2 degrees, and that emissions reductions of 80 per cent or more are necessary to have a reasonable chance of avoiding 2 degrees. Recent research paints an even more challenging picture, namely that CO_2 emissions must be phased out completely by 2050 in order to have a 70 per cent chance of avoiding 2 degrees (that is still a high risk of failure!).

In July 2009, during the EU ministerial meeting in Åre, I tried to recommend that the EU and the Swedish Presidency should not follow in the G8's footsteps, by establishing a halving of CO_2 emissions as sufficient to achieve the 2 degree goal. Instead, the EU should build on the most recent science and add a more ambitious target of 80 per cent reductions (one still associated with high risk according to recent research). The political reaction was fierce and immediate. EU Commission President Barosso was furious and stated that this was an unfounded attack on the EU's scientifically based climate policy (which of course is not correct). The Swedish government was extremely concerned and challenged me, saying 'Why are you now, when we are so close to a consensus, risking EU unity?' Yes, but consensus on what? Just because EU leaders did not believe that we could afford to solve the climate problem, we should not bury our heads in the sand and pretend that the problem is being solved!

This winding trail of compromises descends ever further down a slippery slope. When climate deniers such as Bjorn Lomborg are squeezed into a corner by science, the final argument (against the scientific consensus) is always compromise, often disguised in economic terms. The cost of solving environmental problems is considered too large in comparison to the benefits that environmental measures are thought to provide. This is how it has been over and over again, ever since Rachel Carson in the 1960s, in her legendary book *Silent Spring*, provided evidence of the harmful effects of chemicals and heavy metals, during the debates on the dangers of smoking and the damage to climate change caused by 'acid rain'. When the economy goes into recession, as in recent years, climate mitigation objectives are relaxed even more. Suddenly the ultimate foundation of welfare and prosperity – the natural systems – is less important, because we have to focus all our energy on – what? Well, human welfare. The failure to understand the linkages is nothing less than a disaster. After Copenhagen, the prospects for a climate treaty were dimmer than 10 years earlier, and we are moving steadily towards a global warming of more than 3 degrees.

However, the dilemma does not end with compromises at the level of politics; again, these are to be expected, it's the politician's role, but they should have been more honestly communicated. Instead of pretending that the measures suggested were sufficient, EU leaders should have acknowledged that it was a political compromise – not something condoned by science. The problem is also about science's own shortcomings. Here we have two major challenges that I keep struggling with: science's tendency to compromise and its' inability to grasp an understanding of systems.

The compromising within science is in a way even more serious than that within politics. My conclusion, which may surprise many, is that science's current inability to 'stay by the science' is not predominantly about scientists exaggerating the risks – as they are normally portrayed by deniers and the media – but rather about scientists tending to tone down risks and compromise with their own research. The process leading up to COP 15 is an example. Throughout 2009 there was an informal intra-science discussion about what strategy was the best to obtain a binding agreement in Copenhagen. Was it better to play down the risks and assent to a compromise goal (such as a 20-30 per cent reduction in emissions by 2020 and 50 per cent reduction by 2050) in order to get an agreement and therefore a positive development (which could later on be matched by a higher level of ambition)? Or should science continue to convey sincerely the complexity of the research, the risk profile and the need for a much more stringent goal?

In hindsight we know that the compromise strategy won out. In the end only a very few scientists continued to convey the full scope of the challenge: that CO_2 emissions must now be reduced by at least 80 per cent; that CO_2 represents only 60–70 per cent of emissions and that other gases present an equal or greater risk; in addition, that we risk undermining the major carbon sinks on Earth – the oceans and terrestrial ecosystems; that taking into account population growth, poverty, and the right to development in emerging economies, there was absolutely no chance of stabilising the climate below 2 degrees unless the rich countries phased out their emissions well before 2050.

This way of compromise within the scientific community is probably why the reaction was so strong from the EU leadership in July 2009, when I made the point publicly that the climate problem was more serious than we previously thought and that emission reductions were required to go much further than a G8 meeting had proposed. Only a few other scientists in the world put the facts from the scientific data sheets into their mouths and spoke clearly. It was so bad that the possibility cannot be excluded that politicians actually acted in good faith! For example, just weeks before the G8 meeting in June 2009 a number of scientists published a message in the form of a large advertisement in the *International Herald Tribune* and recommended (1) that the G8 adopt as a target staying within two degrees of warming, and (2) that a 50 per cent emissions reduction by 2050 was an appropriate initial target. The scientists signing this article clearly knew that neither 2°C nor 50 per cent would stand the scrutiny of science, and that the plea was simply an effort at 'getting the climate ball rolling'; the advertisement was clearly compromising to science and created a lot of confusion among the public.

Basically, this incident also captures the IPCC's dilemma. If the IPCC is open to criticism, it's not that the panel exaggerates the climate problem. Rather the opposite, not least in underestimating the risks of sea-level rise and tipping points and the feedbacks and amplification effects on the oceans, forests, soils. This critique is not primarily directed at the IPCC working group reports, but rather at the summary documents for policy makers, where the language goes through a thorough negotiation process that sometimes puts the integrity of the science at risk. This is one of the great challenges of science: to be completely free from external influences and not to be drawn into the political process.

The second scientific challenge that I (and many colleagues) keep struggling with is the great, if not urgent, need for a systemic perspective and an integrated approach to solving the complex problems facing humanity. My own scientific journey began at the Swedish University of Agricultural Sciences, where, as an agronomy student, I realized early on that the university's watertight bulkheads between scientific disciplines did not lend themselves to solving many of the problems in real life. This was markedly the case (and still is) in the environmental field. Sustainability has too long been an isolated phenomenon among ecologists, biologists, botanists, zoologists, and so on, with essentially a natural science focus within a rather narrow sub-component of the complex and interconnected Earth system. Moreover, research on 'living systems' of the biosphere has been separated from research on natural resources (such as geology) and how the planet works (such as the physical science of the climate system or chemical research on chemical processes in oceans, land and air). There are indeed interdisciplinary approaches in the sciences, such as biogeochemical research, but an extremely large gap remains in linking the biological and physical processes on the planet, which closely interact and thus together determine the planet's stability; how, for instance, do the world's ecosystems affect the climate?.

This in itself is a major challenge: the realization that the way we have structured research and organized universities is not consistent with how reality works. We cannot hope to solve major environmental problems such as climate change, with today's fragmented and isolated scientific disciplines. Instead, research needs to be organized on a much broader understanding of systems. An even greater problem is that despite a greater understanding of how the planet works and what risks we are taking, we still are not making any significant progress towards a more desirable sustainable future. What we need is an interdisciplinary science that focuses on solving problems. We see more and more research emerging that really tries to integrate social sciences, humanities and natural sciences, but an incredible amount of work remains, and it's hard! I myself direct two multidisciplinary environmental research organizations – the SEI and the SRC – and in both cases I wrestle with the challenge of hiring and working with scientists who truly respect and understand the social dimensions, and also with the difficulty of finding economists, political scientists, anthropologists, philosophers, etc., who truly understand the complex dynamics of the biophysical systems of the Earth. We simply have to recognize that at this crucial stage in human history, when major decisions must be taken to change the course of world development, science is not really on track with systems-based solutions.

Why? Because the sciences and universities are stuck in the disciplinary status quo they have been in for centuries. Such a singular focus is now obsolete. Since 2009, I have led an international process under the ICSU (International Council for Science) and ISSC (International Social Science Council) whose task is to set the international research agenda for global environmental changes in the future and how to address them. For 30 years the ICSU has co-ordinated some of the world's foremost international research programmes on global environmental change (World Climate Research Program, WCRP; International Geo-Biosphere Program, IGBP; Diversitas, the research programme on biodiversity and ecosystem services; International Human Dimensions Program, IHDP; and the Earth System Science Partnership, ESSP).

In our work, which started with a two-year visioning process of consultations with thousands of scientists around the world, it was concluded early on that more research in the same traditional manner would not be sufficient, i.e., that 'business as usual' in terms of research organizations and today's disciplinary scientific focus will not be able to generate a deeper understanding of the major global risks humanity now faces and the necessary solutions. Climate science cannot be isolated from research on ecosystem services and functions, and on how people, communities and the international community react and act on issues of environment and development. The new research agenda for the next ten years, which we are now developing, demonstrates that we need no less than an Apollo-like programme in order for science to provide insights and solutions for a rapid transformation of world societies towards sustainable development. The challenge is to continue to support basic disciplinary research while also investing in interdisciplinary research that can provide answers to complex – and interlinked – social and ecological challenges confronting humanity. This requires a reorganization of the currently fragmented research community, towards more integrated and problem-solving programmes.

My belief is that interdisciplinary science emerges quite naturally from a focus on problem solving. The problems we face are so complex that they require collaboration across disciplinary boundaries. I often point out, for example, that we can no longer talk about strictly environmental problems; what we face are developmental problems. The environment – our biosphere and its ecosystems – is the foundation of welfare and prosperity and therefore of our development. While we cannot negotiate with nature, we will be able to compromise among ourselves, with our aspirations, the demands and rights we espouse at our local and regional communities, and also with the relationships between the countries of the world. A focus on solving problems such as climate change (a relatively easy problem compared, for example, to the closely related problem of loss of biodiversity) compels collaborations across disciplinary boundaries.

I have always been involved in problem-oriented research, from finding innovative solutions to water problems in Africa to the methods that can lead to a new, sustainable green revolution in the poor tropical regions of the world. I have several of the intellectual heavyweights of the Swedish interdisciplinary sciences to thank for this, such as the late Erik Arrhenius, who as Professor of Natural Resources at the University of Stockholm adopted me as a graduate student in the early 1990's; Uno Svedin, then head of the Research Council committee that granted my first research funding for interdisciplinary research on water, land and development in the drought-stricken Sahel region of West Africa; Carl Folke, one of the world's leading interdisciplinary environmental scientists, who early on gave his full support for my research; and, of course, Malin Falkenmark, the leading – and one of the most recognised – international hydrologists, who in the spirit of George Borgstrom has led the research on water and sustainable development. Malin was my advisor as a Masters student at Ultuna and again during my PhD years, and is to this day one of my closest research colleagues and certainly my most important mentor. This privileged interdisciplinary training provided me with the opportunity to intimately connect science and the real world, not only in practical research work, such as building dams to protect irrigation under the hot sun in Niger in order to assess the water balance and crop development in small millet agriculture, but also sometimes stepping out of the research role and developing and applying practical knowledge in acute relief situations.

Immediately after the horrific genocide of some 800,000 Tutsis and moderate Hutus in Rwanda, I was asked by the Swedish Red Cross to lead a team of water experts and engineers on behalf of the International Red Cross Committee (ICRC), with the task of repairing bombed and destroyed water supply systems in northern Rwanda. In the final stages of the genocide, nearly one million Rwandans had fled across the border into what was then Zaire (now the Democratic Republic of the Congo, DRC), creating the world's largest refugee camp in Goma, on a still active volcano slope. Our task was to ensure that the water supply would work so that these refugees could come back to Rwanda as soon as possible. This mission, which I was asked to lead in the midst of my PhD studies in West Africa and France, was without question a challenge I had to take on, not only because it was an opportunity to make a 'real' difference and nurture my own research with a real-world application, but also because it was the Red Cross that called. From my first year of studies at Ultuna in 1986, I have had a great admiration for the Swedish Red Cross and in particular for the leadership of Anders Wijkman' as Secretary General of the Red Cross during the middle and late 1980s). Anders' engagement, not least his persistent efforts to build up the capacity to prevent disasters instead of investing more effort in Disaster Relief, on the premise that 'prevention is better than cure', was a great inspiration, completely in line with my own approach to environmental and sustainable development.

My assignment in Rwanda was an incredible experience. The day to day challenges (which were followed by several missions for the Red Cross in Tanzania and Zaire) were also very humbling, as we tried to solve environmental problems in a sea of social problems and in the face of sudden surprises such as huge influxes of refugees. This practical experience has always had its immediate counterpart in research , where awareness of the risks of sudden, unexpected events such as drought and flood have been and are also significant.

In this work, both in research and application, I have come to realize that there is much we do not understand, especially the risk of threshold effects – rapid and often irreversible changes in the social and ecological systems – and how local systems (such as an agricultural system or a city) are interconnected and scale up to the global level. This is a new situation, a new realization that we have entered the global era of sustainable development, where the daily conditions for an African farmer (such as the probability of rain) are directly linked to the consumption patterns in a country like Sweden. We must therefore do the theoretical research needed for new insights into how our social and ecological systems interact and work. But we do not have the luxury of doing just 'curiosity driven' research on issues related to the major environmental challenges. We must speed up and increase investment so that we can quickly find new insights and then dare to experiment with new solutions.

It is in this context that perhaps our most difficult scientific challenge comes to light. There is no doubt that we need a new interdisciplinary revolution in our schools and universities, to train the next generation of global problem solvers. But this takes time. We cannot wait until we have educated a new generation of economists and political scientists who understand that healthy ecosystems are the basis for human welfare. Parallel to this revolution in science and education, we must quickly find solutions to the many global environmental and developmental problems of today. This must be done in today's fragmented – and in many ways obsolete – economic and institutional realities. How this will be done, before it's too late, is anybody's guess.

4 From Copenhagen to Durban

> 'There's really only one label for the pathetic exercise we've just witnessed in Durban: deceit. The whole climate-change negotiation process and the larger political discourse surrounding this horrible problem is a drawn-out and elaborate exercise in lying – to each other, to ourselves, and especially to our children. And the lies are starting to corrupt our civilization from inside out.'
>
> Thomas Homer-Dixon, 12 December 2011

The international climate change negotiations are organized in ways that can drive even the most patient to despair. It is now twenty years since the United Nations Framework Convention on Climate Change (UNFCCC) was signed at the UN Environmental Conference in Rio de Janeiro in 1992, but no climate treaty to speak of is on the cards. Emissions of greenhouse gases continue to increase – at an ever-faster rate over time. Between 1970 and 1995 global emissions increased by an average of 1.7 per cent annually. During the next decade the increase was by 2.5 per cent a year. In the following years (2009 excluded) emissions increased by nearly 3 per cent a year. 2010 was unique: global emissions grew by a staggering 5.9 per cent, and still the climate negotiations slither along at a snail's pace.

Copenhagen: a missed opportunity

After years of largely fruitless negotiations, expectations were high for the 2009 climate summit in Copenhagen. The UN scientific panel, the IPCC, had sharpened the tone of its report in 2007. At the same time leading economists, under Lord Nicholas Stern's leadership, had convincingly shown that the consequences (not least economically) could be disastrous if measures to reduce greenhouse gas emissions were postponed.

Activity was high before the Copenhagen climate summit – among governments, scientists, industrialists and civil society. It was now or never! The goal was a binding climate agreement. Unfortunately the final result ended up far from it: a political declaration, the Copenhagen Accord, with which few were satisfied.

Both the authors of this book took part in the Copenhagen conference. Conditions were at times chaotic. Poor communication between the UN and the Danish hosts resulted in twice as many delegates as the conference centre could accommodate, with most of us spending long hours queuing in the snow and cold before we could be admitted. Many thousands of delegates did not get in at all. When the outcome of the meeting was a 'flop', it confirmed for many the image of poor leadership on the part of both the UN and the Danish government.

Despite the failure some progress was made. Developed countries made promises of financial support for climate action in the poorest countries: 10 billion dollars per year between 2010 and 2012. At the same time they expressed the goal of increasing this support step by step, reaching $100 billion per year by 2020. However, the need for support for both adaptation and investment in low carbon energy systems in low-income countries is deemed to be many times larger than the amount pledged. But the promise of climate aid was still a breakthrough for a new way of thinking.

Another positive outcome of the Copenhagen Accord was the progress achieved in the efforts to limit deforestation. After many years of negotiations, agreement was reached in principle for a system of financial support for the protection of tropical forests.

Comments after the Copenhagen conference varied greatly. When President Obama returned to the States he was hailed as something of a hero. Even in China and India the agreement was seen as a success. The reason was simple: none of these countries would commit to the obligations of an international agreement. In Europe, however, the comments were consistently very negative. 'Failure', 'disappointment', yes, even 'disaster' were the words used.

However one views Copenhagen, the meeting at least to some extent confirmed that climate change is a serious problem that requires bold steps. The centrepiece of the Accord was that countries confirmed their ambition to avoid a rise of more than 2 degrees in the average temperature on Earth. This goal, which has been discussed since the mid 1990s, is a political target set at the EU level of governance – not a target based on climate science. Still, it has emerged as a reasonable goal for the international climate effort. A temperature rise of up to 2 degrees should be possible to manage in terms of adaptation, so the reasoning goes.

Criticism of the Copenhagen meeting centred on the fact that nothing was said about how this goal was to be achieved. Instead of a binding agreement on emission cuts, the vast majority of countries submitted declarations of intent to the UN of how much they planned to reduce emissions by 2020. Pledges of emission reductions are obviously better than nothing, but when you add up those promises, you quickly realize that the chances of avoiding the 2 degree target are zero. The emissions curve based on these government pledges points to a temperature increase of between 3 and 4 degrees. 'A different planet', to quote climate scientist James Hansen.

An examination of the outcome of Copenhagen was published in the journal *Nature* in April 2010 by Joeri Rogelj, Malte Meinshausen and other scientists from the Potsdam Institute for Climate Impact Research. Their conclusions were anything but encouraging. Without a binding agreement most countries are not expected to meet even the moderate pledges made to the United Nations. One important reason is that countries can 'save' emission allowances from the period of the Kyoto Protocol until after 2012. Various industrialized countries are expected to bring emission allowances, equivalent to more than 12 billion tonnes of CO_2 (almost three times the EU countries' emissions in a single year!), into a possible new climate treaty.' Another reason for the expected limited outcome in terms of emission reduction concerns the generous rules on how Kyoto signatories can use growth in their forests to offset real emissions. The likelihood is therefore high, according to the Potsdam study, that the result of Copenhagen will be an increase of global emissions by at least 20 per cent by 2020. Translated into temperature this means a significant risk – more than 50 per cent – that the average temperature on Earth will increase by more than 3 degrees by 2100 as a consequence of the pledges made in Copenhagen. According to most climate scientists this is a disastrous outcome.

Cancún did not save the climate

The next Climate Change Conference was held in Cancún, Mexico, in November-December 2010. After the failure of Copenhagen, expectations were low. The negotiations had long been stalled, not least because Canada, Russia and Japan made a common pact with the United States and refused to discuss a renewal of the Kyoto Protocol. At the same time the group of developing countries demanded an extension of the Kyoto Protocol. But the combination of skilful negotiation tactics by the Mexicans and a desire among many of the participating countries not to go home empty-handed meant that the conference did yield some positive results. This, however, came at a cost: the issue of emission reduction was postponed. The key decisions were:

- A repetition of the goal to keep global temperature rise below 2 degrees. In addition – and as a concession to the small island states – it was decided that, in the future, lowering the temperature target to 1.5 degrees Celsius would be considered.
- The emissions reduction pledges made at the Copenhagen meeting, which were not binding and clearly inadequate, will nevertheless be part of the UN treaty process.
- It was decided to establish a Climate Fund to support climate action in low-income countries.
- A framework agreement, REDD+, was created to reduce deforestation and provide incentives for sustainable forestry in developing countries.

However, concrete measures as to *how* greenhouse gas emissions would be reduced, as well as the year when emissions would peak, were put off to a later date. Comments after Cancún expressed everything from great satisfaction by many heads of government that the UN process could, after all, continue, to deep disappointment among many climate scientists and environmentalists that nothing much was achieved to start reducing emissions. A common comment was that 'The decision in Cancún rescued the negotiation process within the UN, but hardly the climate.'

After Durban: a glimmer of hope

In the debate that followed Cancún many commentators seemed prepared to write off the whole UN process. But such a move would have been very unfortunate. The goal of a binding agreement at international level cannot and must not be abandoned. It is more important today than ever before to keep negotiations going. The fact that it may take many years to achieve a binding agreement is a different matter.

Nothing but a significant reduction in greenhouse gas emissions can bring about a stabilization of the climate system. Science is totally clear on this. Seen from this perspective, it is abundantly clear that the world's major economies do not take climate change seriously; or, to put it differently, that they make the great, if not disastrous, mistake of compromising away a solution to the climate problem in return for perceived short-term economic benefits.

A few weeks before the Climate Change Conference in Durban in 2011, the World Energy Outlook report (WEO) 2011 was presented. The WEO is compiled annually by the International Energy Agency (IEA) and is regarded as one of the most authoritative analyses of energy. The report's main objective is to make energy forecasts – everything from demand and available reserves to new technologies and costs. The WEO 2011 paid particular attention to climate change. The report notes that the door to achieving the 2 degree target is rapidly closing. As energy usage is now tracking, a long-term rise in average temperatures in excess of 3.5 degrees is likely. The report calculates that '80 per cent of the cumulative CO_2 emitted between 2009 and 2035, according to a scenario to stay within the 2 degree target, is already "locked-in" by capital stock – including power stations, buildings and factories – that either exists or is under construction and that will still be operational by 2035, leaving little additional room for maneuvre'. This means that any new infrastructure from 2017 onwards must in principle be 'zero carbon' to meet the 2 degree target. As the IEA's chief economist put it: 'If we do not have an international agreement, whose effect is put in place by 2017, then the door to holding temperatures to 2 degrees of warming will be closed forever.'

One would have expected the IEA report to act as an energizer for the negotiations in Durban. But that did not happen. In the wake of the IEA report's dismal findings, the agreements in Durban stand as a very poor compromise. Instead of immediately beginning the work of levelling and bending back the global emissions curve, well ahead of 2020, the negotiation process will instead continue until 2015 in order, if successful, to have a binding treaty in place by 2020. In practice this means that the necessary transformation of the infrastructure and our production and consumption systems, especially energy, will in all likelihood be postponed for at least a decade.

Yet, from the point of view of the realist whose expectations were low, Durban was after all a step forward. At both Copenhagen and Cancun, the result was a big question mark for global co-operation. There the emphasis was on voluntary action at country level. This is of course extremely important, but completely inadequate if the world is to have a chance to avoid dangerous climate change.

The difference, compared to Copenhagen and Cancún, was that Durban was able to obtain agreement among world governments that the main objective for negotiations in the future should be a legally binding treaty. A starting point as late as 2020 is deeply worrying, but the deadlock has been broken. Countries like the United States, China and India, which had so far refused to discuss binding agreements, did agree to the principle, which must be seen as a breakthrough. Whether the US Senate ultimately succeeds in mobilizing the 67 senators needed to approve such an agreement remains uncertain. Similarly, there is no guarantee that countries like China, India, Brazil or South Africa will join. Everything depends, of course, on the content of such a future agreement, not least how the wording in the climate convention of 'common but differentiated responsibilities' will be interpreted. The emerging economies certainly recognize that the world needs a common agreement on climate change, but they are adamant on the principle that the responsibility must be tailored both to the historical emissions of countries and their financial ability.

One success in Durban was that the Kyoto Protocol was kept alive and will now remain in force until either 2017 or 2020. The value of this is unclear, however, because so few countries feel bound by the Protocol. The situation was not helped by Canada dropping out of the Kyoto Protocol just days after the Durban meeting on the pretext that the country cannot afford to live up to its commitments. Canada's decision was extremely provocative, especially because the main reason for it was the country's decision on a large-scale exploitation of the deposits in the oil sands. Extraction of oil from these leads to substantially higher CO_2 emissions than the extraction of crude oil, and will thus make the climate change effort all the more difficult.

In Durban the new Green Climate Fund was formally established, with the aimof supporting investment in measures for mitigation and adaptation in developing countries. The fund, which will have a capital base of at least $100 billion, has so far only received pledges of support from a few countries, among them South Korea, Denmark and Germany.

Overall then, Durban took a few steps in the right direction. But agreement is fragile. Consensus was reached in the last trembling minutes of negotiations. The agreement was driven through by a coalition of the European Union, the world's poorest countries (the LDC group) and the small, low-lying island nations ('small island states'). The US, Brazil, India, China and South Africa resisted until the very end and yielded only under heavy pressure. Above all, India was pressed extremely hard to agree to a negotiating track whose main purpose is to 'force' all countries into commitments for emission reduction. The question remains how resilient the agreement from Durban will be during the difficult economic situation now being experienced by many countries, in which the main priority seems to be to stimulate economic growth at any cost. In such a situation it is very likely that climate measures will be incorrectly seen as an obstacle and therefore given a lower priority.

Our conclusion is that Durban confirms the increasing divide between what science shows needs to be done and what politics thinks is possible to do. To launch a global climate deal only after 2020 is of course irresponsible, given the risk panorama conveyed by science. At the same time, we now have a global straw at which to grasp. If combined with regional and national measures, alongside the UN process. then progress could be made. We can only hope that technology breakthroughs, in combination with effective policy measures in individual nations, will help pave the way for more concerted action.

Experiences from the recent conferences clearly indicate that efforts to stabilize the climate system must be significantly broadened. The current strategy, with a 'top-down' process that implies a binding agreement for every country, must be complemented by other actions that are more 'bottom-up', i.e., measures that can be initiated at national level and eventually lead to a real reduction of greenhouse gas emissions. The challenge will be to use the fragile agreement in Durban as a stepping-stone to a global climate treaty, and – parallel to that – to do everything possible to accelerate the bottom-up work towards a low carbon economy in a variety of countries. In fact there are already quite a number of positive examples, both in terms of technology developments and policy measures, that are starting to bend the curve in terms of carbon emissions. In later chapters we will describe many of these examples.

In addition, there are many actions that governments can consider that, although not directly motivated by climate change concerns, would nevertheless benefit climate change mitigation. Such actions make sense even if the threat of climate change should prove to be much less serious than science tells us. In the US such actions are referred to as 'no regrets policies'. One obvious example is efforts to enhance energy security. In most countries measures to reduce energy dependence will consist of major investment in energy efficiency and the development of alternative energy –policies that would also contribute to the reduction of CO_2 emissions.

The many health and environmental problems directly linked to the burning of fossil fuels are another type of 'no regrets policy' and an important argument for bringing about a reduction in their use. Air pollution from tens of thousands of coal plants around the world and the exhaust from more than 700 million cars imposes clear dangers to human health and the environment. A study in 2005 by the US Science Foundation estimated that the health-related costs alone in the US from air pollution from coal and car traffic added up to over 120 billion dollars per year. Studies in other regions have come to similar conclusions. The harmful health effects of coal use in China have been estimated in various studies to exceed 5 per cent of its GDP.

We could easily suggest other instances of a 'no-regrets policy'. But the examples already highlighted are more than enough to show that the UN climate negotiations could – and should – be supplemented by other proactive measures. In the end, the kind of efforts proposed here could contribute a great deal to the lowering of greenhouse gases. As long as an international agreement may at best not become a reality until 2020, other avenues need to be explored as much as possible.

5 Respect the planetary boundaries

> We travel together, passengers on a little space ship, dependent on its vulnerable reserves of air and soil; all committed for our safety to its security and peace; preserved from annihilation only by the care, the work and, I will say, the love we give our fragile craft.
>
> Adlai E. Stevenson, 1965

A primary purpose of this book is to increase understanding of how natural resources (such as minerals and water), biophysical processes (climate system) and the living ecosystems (such as a savanna or wetlands), which we refer to collectively as natural systems, function and interact, as well as contribute to the very basis of our livelihoods and welfare.

The relationship between the climate and the ecosystems is a complex one. A warmer and less stable climate system is a threat to many ecosystems and to biodiversity. At the same time, both marine and terrestrial ecosystems constitute important components of the climate system. The systems interact closely. The conclusion is clear: first, the issues of climate, ecosystems, natural resources and economic growth cannot be treated separately. They are closely interlinked and must be dealt with as a whole. Second, the climate crisis can only be resolved through a simultaneous reduction of greenhouse gas emissions and a far more sustainable management of global ecosystems.

There are already alternatives to oil, gas and coal that make it possible for us to gradually reduce carbon dioxide emissions. The costs of various forms of renewable energy, particularly solar, are falling rapidly. With the right kind of support mechanisms, a transition to a fossil-free energy system is both possible and desirable. It will take diligence for several decades, but it can be done.

When it comes to the protection and regeneration of the services provided to us by forests, farmland, fisheries, biodiversity and fresh water resources, the challenge is far more difficult. The continued rapid growth of both populations and economies around the world makes the task extremely difficult. The pressure on natural systems is constantly intensifying and it requires a radical rethink of our approach to the way the economy is organized to prevent a further rapid erosion of many of the most important ecosystems.

Few people think about it, but we have now reached a point in our development where the influence of human activity has so altered the world that we may have entered a new geological age, the Anthropocene. The atmosphere is just one of several interacting systems on Earth that are exposed to the negative impact of humans. Life on Earth depends on an intimate interaction between the troposphere (the lower layer of air around the Earth), the stratosphere (the upper atmosphere with its protective ozone layer), the biosphere (the living part of the Earth and its land-and water-based ecosystem), the geosphere (the solid part of the Earth) and the cryosphere (the large temperature-regulating ice biotopes).

The evidence is now clear. It is not only greenhouse gases, with their impact on climate, – that have shown an accelerating and negative trend over the past fifty years. The same curve of development, which is often likened to the blade of a hockey stick, also characterizes most natural systems. As expressed by Will Steffen, the Australian researcher: 'The time period after World War II can be described as the great acceleration.' In this short period of time, the pressures on key ecosystems have increased exponentially. Key indicators of the planet's state are higher levels of carbon dioxide in the atmosphere; large dead zones in coastal areas caused by phosphorus extraction and fertilizer production; melting sea ice, polar ice sheets and Arctic permafrost; rising sea levels and ocean acidification; biodiversity loss; land use changes; and growing consumption of freshwater supplies and energy by a growing global population in which billions of people still lack even the most basic elements of well-being.

Some disturbances in the environment, such as emissions to air and water, can be observed directly. Others, such as the loss of biodiversity and soil degradation, build up over time. Human impact can be expressed in several ways. A simple starting point is the concept of the ecological footprint. This concept, launched in the 1990s, is an attempt to explain the proportion of the biologically productive area that a given population consumes in order to meet its need for raw materials and to take care of its wastes. Humanity's combined footprint has increased rapidly, especially since World War II. The world's population is growing. Its economies are growing. The only problem is that the Earth is not growing. The only resource that is continuously added is solar energy and we can certainly make far better use of it than we do today. But for most other resources there is a limit to how much people can take out. And this we cannot continue to ignore.

Humanity is facing an unprecedented challenge. Until recently, we relied upon the myth that the Earth was infinitely large and that it was not within human capacity to disrupt its life-sustaining processes. But we find more and more evidence to the contrary. Nobel Laureate Paul Crutzen, whose research helped to identify threats to the ozone layer and protection against ultraviolet radiation, has described this development as a new geological era – the Anthropocene – in which humans are the largest geological force on Earth. This is an astonishing view, suggesting that the impact on the Earth as a whole of seven billion people and our consumption patterns is stronger than the natural biophysical and geological processes.

A typical argument often heard in the climate change debate: 'It is hubris to believe that humans in any way have the potential to influence climate.' But that is exactly what happens to the atmosphere through our emissions of greenhouse gases. The same applies to other important natural systems on Earth. Greater awareness of these facts ought to lead to an awakening among the general public, companies and, not least, politicians.

The interaction between the atmosphere and biosphere

Awareness of the risks of climate change is reasonably large today. But understanding of the interactions between the atmosphere and the biosphere and the risks of deforestation, overfishing of the oceans, loss of agricultural land, overuse of fresh water and biodiversity loss is much more limited. This lack of awareness is particularly worrisome in the present precarious situation. People need to realize that the geological phase in which human beings have lived for the past ten thousand years – the Holocene –has provided a stable and, for humans, very favourable state in Earth's history. Without the stable climate conditions that have prevailed during the Holocene, the development of today's modern society would never have been possible. People also need to be aware that ecosystems and their services to human beings, such as both the regulation of the climate system and the buffering of our impact on the climate, the production of food, clean water and clean air, pollinated plants and the formation of topsoil, constitute the very basis of human welfare and social and economic development. If ecosystems fail, the foundation for humanity's sustenance, and thus the entire economy, will be jeopardised.

The Earth is a complex and self-regulating system with an inherent resilience – a resistant force – to meet different types of disturbance. This resilience is maintained through a complex interplay between the atmosphere, oceans and terrestrial ecosystems. As these systems are subjected to negative influences caused by humans, the resistance also changes when confronted by various shocks such as changes in the climate. The cumulative impact of human emissions of greenhouse gases is therefore determined, not only by the level of emissions, but also by the way the biological systems on Earth have evolved and respond to human influence. We need to acknowledge the risk of surprises, tipping points, or threshold effects. Both climate and ecosystems are variable systems that are characteristically nonlinear. An abundance of research underlines the risk of various biological systems on Earth responding to a warmer climate by rapid and probably irreversible changes. Examples of such systems are the Arctic, the

Greenland ice sheet, monsoon rains, and the great rain forest systems in the Amazon and the Congo. These systems risk crossing thresholds, leading to runaway climate change, drastically decreased food production, and so on.

Holocene: a desirable state

One important reason for the growing concern over climate and our environmental predicament is the progress made in paleoclimatological research. This refers to research on the state of the Earth during historically long periods of time. The figure below shows the conditions for life on Earth during the last hundred thousand years, illustrated by calculations of the variation in air temperature in the northern hemisphere. The last hundred thousand years are particularly interesting for us humans, as they represent about half of the time we have existed on Earth as a modern species.

As we can see, most of the period was a very turbulent journey in and out of extreme temperature variations. Research indicates that humans left Africa about eighty thousand years ago during a cold period when large parts of Africa were subjected to drought. Humans reached Australia around sixty thousand years ago and, through Asia, reached Europe about twenty thousand years later. The primary cause of human migrations may have been the difficult climatic conditions.

The latest warm interglacial period began about ten thousand years ago. This has turned out to be an extraordinarily stable period in Earth's history. After only a few thousand years in this geological phase – called the Holocene – humans invented and developed agriculture. People settled down, tamed animals, cultivated plants and started the journey of civilization as we know it. From being a total population of a few million hunters and gatherers for more than two hundred thousand years, different cultures then succeeded each other during Holocene: Mesopotamia, Pharaonic Egypt, Mayan culture, Ancient Greece, the Roman Empire, China's great period, early Islam, African civilizations, the Renaissance and, most recently, the industrial society.

The population increased century by century, but very slowly – about 0.1 per cent per year. By 1820 world population had reached the first billion. Then the population began to increase rapidly, thanks to the combination of better diet and hygiene. Two billion was reached in 1928, three billion in 1960 and six billion in 2000. Now in 2012 the level has reached seven billion. How this development progresses depends on a number of factors to which this book will return. But there are many indications that the population on Earth will be between nine and ten billion by 2050.

The rapid rise in both population and economic growth would never have been possible without the stable geological characteristics of the Holocene. It is no exaggeration to say that conditions in this period have represented an ideal state for human beings. As a species we managed and survived for a very long period before the Holocene, but then it was a very small population who lived in very difficult circumstances.

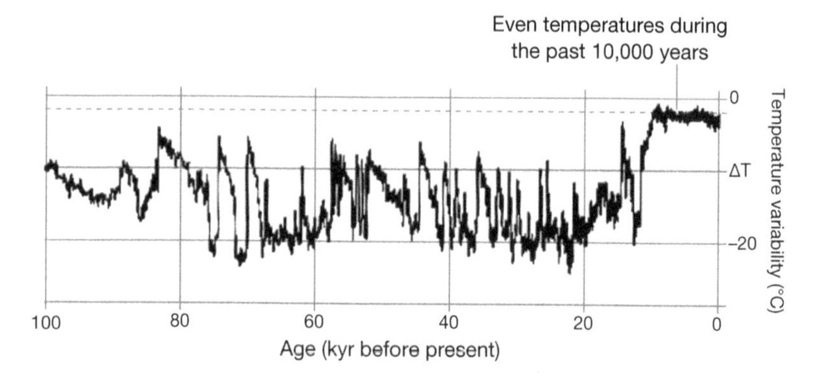

Figure 5.1 Temperature curve based on data from the Arctic, which exhibits greater temperature fluctuations than the Earth in general. When the Earth goes in and out of ice ages the Arctic shows oscillations of nearly 20 °C, while for the Earth in general the temperature change is about 5 °C. Therefore it is not surprising that the Arctic is today warming up twice as fast as the rest of the world.

Against this background, we have good reasons to do everything we can to preserve the general conditions for life and development that the Holocene offers. But in reality we do just the opposite. We expose the soil to enormous pressures, both through our impact on climate and the over-exploitation of forests, farmland, fresh water and marine resources.

Even earlier in the Holocene there have been periods when the Earth was under great stress. Examples include the medieval warm period around the year 1000, the Little Ice Age around 1600 and the Pinatubo volcanic eruption in 1991. But each time, after a period of wavering – such as the multi-year drop in temperature after the Pinatubo eruption – the Earth returned to its position of equilibrium. All research indicates that without the threats by humans we would have a good chance of enjoying similar conditions for several millennia to come. The Holocene is therefore our period of grace, providing the ideal conditions for the extraordinary development that human society has undergone. Our wellbeing, welfare and prosperity on Earth are completely dependent on the stability and capacity of the biophysical systems.

Ecosystems are the basis for humanity – and the economy

Even without climate change, we are facing a gigantic challenge in terms of the future development of society. Earth's ecosystems, from glaciers to rain forests, farmland and wetlands, generate functions (such as regulation of climate and water and pollination of a multitude of plants) and services (such as clean water and food) that form the very basis of social and economic development. In 2005 the UN's assessment of ecosystems, the Millennium Ecosystem Assessment (MEA), showed that two-thirds of the most important ecosystems are exploited beyond their capacity. This is an untenable situation. It means that today's citizens are eroding the prospects for their children and grandchildren's welfare. The economy is eating into the natural systems and reducing their ability to deliver services in the future.

The problem is further complicated by climate change. A warmer climate is a threat to many species. Both the IPCC and MEA have estimated how biological diversity will gradually decrease in a warmer world. One effect is that resilience weakens in a situation where we will need the best possible resistance in biological systems in order to balance and buffer the emissions of greenhouse gases that humans generate. Instead, the planet is exhibiting its weakest ecological condition since industrialization began in the late 1700s. Ever since Darwin, science has been absolutely clear about one thing: humans are an integral part of nature and our welfare depends on the functions and services generated by the Earth's ecosystems. This insight has been difficult to disseminate, however. Many economists act as if economic development is independent of the natural systems –as if nature is a constant.

In its report in 2005 the MEA stated that the depletion of the world's ecosystems has never been as rapid as during the last fifty years. At the same time, the MEA emphasized the fundamental role played by ecosystems and the services they provide to the welfare and wellbeing of society. The MEA has been followed up by several key initiatives to try to integrate the values that ecosystems represent into the economic framework both at macro and micro levels. A project launched by the UN Environment Programme (UNEP), The Economics of Ecosystems and Biodiversity (TEEB), is one important example. Through empirical studies and policy analyses, TEEB has provided a basis for the urgent need to give ecosystems and their functions a value both in national accounts (a value that is absent today) and at company level (TEEB's reports in 2009, printed in book for in 2010).

The EU Commission did launch a parallel initiative, Beyond GDP, with the aim of complementing today's national accounts with indicators that would provide a more accurate picture of society's development. French President Sarkozy further expanded the EU's work by establishing a task force on the measurement of welfare and wellbeing, led by Nobel Laureate Joseph Stiglitz. Their work resulted in a report in September 2009: 'Measurement of Economic Performance and Social Progress' (Stiglitz *et al.* 2010). The report highlights the shortcomings of today's national accounts, including the fact that changes in natural capital are completely neglected. One important result from initiatives like TEEB, Beyond GDP and the Stiglitz report is that issues like the valuation of natural capital and biodiversity can no longer be ignored. But we still have a long way to go before appropriate valuation becomes fully integrated into the economic policy frameworks.

An important step was taken in June 2010 at a UN meeting in South Korea. A decision was made to establish an equivalent scientific body to the

IPCC in the field of biodiversity and ecosystem services: The Intergovernmental Platform on Biodiversity and Ecosystem Services (IPBES). The UN General Assembly reaffirmed the decision in the autumn of 2010. Now the work of fostering a new understanding can go forward, so that ecosystem services, from the local pollination of plants to the regulation of the climate on Earth, can become part of the framework of the economy.

The Earth buffers our emissions

A prominent example of Earth's resilience is the way oceans and terrestrial ecosystems have buffered human emissions of CO_2 for the past fifty years. About half of man-induced emissions have been absorbed by the biosphere (Canadell et al. 2007).

Understanding that the Earth is a complex interacting system – a kind of player piano – is in itself a strong call for caution with regard to climate. Future warming will be determined by the strength of the feedback mechanisms on Earth and not just by the greenhouse gases on their own. This, by the way, explains the difficulties experienced by science in determining the more specific increase in the average temperature on Earth at a given increase in the concentration of greenhouse gases.

To date, the Earth has acted as humanity's best friend. By mobilizing the biological systems such as carbon sinks, the temperature increase has been restrained. Now there are signs that both marine and terrestrial ecosystems may not be able to keep absorbing as much CO_2 as before. When the oceans become warmer and more acidic they absorb less CO_2, the uptake of CO_2 by vegetation is reduced, and for some types of vegetation this may trigger the transition from being a carbon sink to a carbon source. Thus the magnitude of climate change depends not only on how successful we are in reducing greenhouse gas emissions, but equally on our ability to manage Earth's ecosystems well.

No one knows with any certainty how long Earth's capacity for resilience with regard to greenhouse gases will last. The real drama lies in the extent to which the Earth's response to human emissions of greenhouse gases will shift, from being negative and cooling to being positive and warming. The realization is growing that various biophysical systems on Earth – from the oceans through local wetlands and lakes to regional savannahs, monsoon systems and the large ice biomes such as Greenland, the Arctic and parts of Antarctica – may be associated with threshold effects. Suddenly a level is passed that triggers sudden and (at least from a human perspective of time) irreversible changes.

The Arctic is an example of an ecosystem where sudden threshold effects appear to be thoroughly realistic. For decades the scientific community has been greatly concerned about the melting sea-ice in the Arctic. Polar regions are far more sensitive to climate change, warming up at least twice as fast as the Earth in general. A contributing factor is that the Arctic ice is exposed to the fallout of various air pollutants, meaning that white surfaces turn darker and therefore absorb more solar energy than before.

There are many indications that a threshold effect in the Arctic may be imminent. No climate scientist had predicted what happened in the summer of 2007, when the extent of summer sea-ice declined rapidly, by nearly 30 per cent in a few months. In one of the IPCC scenarios, the assessment had indeed been made that the Arctic could be ice-free during the summer season within the time frame of 2060-2070. But the very rapid ice-melt in 2007 took everybody by surprise. In the next two summers the melting was certainly less, but the summer sea-ice in 2010 declined nearly as much as in 2007 and the same happened in 2011. We will come back to the specific problems of the Arctic and the rapid melting that is happening there in Chapter 12.

What is happening now before our eyes in the Arctic must be seen as a red warning flag. However, it is a completely different kind of red flag to the one the Russians planted from a submarine at the bottom of the North Pole a few years ago. The Russian's flag was used to stake a claim on the potential oil and gas discoveries, as part of the absurd scramble for fossil fuels that is going on in the Arctic. The incident shows, if anything, how far we are from a global meeting of minds to actually solve the climate problem.

Knowledge of the risks of threshold effects caused by human emissions of greenhouse gases is quickly expanding. The feedback loops that can cause threshold effects are always to be expected in the biosphere. An important synthesis of this problem, with a focus on the large-scale systems in danger of crossing thresholds due to global warming, was presented a few years ago in the American scientific journal *PNAS, Proceedings of the National Academy of Sciences* (Lenton *et al.* 2008; Schellnhuber 2009).

Where are the Earth's boundaries?

So far our assessment of the science has intended to show that stabilization of the climate system in the future is a far more complex issue than just curbing the level of human emissions of greenhouse gases. Both the productivity and resilience of ecosystems are critical factors. The same can be said for probable threshold effects. We find ourselves in a new situation. From being mainly local impacts on air, land and water environmental problems have now become global. A city like Stockholm, for example, has a far cleaner environment today than it had fifty years ago. But that does not mean that the residents of Stockholm can rest on their laurels. Their lifestyles and consumption patterns affect the state of the environment in other parts of the world – including the climate balance – in an increasingly negative way. An example of the closely-knit relationships within the global economy is the finding (according to the Centre for Climate and Environmental Research in Oslo) that half the increase in China's CO_2 emissions between 2002 and 2005 was linked to the export of goods to the US and Europe.

Increasingly, environmental problems have become global, as the final statement at the Planet under Pressure Conference in London in March 2012 recognised:

> In one lifetime our increasingly interconnected and interdependent economic, social, cultural and political systems have come to place pressures on the environment, that may cause fundamental changes in the Earth system and put future welfare and wellbeing at serious risk.

There is strong scientific evidence that human beings, through their increasingly unsustainable production and consumption systems, generate such negative impacts on Earth's systems that the preconditions for human life are put in question. Hence the challenge must be to safeguard Earth's natural processes in order to ensure the wellbeing of both today's people and future generations. The unambiguous message from science is that the conditions that prevailed during the Holocene are the only known conditions for stable human societies.

Planetary boundaries

The question naturally arises, what would be required to remain in the Holocene and thus avoid the possibility of threshold effects on a large scale? To try to respond to this question, a number of leading scientists decided to try to develop a new conceptual framework, the planetary boundaries. This new concept takes its inspiration from a lot of previous research efforts, not least from institutions like the Club of Rome and the Global Footprint Network. The initiative was inspired by work within the Tällberg Foundation, and by its founder, Bo Ekman. Another person who was instrumental in the formulation of the concept was Tariq Banuri, the former director of the Department for Sustainable Development at the United Nations. The importance of identifying ecological boundary conditions for humanity had been a recurring theme in the Tällberg Foundation, and was already raised as a topic at the Tällberg Forum in 2005. Thanks to the conversations within the Foundation, science was stimulated to take a more holistic approach, going beyond the concept of climate boundaries.

The concept of 'planetary boundaries' is quite simple. The task was, on the one hand, to define the biophysical processes that are crucial for a stable development on Earth, and, on the other hand, to determine the risk of threshold effects relative to these processes and identify the key drivers that could lead to them. Based on such an analysis, it was reasoned that it should be possible to define a safe environmental space ('safe operating space') for human development on Earth.

Defining the critical biophysical processes is one thing. Far more difficult is determining the risks of threshold effects such as the concentration of greenhouse gases that threatens to trigger an irreversible melting of the Greenland ice sheet. The method chosen was to define the boundary limits well below the estimated thresholds within each area. By applying the precautionary principle the attempt was made to create a 'safe space' within which the future development of our societies can take place.

Introducing the notion of 'planetary boundaries' will change the prerequisites for how society deals with various environmental and developmental challenges. Instead of focusing all interest on monitoring various environmental impacts such as greenhouse gas emissions and biodiversity loss and making efforts more generally to minimize such impacts, the concept of planetary boundaries provides an opportunity to develop *a game plan for human development on a planet that has limits*. In this game plan a number of different alternatives for development should be possible.

Economic development today is managed as if we are on a straight highway into the future. To use a metaphor, humanity is rushing ahead on this highway like a vehicle with an oversized engine and the headlights turned off and there are no guardrails. By defining the boundaries for human development on the planet, the aim is to turn on the car's headlights (to be able to assess the risks) and to equip the road to the future with guardrails. Such guardrails should be designed to minimize the risk of undesirable changes in the conditions for human development in the future.

The new concept was launched in an article in the scientific journal *Nature* in September 2009, suggesting that human development is dependent primarily on a total of nine biophysical processes (see figure on next page) (Rockström *et al.* 2009a; Rockström *et al.* 2009b). Climate stability is one of the boundaries, but the message was very clear: a stable climate is *but one* of a number of biophysical processes that we need to manage carefully.

The planetary boundaries differ in character. Three of them are truly global in nature: maintaining climate stability, protecting against stratospheric ozone depletion, and the prevention of acidification of the oceans. In addition to these three boundaries, the article in *Nature* points to four critical biophysical processes/systems, also with global dimensions, that regulate the function of biological systems and will thus determine Earth's resilience to future shocks and possible threshold effects. These are the nutrient cycles of nitrogen and phosphorus, the loss of biodiversity, the degradation of land resources and the over-exploitation of freshwater resources.

The article in *Nature* suggests limits for these seven areas, all with the goal of creating a 'safe space' for human development. For the two remaining areas of concern, namely the concentration of pollution from toxic chemicals and aerosol concentration (air pollution by both warming soot particles and cooling particles such as nitrate and sulphate), the boundary values could not yet be determined. More research is needed. However, it is beyond any doubt that human beings must develop detailed strategies to prevent the increasingly negative impacts of both these phenomena.

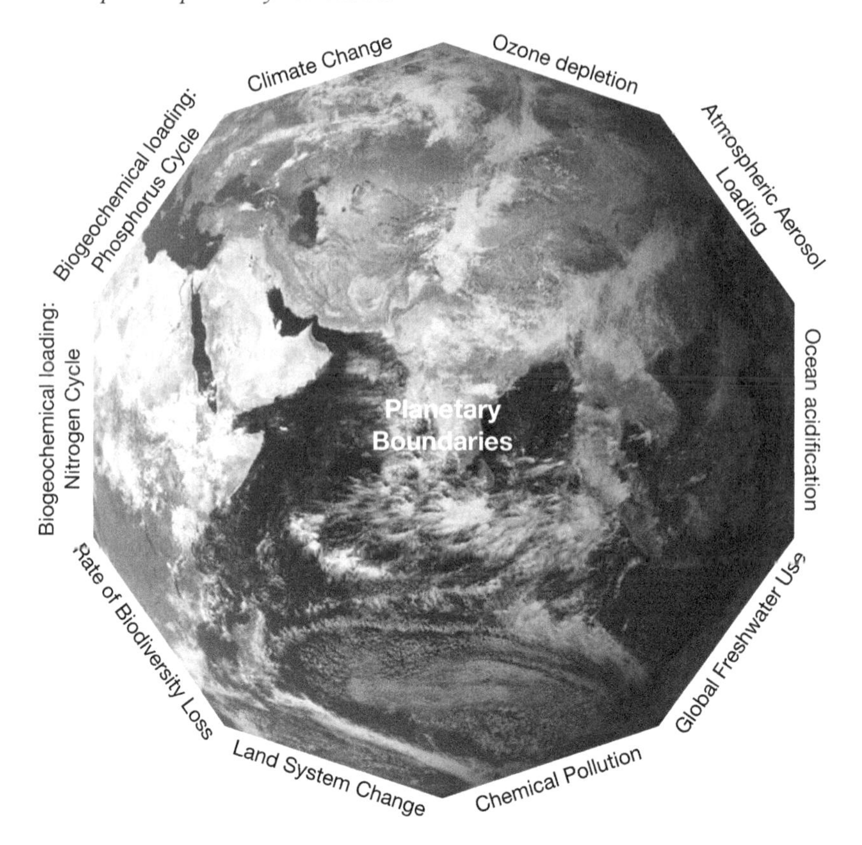

Figure 5.2 Planetary boundaries

The analysis presented in *Nature* suggests that humanity has already exceeded three of the boundary limits proposed as on the safe side of unwanted consequences. These three include climate stability, where the concentration of CO_2 already exceeds 390 ppm CO_2, equivalent to nearly 440 ppm CO_2-e, and where compelling reasons exist for aiming at a significantly lower concentration of greenhouse gases in order to prevent catastrophic climate change.

The second area where the limit value for a safe game plan is exceeded is the loss of biodiversity. Extinction of species is occurring at an alarmingly high rate and is considered to be between one hundred and one thousand times higher than the natural loss of species. This is deeply worrying at a time when we know that the protection of biodiversity goes far beyond the safeguarding of individual species.

The third area where the limit value has been exceeded is the human impact on the global nitrogen cycle. Humanity today adds considerably more nitrogen to the cycle than the natural flows. The major contribution is from the use of fertilisers in agriculture, but nitrogen oxide emissions

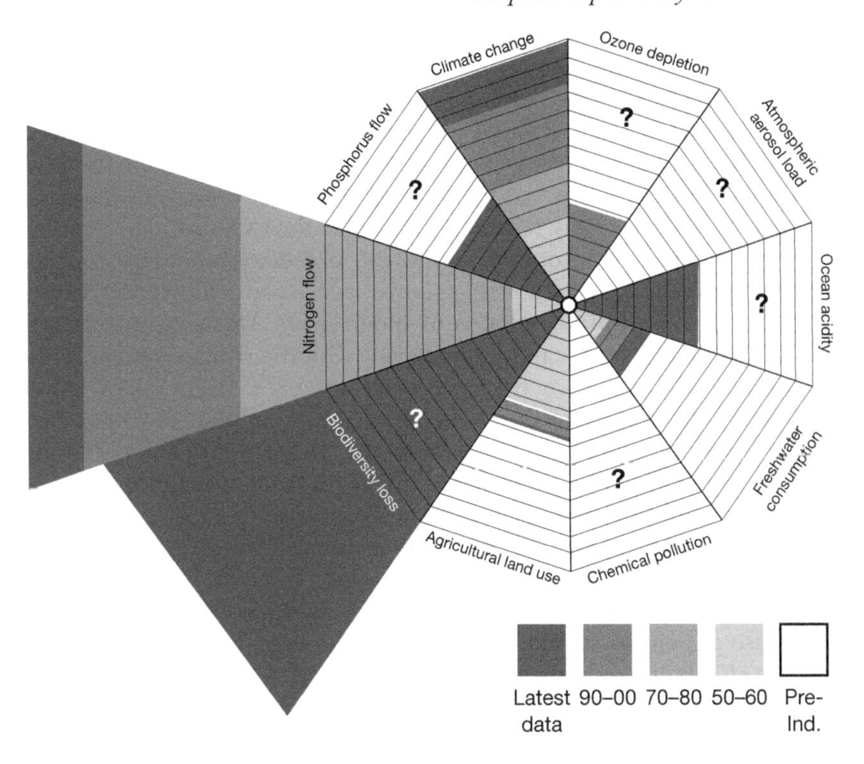

Figure 5.3 Society and the planetary boundaries

from transport also contribute. The adverse effects of all the excess nitrogen are extremely serious, such as water and air pollution and eutrophication (the depletion of oxygen in water).

Interrelated problems

The analysis underlying the definition of the planetary boundaries should first and foremost lead to a fundamental change in the discourse on sustainable development, from a focus on limiting the negative impacts of individual pollutants to defining the safe space for human development based upon the Earth's biophysical capacity. But equally important is the need to formulate a far more proactive climate policy. All the biophysical processes within the concept of planetary boundaries interact. We can almost talk about a Three Musketeers behaviour: one for all and all for one.

A clear example of this is the buffering of CO_2 emissions by the oceans and terrestrial ecosystems. With rising temperatures the oceans become more acidic and their ability to absorb CO_2 is reduced. This increase in acidity reduces the supply of carbonates, which form an important building block for the shells and skeletons of animals, fish and coral formations. Acidification of the oceans, caused by human emissions of fossil fuels, thus pulls the rug out from under marine life. The connection is crystal clear and provides a strong enough argument for swift reductions of CO_2 emissions, regardless of the risks of a warmer and less stable climate.

In addition to the fact that the pH value of the oceans has already dropped significantly, the latest research also shows that the combination of overfishing, eutrophication and the warmer ocean water weakens the coral reefs, reducing their ability to function as sinks for CO_2. So here we have four of the biophysical processes within the planetary boundary concept interacting vigorously: greenhouse gas emissions, ocean acidification, excess nitrogen and phosphorus and loss of biodiversity. This example clearly illustrates the dilemma. Human interference with the climate system is just the trigger for a series of processes that may have dire consequences. Other examples of the close interaction between the different planetary boundary areas are the release of methane into the atmosphere from thawing permafrost in the Siberian tundra, and the death from insect infestation of large areas of forest in the northern US and Canada.

An important conclusion therefore is that climate change must be viewed in a broader context than hitherto. The close interaction between the climate system and many ecosystems makes it impossible to focus on greenhouse gas emissions alone. No one knows exactly where the various threshold effects are and how other biophysical processes will respond. The interaction between the atmosphere and the biosphere is so intimate that climate change mitigation is as much a question of the management of the Earth's ecosystem as the reduction of greenhouse gas emissions.

Here is yet another cause for disappointment in the UN negotiations on climate change. If the oceans, forests and soils gradually lose their capacity to absorb greenhouse gases – going from being carbon sinks to being carbon sources – the consequences will be extremely serious. The only conclusion is to broaden climate policy and bring the management of oceans and terrestrial ecosystems into the picture. Ever greater safety margins are needed in the future to reduce the risk of unpleasant surprises. This is the most important lesson learned from the work on the planetary boundaries.

6 A triply green revolution

> The environment is not just pretty trees and tigers . . . It is literally the entity on which we all subsist, and on which the entire agricultural and industrial development depends.
>
> Anil Agarwal

To feed the Earth's increasing population is almost certainly the biggest challenge we face as a consequence of climate change. The paradox is that agriculture is the sector of the economy that contributes most to climate change: around a third of greenhouse gas emissions originate from agriculture and are therefore directly related to what we eat. At the same time agriculture is the first sector to be hit by climate change. Since the vast majority of the population in low-income countries gain their livelihoods from agriculture, a more unstable climate poses serious threats to both food supply and economic and social development in general.

Nothing less than a second green revolution will be required to improve nutrition for at least one billion chronically undernourished people in the world of today and in addition provide enough food for an estimated increase in the world population of two to three billion people over the next thirty to forty years. The challenge is made all the greater because almost all the population increase will take place in the poorest countries of the world. Recent estimates indicate that food production needs to increase by 70 per cent until 2050 in order to adequately feed a growing world population (IAASTD 2009). This task will be extremely difficult, irrespective of climate change.

In modern times we have already experienced a green revolution, which brought about a doubling in the production of staple cereals such as rice, corn and wheat. It occurred in Asia in the 1960s, the result of a new, modern 'farming package' with refined hybrid seeds, commercial fertilisers, diesel pumps for irrigation, and pesticides. The new farming methods were the basis for a spectacular increase in food production, especially in India. An important factor was the safe supply of water, based on stable climate conditions and good monsoon rains.

Today, humanity faces a challenge of similar dimensions, with the focus now primarily on Africa. But conditions have changed substantially. To begin with, a second green revolution must be environmentally sustainable. The earlier green revolution had a number of negative side-effects, such as falling water tables, eroded soils, extensive chemical pollution from pesticides and nutrient overload from fertilisers. Over time, these adverse effects gradually risk eroding what was achieved.

A green revolution in a changing climate

Climate change makes a second green revolution doubly difficult. In many parts of the world agricultural production is controlled primarily by the availability of water. Compared with countries in the temperate regions of the world, such as Sweden, the difference is great. In our country it is mainly the low temperature and to some extent the lack of light that limit the size of harvests. Various studies estimate that a warmer climate will lead to reduced rainfall in some tropical regions, resulting in reduced production of food. The FAO, for example, has estimated that Africa's harvests may be reduced by 20 per cent as early as 2020, as a result of a warmer climate.

Climate change affects regions differently. For example, in temperate regions an increase in crop yields in the short term is expected, thanks to a warmer and more humid climate. In the medium term, however, yields are likely to fall because of increased disease infestation. Several regions in the world will gain a short-term benefit from 'carbon fertilisation', because increased levels of carbon dioxide (CO_2) in the air actually benefit plants. More CO_2 in the atmosphere will especially benefit cereals such as wheat, rye, oats and barley when grown in temperate climates. Regions expecting lower rainfalls, however, are going to fare badly.

It is striking that the future supply of food seems to be yet another area with profoundly unjust consequences. The countries that have so far been the major cause of climate change tend to be affected only marginally or not at all, at least in the short term. The exceptions are Australia and the south-western United States, which are likely to be hit hard by more extreme weather. In the poorest regions of the world, where contributions to climate change are the least, climate change is expected to hit agriculture badly.

Vital water

The warmer climate is primarily a threat to water supplies. Too much or too little water, at the wrong time. A shortage of ground water as the glaciers melt, prolonged droughts, unusable coastal areas as sea levels rise, extreme weather events such as tornadoes and floods that become more and more powerful. In studying the various estimates of climate change in the future, it is difficult to assess in detail the impact on freshwater availability. But some 'hot spot' regions emerge where climate models clearly predict that water availability will decrease. These include southern Europe and northern Africa, parts of western Africa, southern Africa, southern Australia, the north-eastern parts of Latin America and parts of western North America.

Already we have seen signs of the impact of climate change on weather patterns, such as the decade-long extreme drought in Australia that was interrupted in 2010 by unprecedented floods. As shown by the recent special report on extreme weather events by the IPCC (IPCC 2011), there is growing empirical evidence, despite remaining uncertainties, that rainfall has become more erratic over the past decades. For example, some regions of the world have experienced more intense and longer droughts, in particular southern Europe and West Africa.

The big concern about the impact of climate change on freshwater availability is mainly linked to the increased demand for food in the world. Agriculture is by far the largest water user. Each day, a normal use of water per person in a rich country amounts to a staggering 3000-4000 litres just from the food consumed; this represents roughly 90 per cent of our total water needs. Securing food for one person for a year requires a minimum of 1,300 cubic metres of water. All this is the sum of the water that roots take up through the soil and the water that evaporates from the fields, which is often the main part. When agriculture suffers from water scarcity, society suffers from food scarcity.

Approximately 70 per cent of the water we take from our lakes, rivers and groundwater goes for irrigation. For part of the year about a quarter of the world's great rivers do not reach the sea anymore, as a result of freshwater resources being over-exploited to produce food. Even here humanity is up against limits. This is why research increasingly points to the need to redirect our focus from runoff water or blue water, where we tap river flow and groundwater for irrigation, to green water flows, which in many parts of the world still present a large, untapped potential. Green water consists of the rain that infiltrates soils and forms soil moisture, and that flows back to the atmosphere in the form of evaporation (from soil and canopy surfaces) and transpiration (plant uptake). It is the water that sustains all rain-fed agriculture in the world, practised on approximately 80 per cent of the world's agricultural land. For many farming systems in the world, less than 50 per cent of the total available green water in soils is used productively (Falkenmark and Rockström 2004).

Calculations show that the approximately 7,000 cubic kilometres (km^3) of fresh water that are today used annually for food production will probably have to increase to more than 9,000 km^3 by 2050 in order to feed a world population of nine billion people or more. At the same time, as already mentioned, we know that climate change in some regions will be a major threat to water availability. A far more efficient use of water is therefore an absolute necessity.

Agriculture in the context of the planetary boundaries

Food security is in many ways in a more precarious position now than in the 1960s, when Asia was threatened by mass starvation. Today, agriculture must deliver not only a second green revolution in terms of rapidly increased production but also, as pointed out by Gordon Conway fifteen years ago (Conway 1997), a revolution that is truly green, i.e., environmentally sustainable and, moreover, based on management practices that are adapted to a warmer climate and more resilient in the face of growing risks of shocks. The research at the Stockholm Environment Institute and Stockholm Resilience Centre, supported by many research groups around the world, in fact shows that this new 'doubly green' revolution must in fact be 'triply green', as it must largely depend on the improved use of green water.

In terms of the 'green' in environmentally sustainable agriculture, however, it is no longer enough to 'only' aim for reducing the environmental impact of modern agricultural practices. Agriculture is closely associated with several of the planetary boundaries. It is the world's single largest contributor to climate change and loss of biodiversity. It is the world's single largest consumer of both water and land on Earth. It is also the key driver behind the use of nitrogen and phosphorus, and contributes to chemical pollution. In order to meet the planetary boundaries, the world's agriculture will be specifically required to:

- transform agriculture from being a carbon source to becoming a carbon sink;
- achieve a green revolution in virtually all existing farmland in the world;
- reduce the use of water in many of the world's river basins;
- reduce eutrophication resulting from excess nitrogen and phosphorus;
- drastically reduce the loss of biodiversity.

This is a difficult task that in the future will require a lot of support and backing from governments all over the world.

Agriculture accounts for about one-third of global greenhouse gas emissions, especially if we include deforestation, soil erosion and the entirety of production, including livestock. If deforestation is disregarded, agriculture is estimated to account for about 17 per cent of greenhouse gas emissions. Since we are already in a danger zone, given the concentration of greenhouse gases, measures to transform agriculture cannot wait.

One particular challenge is that the necessary transformation must take place without claiming a lot more land. Having converted nearly 35 per cent of the surface of the Earth to some form of farming practice, agriculture is already the world's largest land user. We have probably come to the end of this strategy and can only use marginally more land to produce food in the future. Earth's ecosystems, excluding agriculture, represent a considerable carbon sink: nearly 25 per cent of anthropogenic CO_2 emissions are absorbed by forests, marshes, wetlands and grasslands. To clear additional forest land to produce food would greatly endanger this sink capacity.

Modern agricultural success depends to a very large extent on the availability of cheap oil. Fuel for tractors and other pieces of equipment, but in addition, as a source of energy to produce fertilisers. Fertiliser production removes more nitrogen from the air – which is then injected into the biosphere – than does the entire natural global nitrogen cycle. While commercial fertilisers contribute to increased harvests they have several downsides: high nitrate runoff into rivers, lakes and oceans and high greenhouse gas emissions – from fertiliser production but, as well, from the rapid increase in livestock production (a significant share of world grain production is used as fodder).

To be able to stabilize the climate, nitrogen and phosphorus leaching must be rapidly reduced. In particular, nitrogen leaching must be reduced dramatically, by about 50 per cent. Reducing use of nitrogen and phosphorus is also of critical importance in order to reduce the risk of catastrophic tipping points in aquatic ecosystems, where overloading of nutrients can induce abrupt regime shifts, e.g., from clear to murky lakes.

Phosphorus is, like oil, a 'fossil' resource and thus limited in supply. Similar to 'peak oil', there is increasing concern about 'peak phosphorus'. The world's major phosphorus resources are mainly concentrated in three countries, China, the US and Western Sahara (controlled by Morocco), causing concern for 'phosphorus wars' in the future. The phosphorus challenge is large and complex, with constraints both in access to the finite rock phosphate resources in the world, and its impacts on ecosystems. In the original analysis of planetary boundaries the concern about phosphorus overuse was primarily the risk of inducing catastrophic tipping points in marine environments, causing major dead zones. However, in a recent critique of the proposed phosphorus boundary (set as the total amount of phosphorus allowed to reach the ocean each year, at ~ 10 million tonnes of phosphorus [Mt P] per year), Steve Carpenter and Elena Bennett rightly point out that leaching of phosphorus in our landscapes generates a lot of damage to ecosystems before it reaches the ocean. Moreover, they show in a robust analysis that aquatic ecosystems on land are more sensitive and subject to the risk of catastrophic tipping points, at much lower rates of phosphorus flows, than what would be needed to induce large dead zones in the marine ecosystems. Therefore they suggest a dual boundary for phosphorus, one for freshwater systems on land and one (the original) for marine systems in the oceans. In so doing, they show that humanity has already transgressed not only the nitrogen boundary but also the phosphorus boundary (Carpenter and Bennett 2011).

Nutrients for the global food supply therefore present a major problem. A particular difficulty is that a 'second green revolution' in tropical regions will require increased use of nitrogen and phosphorus. While European farmers use on average close to 200 kilograms of fertiliser per hectare and per year, the equivalent average in Africa is about 7 kilograms. There is, no doubt, room for redistribution. Modern farming in industrialised countries uses far too much fertiliser. The opposite is the case in Africa, where giving depleted soils a nitrogen and phosphorus boost is absolutely essential.

More problems

The great dilemma that comes with life in the Anthropocene is that there are so many processes in nature that affect us. One serious factor affecting agriculture is the increased concentration of tropospheric ozone. This increase is directly related to our use of fossil fuels. While the stratospheric ozone layer is a protective shield against harmful solar radiation, ground level ozone is a poison that, among other things, reduces crop yields in agriculture. It also represents both a health risk and a powerful greenhouse gas. Research shows that rice harvests in Asia, the world's largest and probably single most important food crop, could fall by 25 per cent as a result of ground-level ozone.

A worrying picture now emerges. Climate research suggests that crop yields in tropical regions could shrink by 25 to 50 per cent over the next fifty years as a result of warming. Research on plants in atmospheric chemistry indicate similar risks due to ozone. Other research reports stress that continued soil erosion could steadily undermine harvest results. What will happen when these three negative factors interact – which of course they do in reality – is anybody's guess. That agricultural systems in some regions may collapse can no longer be excluded, and then we shall suddenly be light years away from the new green revolution we need. We already see indications of this, with reports of collapses in parts of Syria and Iraq as a result of many years of drought combined with lack of soil conservation. There are also reports of great difficulties for farmers in south-eastern Australia, after several years of drought that drained the irrigation reservoirs. Humanity has clearly pushed itself into a corner. It will take extraordinary measures, particularly in agricultural research, for the world to have a chance to meet the food supply needed for nine to ten billion people in the middle of this century.

Opportunities abound

Even if we put climate change aside, the challenge is gigantic; lifting at least one billion people out of hunger today and also providing food for an additional two to three billion people within forty years will not be easy. Our purpose here is not to provide a complete programme of the measures necessary to achieve this goal. Instead, we want to draw attention to some promising paths towards a more sustainable use of land, water and nutrients.

Several recent broad scientific reports point to new ways of producing food in a sustainable manner. An important example is the International Assessment of Agricultural Knowledge, Science and Technology for Development (IAASTD), launched by several UN agencies and the World Bank, and presented in 2008. Another is the UN World Water Development Report, *Water in a Changing World*, published in 2010, which specifically highlights the challenges in securing water supplies for agriculture in a world subject to rapid climate change. An important complementary global study that focuses on solutions, known as the Comprehensive Assessment (CA), was carried out by the CGIAR system and represents a scientific evaluation of different methods for efficient water use in the world's tropical agriculture (CA 2007).

In 2011 the FAO released another important synthesis report on the challenges and opportunities for sustainable intensification of world agriculture (FAO 2011), followed by a forward-looking summary by IDDRI and TERI, *Towards Agricultural Change?*, which highlights the importance of agriculture for sustainable development globally and specifically analyses the opportunities for investment in sustainable agriculture (Jacquet *et al.* 2012).

All of these reports emphasize the need for major investment in agricultural development. At the same time, paradoxically enough, the necessary financing could be difficult to obtain as environmental and climate risks increase and agriculture is thereby perceived as a more risky investment. One complicating factor is that agricultural investment has to be different in the future. An increase in productivity cannot and will not primarily be accomplished in the 'usual' manner, through intensification and the use of more inputs such as fertilisers, soil and water. Instead, two complementary approaches are needed.

The first strategy is to fully evaluate the multi-functionality of agriculture. Farmers don't only produce food and energy. When farming works well, it generates a host of ecosystem services, such as management of open space, preservation of biotopes and 'delivery' of good quality fresh water for downstream users, as well as the potential to sequester carbon and other nutrients in the soil. Production and multi-functionality must be integrated within a single business model and valued – even financially, to allow the necessary investment in research, development and improved agricultural methods.

The second strategy involves an even more integrated scientific approach. The development of new crops, cultivation methods etc., will have to be combined with local 'know-how' and traditional knowledge in order to meet social needs in rapidly changing global and local environments.

Even if the challenges are colossal – the world must increase food production by at least 70 per cent by 2050 to feed a population of nine billion people or more – there is guarded optimism among many scientists that food production can meet the demands in a sustainable way. Evidence of this was summarised, for example, in an important scientific paper published in Nature in late 2011 ('Solutions for a Cultivated Planet', led by Jon Foley of the University of Minnesota with, among others, Johan Rockström as co-author). The paper (Foley *et al.* 2011) presented an overall study of whether the world can support a rapidly growing population while living up to fundamental environmental objectives. The conclusion, based on a global analysis of the gap between actual and potential yield levels in today's agriculture, was that it ought to be possible to provide food in a sustainable way even for a population of nine billion people. This is mainly due to the large unused agricultural potential in many of the world's tropical regions. Added to this picture, of course, is the need to reduce the proportion of food production that is either destroyed on the way to the consumer through lack of storage, processing and transportation or discarded at the consumption stage. The amount of edible food thrown away today in American or European homes is by some estimates close to 30 per cent.

Industrial agriculture must be reformed

There is no doubt that modern agriculture, through both Asia's green revolution and Europe's industrialization, has been a source of considerable social and economic benefit. Modern plant breeding, combined with production systems based on fossil energy (tillage, transportation and production of fertilisers), has enabled a phenomenal increase in productivity – an absolute prerequisite for the provision of affordable food for an increasing world population.

As we have already pointed out, however, a series of cracks in the facade of success are emerging. 'Simplification' of our landscape is one, when originally mixed farming, with a large diversity of plants and animals, is transformed into a monoculture, and also the weakening of the resilience of farming systems to manage disruptions in the form of disease and pests, torrential rains and drought. Modern seeds can produce large harvests, provided water supply is good, but they are often more vulnerable to droughts compared to traditional varieties. Modern plant breeding, biotechnology and genetic modification of crops can produce major improvements (resistance to disease, drought and so on) but they may also increase vulnerability to fluctuations in water availability, the effects of ground-level ozone, or attacks of emerging diseases in a warmer world. If a systems perspective is missing, there is the danger that modern agricultural development will, indeed, solve some problems but at the same time create new ones.

A general lesson from systems research in ecology and agriculture is that biological diversity provides resilience and strength, while monocultures increase vulnerability. The goal must be to nurture agriculture so that it can deliver services while resisting disruptions. This places new demands on agricultural science, which can no longer solve one problem at a time, but rather must resolve several problems simultaneously.

To generate carbon sinks, we should strive to develop perennial grains, i.e. grains that need not be sown each year. Such a breakthrough, on a large scale, would bring about crop systems where soil cultivation is minimized (which requires less oil), the structure of soil carbon is maximized (because ploughing is avoided), water retention in the soils is increased and crop resilience is strengthened significantly (for example, by deeper and stronger roots that can use water more efficiently).

As already stressed, we also need a 'revolution' in the use of water. Over-exploitation of water resources is already a major problem. One approach would be to use precipitation more efficiently. Over 95 per cent of Africa's agriculture is supported by rain. The world's most vulnerable regions in terms of water are first and foremost the savannahs. The opportunity here is that these areas are characterized by excessive water loss, especially through rainwater evaporation. There are many successful examples from all major continents that point to a large, untapped potential to exploit rainfall more efficiently, thereby significantly increasing the production of food. Research shows, for example, that crops in different areas in Kenya can easily be doubled by small-scale protective irrigation and, above all, that food production can be sustained even in years when drought typically wipes out agriculture altogether.

Innovations in water use must be combined with a more sustainable use of the soils. Probably the most important measure is to abandon the plough in favour of different methods of plough-free cultivation. In particular, the use of the plough in the tropics contributes to massive losses of carbon from the soil, as organic material comes into contact with the air and heat too quickly and becomes CO_2. Ploughing also causes major problems in the form of soil erosion and various degrees of plough pans that hamper the access of roots to water.

In addition, there must be a revolution in the management of nutrients. Without the supply of nitrogen, phosphorus and potassium the soil cannot produce higher yields. It is exciting to follow the development of organic/ecological farming, particularly regarding nutrient management. More and more evidence shows that organic farming, even on a large scale, can ensure roughly the same amount of nutrients in crop production as does conventional agriculture using chemical fertilisers. This is achieved by a good balance between crop and livestock production (producing manure) and smart crop rotation with legumes that capture nitrogen from the air and transform this into organic nitrogen in the soil. But these examples are from the cold and wet regions of the world, like Britain and Sweden. The question remains how sustainable these practices are in the long run (for example, the phosphorus supplies in pastures and farmland will be depleted in the end if no phosphorus is applied).

Tropical regions do not have the same amount of biomass, nor the same ability to transfer manure from grazing animals to the fields; neither do they have the same opportunities for large-scale composting and the use of crop rotation that will produce nutrients for the soil. Africa will no doubt need to increase the use of fertilisers for decades to come, to make use of the potential that exists for increased food production. There is no other way to lift the nutrient status in many of the world's tropical soils by a factor of ten, which is what is needed.

The only option

The conclusion is that the world needs a sustainable intensification of food production. The only way to do this and increase world food production by over 50 per cent within 40 years is to increase productivity on existing farmland. We cannot expand land-use for increased food production in the world by continuing to cut down forests, drain wetlands and convert grasslands to croplands. These must be preserved as carbon sinks and sources of ecosystem functions such as the ability to regulate water flows. Sustainable intensification of this magnitude will require technological and biological breakthroughs, new 'management' systems for land, water, food and crops, and new crops.

There is a widespread critical debate in progress on the research and development of biotechnology, including genetically modified crops. Our assessment is that humanity's environmental and food challenges are so great that we must be open to the modern capabilities of biotechnology to produce more resilient and productive crops. Climate change, new patterns of disease, water shortages and scarcity of land mean that in many cases we have to 'expedite' the processing of new crops to face an increasingly uncertain and changing environment. The biological risks – and the ethical aspects – of modern biotechnology must be taken very seriously, however. But they should not, a priori, close the door on new innovations in the effort to secure food supply for the world's population. Like many of the world's most environmentally conscious individuals and organizations, we are concerned about the risk of negative consequences in genetically engineered life forms in nature. At the same time, we are deeply concerned about the world food situation in the long term and this makes it necessary to consider any opportunity to find sustainable and socially responsible practices.

Today, we humans are changing the environmental conditions for crops and plants in the world at a speed that vastly outpaces any normal rate of change. Natural selection processes and conventional plant breeding will have difficulties in adapting crops to the pace of change, which means that it is a responsibility for humanity in the Anthropocene, and in the face of massive increases in food demand, to support state-of-the-art biotech research as one way of meeting the new challenges in productivity, resilience and sustainability facing world agriculture.

In sum, the conclusion is that sustainable agriculture that can feed a world population of nine billion people or more in forty years will require not one but many interacting revolutions: in plant breeding, soil management, water use, nutrient use and landscape management. But as several examples reveal, this task can also yield double and sometimes three-fold gains overall.

7 Energy – the only currency

> To simply add up energy of different values is as wrong as to indicate the cash balance in a number of coins without specifying whether they are one crown coins or five-öre pieces.
>
> Hannes Alfven, Nobel laureate, in *Svenska Dagbladet*, November 18, 1975

Human development has been characterized by a constant quest for new energy sources. Fire made it possible to extract energy from wood to heat homes, but also to melt metals and make ceramics. When humans abandoned the hunter society and settled down almost 10,000 years ago, we learned how to cultivate the soil. Photosynthesis is the very basis of life on Earth. Energy needs in general were satisfied with the help of wood, working animals, wind (for shipping) and human beings' own muscle power. During the initial phase of industrialization, technologies were developed primarily to convert hydropower into mechanical work. This was followed in turn by the use of coal, oil, gas and, towards the end of the 1800s, electricity, which greatly simplified the distribution of energy. With every leap in development – with each new energy source – humans had more energy at their disposal. As a result the standard of living increased, as did the population.

Oil: the secret behind our standard of living

Today it may be difficult to understand what a revolution it meant when oil was discovered as an energy source. When Edwin Drake found an oil well in Oil Creek, Pennsylvania in 1859, it signalled the start of the large-scale use of kerosene and then of a number of other oil products in the US market. Oil proved to contain a high energy content, about four times more per unit of weight than wood. Since oil was also easy to transport and store, as well as being cheap, it quickly became a dominant source of energy.

Hardly any new discovery has had a greater impact on economic and social development than crude oil. Since 1950, oil production has increased more than tenfold. During the same period, world population has grown two and a half times bigger and the world economy has expanded tenfold. Oil currently accounts for just over 35 per cent of commercial energy consumption worldwide. Cheap oil is by far the most important explanation behind the unique and rapid increase in living standards over the last hundred years. True, fossil fuels in the form of coal had been used since the early 1700s, but it was only with the discovery of oil that society's development truly took off. Biomass, muscle and animal power were replaced by oil, and later gas, in every possible activity, from mining and manufacturing to agriculture and transportation.

Oil has had a profound impact on every sector of the economy. In the transport sector the dependence is extremely large: oil accounts for the operation of more than 90 per cent of all cars, boats and aircraft. Agriculture has also become increasingly dependent on oil; calculations in the United States show that every calorie (or joule) of prepared food on the dinner table has needed seven or eight times that amount of fossil energy to produce.

After World War II energy needs, particularly oil-use, increased dramatically. Global energy consumption grew more than threefold between 1949 and 1972. The use of oil grew even more rapidly and soon replaced coal as the dominant energy source. Both the US and Europe went from being self-sufficient coal communities to becoming societies increasingly dependent upon imported oil. Rapidly surging energy usage drove growth. Growth in the economy and the demand for energy followed the same acceleration curves. During certain phases of development the demand for energy even outpaced economic growth. The beginning of a decline in energy intensity in the industrialized countries is a relatively recent phenomenon.

Economic growth over the last hundred years has been accompanied by an almost twentyfold increase in labour productivity. A significant proportion of this increase can be explained by cheap oil. Clever inventions have helped, but we would not have progressed far with the modernization of society without having access to abundant supplies of cheap fossil fuels.

An observation that further illustrates the important role of cheap oil in the economy is that the expansionary phases in the US economy have always occurred during periods of relatively low energy prices. Recessions, however, have been accompanied by, or rather were the result of, higher oil prices.

Energy devours energy

Central to both the supply of energy and the economy at large is the ratio between the energy delivered by a process and the energy used directly and indirectly in that process. The net exchange is reported as EROI, Energy Return on Investment. Crude oil has spoiled us. For much of the 1900s oil production resulted in returns of between 50 and 100 times the invested energy. Gradually, the relationship changed for the worse and oil production now yields less than 20 times. For alternative forms of energy such as ethanol or oil from tar sands, the yields are much lower: for ethanol, produced from maize in the US, the recovery is estimated to be 1.2 to 1; for tar sands in Canada, the yield is estimated to be between 3 to 1 and 5 to 1.

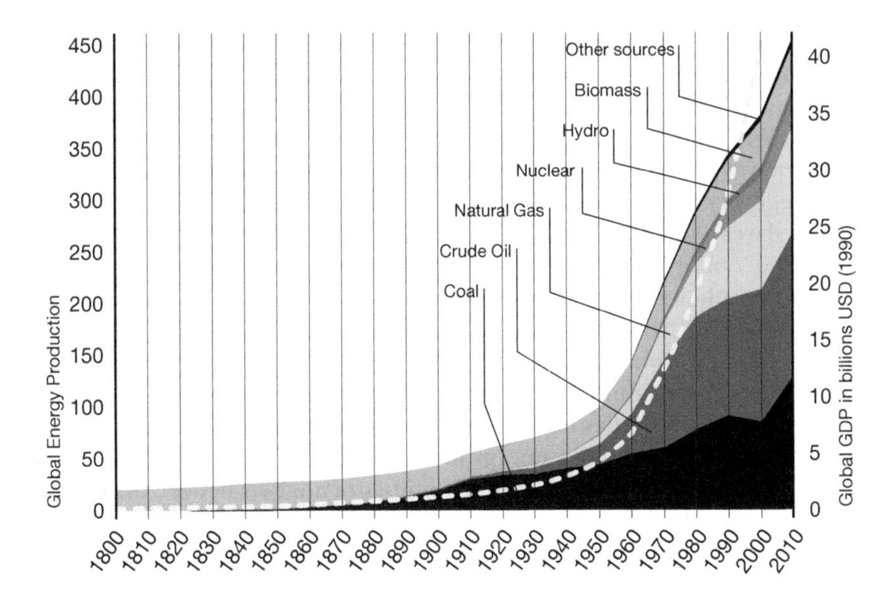

Figure 7.1 Hand in hand
Growth in the global economy and the demand for energy in the world by types of energy. The relationship is almost exactly correlated: more growth requires more energy (research has also documented the reverse relationship, that an increase in energy consumption leads to growth in the economy).

A general assessment is that a net exchange on the order of 5 to 1 is the absolute minimum that a society like ours can accept. Lower yields inevitably lead to economic decline. The reason is that too much of the extracted energy is spent on the process itself and there is not enough left over to drive economic development.

As long as cheap oil flowed, few considered the relationship between the energy invested and the energy received in return. But today, when many scientific reports indicate that we are nearing the point when oil production reaches its peak, the situation is different. The era of cheap oil is over. The central question becomes: Which sources of energy can replace the declining supplies of oil at a reasonable cost and with as large an energy return on investment as possible?

Oil does your job

Oil is a dense energy source. The energy content of one-tenth of a litre of oil is equivalent to the work required to lift a small car to the top of the

Eiffel Tower. Another way to describe the importance that oil, coal and gas have had for development is to express it in terms of human labour. A barrel of crude oil, equal to 159 litres, can accomplish about as much work as the heavy manual labour of twelve people for an entire year – that is, more than 20,000 hours of manual labour. A hard-working person can generate 100 watts of power, perhaps reaching as much as a kilowatt-hour per day. With this in mind, we can calculate how many people – let's call them 'energy slaves' – would be needed to cover our daily needs. For example, every Swede would have the continuous help of more than 100 'energy slaves'. In the US, which is a far less energy-efficient country, the ratio is 200 'energy slaves' per person. With the oil price at $100 a barrel, an American would have to work roughly a quarter of an hour to earn a gallon (four litres) of petrol. That amount of energy is equivalent to roughly 150 hours of manual labour. From this perspective, energy is incredibly cheap, almost free. These comparisons provide an almost eerie sense of what it would mean if oil supplies began to falter and we did not immediately have other sources of high-quality energy to replace it.

As mentioned earlier, a substantial number of analysts believe that 'peak oil' – the point where the total production of crude oil in the world starts to decline – has already been reached or will be reached in the coming years. As demand for oil is expected to continue to increase by several per cent per year, largely as a result of the rapid growth in the emerging economies, the shortfall in the market would quickly amount to several million barrels per day. How such a situation would get resolved, no one knows.

Food is mostly oil

Few sectors have been as strongly affected by cheap oil as agriculture. *After Peak Oil*, a report by the Swedish Royal Agriculture and Forestry Academy in 2006, describes the situation well, discussing the rapid transformation that has occurred in Swedish agriculture since the first half of the 1900s:

> Agricultural holdings have gradually become fewer and larger, more automated and located farther apart. This change involves the entire food chain. Farms, dairies, mills, slaughterhouses, wholesalers, warehouses and storehouses have all become larger and are situated further apart than ever before.

The main driving force behind the change was increasing productivity. Horses and human labour were being replaced by tractors and fossil fuels. Since labour was expensive and oil was cheap, the conversion was extremely fast. The employment rate in Swedish agriculture has gone from nearly 40 per cent in 1930 to less than 1 per cent today. The use of commercial fertilizers, which consume large amounts of energy in their production, and plant protection products (pesticides) has increased tenfold during the century.

The green revolution, based on the use of new seeds, large quantities of fertilizers and pesticides and increased irrigation, meant that global agricultural production increased two-and-a-half times between 1950 and 1984. Without this powerful injection of oil in agriculture, the world's population would have been considerably smaller and the proportion of chronically undernourished people far greater. The US, not surprisingly, is the country that has made itself most dependent on the use of oil in agriculture. Today it takes approximately 1.6 tonnes of oil annually to feed each American. American agriculture therefore lays claim to an estimated 17 per cent of all commercial energy in the United States. This energy breaks down to 31 per cent for fertilizers, 19 per cent for field machines and 16 per cent for transportation and distribution. If the global average is five calories of fossil energy to put a calorie of food on the table, then, as already noted, it is almost double that in the US.

The forgotten energy

Access to modern energy is a given in developed countries. Growth in the economy and energy use has accompanied the modernization of our societies. Knowing this, it is a mystery that such a large proportion of the population in low-income countries are still deprived of access to modern energy. Except for a small number of oil producers and a few countries with large coal reserves, access to modern energy carriers is a distant dream for the majority of the population in developing countries.

More than 1.6 billion people lack electricity. In Africa, 85 per cent of the population are without electricity. In South Asia, the proportion is over 60 per cent. If we look at the energy for cooking and heating, the situation is even bleaker. Nearly 3 billion people rely on solid fuels such as firewood, charcoal, dung or ordinary coal. Cooking with inefficient and poorly ventilated stoves leads to severe health problems: at least 1.6 million people die a premature death each year due to poor indoor air quality. Along with malnutrition, unclean water and unprotected sex, indoor air pollution is the greatest global health risk. Pollution from inefficient stoves also contributes significantly to climate change.

The fundamental importance of the supply of energy has been the subject of a series of studies over the years. A team of researchers from four continents (José Goldemberg from Brazil, Amulya Reddy from India, Bob Williams of the United States and Thomas B. Johansson of Sweden) has produced reams of insightful reports since the mid-1980s on the relationship between energy and poverty. But the response was, for a long time, marginal at best.

Why have not governments and donors, with a few exceptions, given energy issues more attention? Of the nearly $120 billion in total development aid in 2008, barely 7 billion dollars went to the energy sector. This is less than 6 per cent. Even if we include loans from the World Bank, support for the energy sector is a low priority. In Sweden and SIDA's case, the percentage was even lower, fluctuating between 2 and 4 per cent during the past ten years. Aid must satisfy many purposes, yet it is inconceivable that support for energy supplies has received so little attention. The rural poor have been almost completely left in the lurch. One important reason for this is the low purchasing power in rural areas, a phenomenon that also affects access to health care and medicines. To remedy these deficiencies we would need a wisely designed partnership between the public and private sectors. The role of governments would be to mobilize the purchasing power of poor households. Companies would then be able to establish less risky operations in areas where markets do not usually work. Since state treasuries in poor countries are, as a rule, empty, this would be an important area for development assistance, both to improve health conditions and to organize supplies of modern energy.

When the UN General Assembly met in New York in September 2010 a main concern was to evaluate the progress of the Millennium Development Goals (MDGs). Ten years had passed since the Millennium Conference in the autumn of 2000, when the world's heads of governments solemnly agreed to reduce poverty by at least 50 per cent by 2015. On the whole, development in low-income countries looks quite positive. Yet if we exclude China, the goals still remain far off in many countries. One of the main reasons is precisely the glaring deficiency in the supply of energy. As long as people only have firewood and animal dung to meet their energy needs, poverty can never be eradicated. However, when people have access to electricity and modern fuels their lives change radically. Lighting, heating and cooling, together with power for various machines, open up possibilities for everything from young people's education and safe storage of food and medicines to businesses and new jobs.

The MDGs have focused on a number of glaring social gaps and needs, like halving child mortality and infection rates of HIV/AIDS and the proportion of children who do not go to school. What is remarkable is that the MDGs do not include anything specific about strengthening the productive and wealth-generating forces, such as modern energy supplies. Efforts to improve health and education are obvious, but how will the poor countries ever be able to escape poverty unless strong action is simultaneously taken to strengthen entrepreneurship and new jobs? In this context the availability of modern energy is essential. Putting access to modern energy at the centre of the MDGs is the most important thing that could happen to the efforts to realize them. By 2020 we should be cutting in half the number of people living without electricity or forced to cook their food on inefficient stoves. We should equip all schools, hospitals, clinics and municipal buildings with electricity and all the villages with mechanical energy.

Unlike the situation just a decade ago, there are now a large number of renewable energy technologies – modern biomass, wind and solar energy in various forms – which are favourable to many developing countries. There are great possibilities for technological leapfrogging, such as solar power from deserts in China and Africa, wind from the West African coast, biofuels from energy refineries based on sugarcane and second generation feedstock, or electricity from solar cells in poor villages. In Bangladesh alone, in 2010 one million people got their electricity from solar cells. The crux is that the investment cost is usually substantially higher than that for fossil fuels. But in return, the operating cost is low. In addition, investment yields a climate bonus in the form of low CO_2 emissions. This is where the rich countries could have a crucial role to play. A global fund to expand rapidly the supply of renewable electricity and replace inefficient stoves in poor countries would be a powerful way to reduce poverty and to make sure that meeting the energy needs of billions of poor people does not result in a major increase in greenhouse gases.

It is encouraging to note that the UN Secretary General recently made energy access for the poor a top priority. A broad campaign, Sustainable Energy For All, was launched in early 2012 with the aim of providing energy access to all before the year 2030. The campaign is supported by a wide range of stakeholders and represents the first-ever serious attempt to give priority to this critical issue.

Infinite energy demand?

The myth of perpetual growth has been more widespread in the case of energy supply than in most other areas of the economy. For most of the 1900s, forecasts of future energy use pointed straight to the heavens, with little or no regard to the region or country concerned. The cost of energy was low and the basis for most energy planning was the notion that energy demand would continue to grow rapidly. Fossil fuels have had a dominant position in the energy market for almost the entire twentieth century. More than 80 per cent of all commercial energy in the world today comes from oil, coal and gas. The remarkable thing is that the proportion was just as high fifty years ago. A slew of renewable options have certainly evolved, but the rapidly growing overall demand for energy has made the world about as dependent on fossil fuels today as it was before.

The rapidly increasing demand for energy in the postwar period led both the US and most European countries to develop a growing external dependence. For a long time this was taken lightly. It was allowed to happen despite the fact that the regions responsible for most of the supplies of oil and gas were anything but politically stable.

In recent years, however, the perception of energy has changed. Energy conservation is a priority, first in Europe and in recent years in the USA as well. Several factors have played a role. Climate change is an important one. Using energy more efficiently is a key component of any effective climate strategy. Security of supply is another. Europe got a shock when gas supplies from Russia to Ukraine were shut down during a cold January week in 2006. The impact was felt by many EU countries, and it quickly made energy a top priority in the EU.

In the US increasing dependence on imported oil is also seen as a growing burden. From having been self-sufficient in the middle of the 1900s, the US spent more than $400 billion in 2010 buying oil from abroad. If these amounts were used for domestic energy production instead, several million new jobs could be created.

The high import bill and the fact that many of the imports come from very unstable regions (something that recent developments have underscored) was one reason for the large investments – almost a Crash programme – in ethanol production. The basic motive was not to protect the climate, because climate benefits are negligible, but to reduce oil imports. Ethanol is to replace gasoline as a motor fuel. But the road is long. Although numerous ethanol plants have sprouted up, and a significant part of the corn crop goes to its production, ethanol is equivalent to just over 7 per cent of the total consumption of gasoline in the US, which was more than forty billion gallons in 2009. As already mentioned, the energy yield of the process is very low. The impact on food prices is also cause for concern.

How long will oil last?

In recent years, the reserves of oil and gas have come to the forefront. The concept of 'peak oil' is increasingly discussed, representing a radical shift in the debate. Just a few years back 'peak oil' was a marginal discussion among a few experts. The International Energy Agency (IEA), the OECD's expert body on energy, was under the powerful influence of both oil companies and the US government. The mere suggestion that oil could be in short supply was brushed aside. Saudi Arabia, the world's largest producer of oil, has strong objections to the idea that oil could become a scarce resource – objections that seem to be based on a fear that demand will start to decline, that oil demand has 'peaked' This is why Saudi Arabia has no hesitation in demanding compensation in the climate change negotiations for what is called 'non-demand', a perceived consequence of planned climate measures in the OECD countries. This Saudi demand is of course preposterous. Oil is a very valuable resource and it will certainly find a market for a long time to come, regardless of climate policy.

The discussion of 'peak oil' is here to stay. It is as yet barely noticeable in a country like Sweden, but it is growing in scope both in the US and Europe. Research increasingly indicates that the relationship between oil demand and the discovery of new fields is becoming ever more skewed. In addition, investment in new refining capacity is lagging behind. There is thus an obvious risk of a growing gap between supply and demand in the market.

What do we know about oil reserves?

Crude oil has its origin in the sun. It was formed from organic material (plant and animal matter) that for millennia gathered on the sea floor and was covered by huge layers of sediment. High pressure and heat then converted the material into hydrocarbons. The process is ongoing. However, this process is very slow compared to our high consumption, which explains why oil has been termed fossil or non-renewable energy.

Approximately 75 per cent of the crude oil reserves are found in the Middle East and North Africa. Saudi Arabia has by far the largest amount, over 20 per cent. Next are Iran and Iraq with about 10 per cent each. There are approximately 47,000 oil fields in the world, most of them relatively small. Some fields are empty or being emptied, others will soon come into production. A small number of very large fields – the so-called 'giant fields' – account for more than half of global production. The hundred largest fields accounted for 46 per cent of world production in 2007.

The years around 1960 were golden years for the oil industry. Close to 50 billion barrels of crude oil were discovered every year, compared to an annual consumption of only 8 billion barrels. Since then, consumption has grown rapidly and now totals over 30 billion barrels annually. But the discovery of new oil fields has hardly kept pace. More than 80 per cent of all oil consumed today comes from oil fields discovered before 1970. At the same time the volume in existing oil fields is declining fast. A study by the IEA in 2008 showed that the 580 largest oil fields were currently losing an average of 9 per cent of their reserves annually, a rate that can be reduced to between 6 and 7 per cent through investment in so-called 'enhanced recovery'. If no new oil fields begin production, the output from existing oil wells will fall from more than 85 million barrels a day to 30 million barrels by 2030. To compensate for the loss, and to meet the expected increase in demand, new oil fields corresponding in output to those that already exist in Saudi Arabia will have to start operations every three to four years! The question is, how is this going to happen?

As mentioned, a growing number of experts assert that we are now approaching the time when oil production reaches its maximum level: 'peak oil'. An international organization, the Association for the Study of Peak Oil and Gas (ASPO) has been formed to raise awareness of the issues of oil supply. The chairman of ASPO is the Swedish Professor Kjell Aleklett, who leads a prominent research group, Global Energy Systems, at Uppsala University. By looking at how much new oil has been discovered in the last forty years, Aleklett's group made an estimate of the expected new discoveries over the next thirty years. The estimated volume is just over 140 billion barrels of oil. This is double the amount of oil found in the North Sea, for example, but far from the projected need of more than 1,100 billion barrels of oil during this thirty-year period.

While demand for oil is decreasing slightly in most OECD countries, it is increasing rapidly in fast growing economies like China and India. For example, if China adopted the same consumption patterns as South Korea, in fifteen to twenty years' time China alone would account for 70 per cent of all oil demand. Even at a more conservative growth rate, with China doubling its current share of world oil consumption from 10 to 20 per cent, a dramatic increase in world production would be required. China still has a low per capita consumption, but there is no indication that the Chinese will not want to follow the developments taking place in other comparable countries. Korea increased its per capita consumption sixfold in just over twenty years. If there is oil available, the indications are that China will head in much the same direction. Take, for example, the breakneck expansion of its car fleet: sales of new cars rose by 56 per cent during the first half of 2010. If this trend continues, China's consumption of oil will already be at least 20 million barrels a day in 2020. It is against this background that one must see Chinese activity in both Africa and Latin America, aimed at securing long-term access to oil and other commodities.

A dissertation by Frederick Robelius, a member of Aleklett's Global Energy Systems, made a special study of the giant fields, i.e. fields that can produce more than 500 million barrels of oil. As already noted, only about 1 per cent of all oil fields belong to this category, but at the same time they account for more than half of all oil production. Exactly how much oil each field will be able to produce is impossible to calculate, but it is possible to determine a lower and upper limit. The total amount of oil in each field determines how fast extraction decreases. By making different assumptions, based on available information, the extraction can be divided into different scenarios. There is a worst-case scenario and a best case in Robelius' analysis: for the most positive scenario (where recovery from the big fields is maintained at high levels) to be even possible, seven 'giant fields' in Iraq must come into production in the near future. Even in the most optimistic scenario, 'peak oil' would, according to Robelius' analysis, happen no later than 2018.

Aleklett and his team remind us that it is not just a question of finding new oil. There is also the further task of moving from discovery to production. The largest new oil field discovered in the last ten years, the Kashgar field in the Caspian Sea, was initially scheduled to have been in operation in 2005. Today the forecast is that the field will start delivering oil in 2013.

Many warnings about 'peak oil'

When Barak Obama became US president, new opportunities for discussing energy opened up. Now there are references to 'peak oil' in IEA reports and scenarios of extraction of crude oil in the future have gradually been adjusted downwards. In a report in 2005 it was forecast that oil demand in 2030 would amount to 120 million barrels a day. A few years later, the level was adjusted down to 105 million barrels a day. In the World Energy Outlook 2010, the level dropped even further to 98 million barrels per day. But even this level has been considered unrealistically high by many experts. Kjell Aleklett, president of ASPO, has commented that 'we should be glad if oil supply in 2030 reaches up to 70 million barrels a day.'

ASPO naturally has a leading role in reporting and advocacy around the 'peak oil' problem. But recently a number of other organizations have made statements that support ASPO's assessments. The current assessment of the IEA is that 'peak oil' will occur around 2020. In the business world, companies such as Deutsche Bank and Merrill Lynch are making similar projections. A recent report from the insurance company Lloyd's (*Sustainable Energy Security*) challenges businesses to make themselves less dependent on crude oil as fast as possible: 'Prices of $200 per barrel or more are expected soon', which will hit the vast majority of industries hard. In its Spring 2010 report, *The Oil Crunch*, written by a group of business leaders around Virgin founder Richard Branson, the UK Industry Taskforce on Peak Oil and Energy Security (ITPOES) warns of 'peak oil' occurring by 2013.

A report by the American military leadership in April 2010 attracted widespread and warranted attention. It warns that a peak in oil production could occur in 2012. 'We can not rule out a gap in the market between supply and demand of up to 10 million barrels per day in 2015,' was the grim message of the highest-ranking military leadership. In September 2010 a similar document from the German Defence Leadership was leaked. The report and its conclusions were something of a bombshell. In the German study the impact of the supply of crude oil becoming increasingly scarce is discussed in detail:

- Countries with oil will strengthen their position, politically and economically. More and more oil will be traded through political negotiation and agreement, not through deals in the market. The energy sector will become less market-driven, and the consequence will be rationing and administrative decisions of allocation.
- Oil prices will rise very sharply. Since all major sectors are heavily dependent on oil, the economy as a whole will move towards recession and, eventually, collapse.
- Many countries, primarily low-income countries, will have difficulty replacing oil with other fuels. Many economies will fall into crisis, but so will their political systems.

It is highly indicative that it is primarily the armed forces in different countries that strongly emphasize the risks to the supply of oil. While policy in general is decidedly short-term, the leadership in defence and security works from a decidedly long-term agenda. The task for defence policy is first and foremost to assess risk, and the risk panorama today is completely different from that of just a few decades ago. Then, the tension and the arms race between East and West dominated. Today, the main risk analysis is dominated by terrorist threats, environmental threats and climate change, together with shortages and increased competition for vital resources such as water, oil and some metals.

Tar sands, coal for liquids, or shale gas?

If the increasing extraction of crude oil is becoming more difficult, it raises an obvious question: How much of the shortfall can be offset by production from deepwater fields or from so-called unconventional sources such as oil from tar sands, the conversion of coal into fuel, or shale gas ?

Tar sands

The deposits of tar sands are very large, especially in Canada. Production is far from problem-free and no-one knows how large the supply may be. Extraction of oil from tar sands is a completely different technique from drilling for crude oil and uses far more energy. While the net return on energy from the extraction of crude oil today is an average of 15 to 1, the corresponding figure for tar sands is somewhere between 3 to 1 and 5 to 1. Oil from tar sands is thus an expensive and inefficient option from an energy point of view.

Another crucial factor is that the exploitation of tar sands requires large amounts of water and also causes significant damage to nature in the area of extraction. Yet another problem is that the process generates much larger amounts of CO_2 than the extraction of crude oil. According to the US Environmental Protection Agency (EPA) there is an 82 per cent increase in CO_2 emissions from extracting oil out of tar sands compared to crude oil ('from well to wheel'). It is therefore difficult to imagine that these large reserves of tar sands, primarily in Canada, will lead to more than a maximum 4 or 5 million barrels a day in the future. Fuels derived from tar sands in Canada are also not likely to be sold in the EU. The Fuel Quality Directive adopted by the EU sets out progressively more stringent requirements for the CO_2 content of various fuels, which should disqualify tar sands as a source.

Coal to fuel

If we jump to the possibilities of compensating for the reduced supply of crude oil presented by converting coal to fuel, then a similar problem arises. The process uses large amounts of water and the energy spent is significant. Several alternative techniques are possible, however. The experience with one of them in particular, the Fischer-Tropsch process, is well known. The technology, invented in the 1920s, was used on a large scale by the Germans during World War II and was the salvation of the South African apartheid government for many years during the trade boycott.

The question is, how far can the technique be expanded and what quantities of fuel is it possible to produce? There are several limitations. It takes approximately one tonne of coal to produce one barrel of oil. This ratio means that very large volumes of coal must be exploited for this process to have a significant effect on the oil market. Even if as much as 10 per cent of today's coal production were to be exploited, it would only represent a few million barrels of oil a day.

The prospects of replacing crude oil with different types of substitute such as tar sands or fuel from coal looks fine in theory. At the same time the potential is limited by factors related to cost, environmental and climate impact and the inefficient energy conversion involved. Major efforts to exploit tar sands and convert coal to fuel will certainly be made over the next decade. But they will probably only contribute marginally when it comes to replacing the expected loss of crude oil.

Shale gas

Yet another opportunity to replace dwindling crude oil resources would be expanding the extraction of shale gas, i.e. natural gas trapped within shale formations deep under the Earth's crust. Shale gas has become an increasingly important energy source in the US in recent years. Interest in this energy form has spread in other parts of the world as well.

Due primarily to limitations in drilling technology, shale gas was not accessible in the past. However, with the advent of horizontal drilling and hydraulic fracturing, the energy industry has managed to release the gas from shale formations. Some experts predict that shale gas will be a 'game changer', claim that it has made 'peak oil' irrelevant, and refer to huge potential volumes of shale gas. Other experts contend that expectations of future volumes are grossly exaggerated by confusing reserves with resources. A combination of geological realities (shale gas wells are prone to extremely high depletion rates) and environmental concerns (including the risk of methane leaching) will mean that the impact of shale gas on the US energy balance will be marginal.

At present it is difficult to make a balanced assessment. While shale gas no doubt can and will help the US to marginally reduce its import dependency and reduce its reliance on coal for power production, we would strongly advise against making shale gas extraction a priority for US energy policy in the future. Such a move would be equal to a re-carbonization of the US economy in a situation where all our efforts should be focused on reducing our dependence on fossil fuels as rapidly as possible. Given the threat of climate change and the urgent need to reduce carbon emissions, why even consider making shale gas one of the major policy options for the future?

How can we be so poorly prepared?

The discussion so far has shown the fundamental importance of energy supply for a country's development. Dependence on fossil fuels is stunningly large. At the same time we know that this extensive dependence cannot continue. The arguments for a shift are extremely powerful:

- *The climate threat demands it.* According to the latest climate reports, emissions of CO_2 must get down to almost zero by 2050. That in turn means that total global emissions must level off by 2015 and then decline by about 5 per cent per year. Meanwhile we know that emissions have accelerated sharply in recent years.
- *A profusion of environmental and health problems demand it.* Air pollution directly linked to the burning of fossil fuels leads to at least 1.5 million premature deaths each year. In the US alone it is estimated that the additional annual cost, in the form of damage to health from the use of coal and oil, is at least 120 billion dollars (the consequences of climate change are not included).
- *Oil's value demands it.* Oil as a raw material in areas such as chemistry, medicine and food is too valuable simply to burn up.
- *'Peak oil' (and in time 'peak gas') demands it.* Most indications point to scarcity in the near future, primarily for crude oil. The consequences could be very serious, if not disastrous.

What is difficult to understand – no, incomprehensible – is that our preparedness for 'peak oil' is so weak. A shortage in the market would hit most people, including policy makers, like a bolt from the blue. There are no other sources of energy that can quickly replace crude oil in sufficient volumes. We also know that it takes a considerable time to change from one dominant type of energy to another, and as societies we have barely begun the shift. There must be something wrong with an economic system that does not give us warnings much earlier, when the most important resource in our economic and social machinery starts to decline. Without access to high quality energy at affordable prices the economy will move into recession. If one is to believe the study from the German Defence Ministry, the risk of an economic collapse is significant.

For some readers, primarily concerned about climate change, the worry about possible constraints in the market for crude oil may seem strange. Lower oil production means fewer CO_2 emissions, so why bother? The reason is simple: the world economy is so heavily dependent on abundant supplies of oil that any interference would spell trouble. In addition, the risk is obvious that more polluting forms of oil production such as tar sands or liquids from coal – will expand, resulting in higher CO_2 emissions. That is why the oil market must be monitored very carefully and, parallel to that, major efforts be made to speed up the energy transition.

Energy in the long run

Taken in a slightly longer perspective, the energy supply situation looks much better. Although the sun provides about ten thousand times more energy to Earth every day than we use commercially, for a long time the notion was that the sun would only have a marginal impact on energy supplies. The difference in density gave conventional energy sources, such as fossil fuels and nuclear power, a big advantage. The difference in cost also meant a lot. With low prices for oil, given that the users of oil, coal and gas by and large did not pay anything extra for the damage to the environment, health and the climate, it was difficult to see a future for renewable energy. Another factor that worked against renewables – and still does – was the still very high subsidies for fossil energy in many parts of the world. While renewable energy was subsidized by about $60 billion annually, fossil fuels were supported by governments to the tune of more than $400 billion in 2010 (WEO 2011).

In spite of all the barriers, investment in renewable energy is growing fast today. The year 2009 saw something of a trend reversal. For the first time, the total investment in renewable electricity, mainly wind and solar, was greater than investments in conventional electricity. Developments in both solar pV cells and thermal power plants, powered by solar energy, are very promising. Costs have fallen rapidly, far faster than usual for new technologies. Along with developments in wind, wave and modern biomass – and with the addition of geothermal energy in some regions – there is no longer any doubt. Eventually the potential will be there to meet the world's energy demand through renewable energy.

But the transition is by no means easy. There are many obstacles along the way: technical, financial and political, in addition, an often strong opposition from many conventional energy companies. These companies control the energy market today and look with scepticism on the arrival of renewable energy sources and a more decentralized infrastructure in the future.

What does the energy transition require?

Several research studies in the past have tried to calculate what an energy transition would require. In *Peaking of World Oil Production. Impacts, mitigation and risk management* (Hirsch *et al.* 2005) it was judged that it would require at least twenty years of intensive efforts in energy efficiency and alternative energy for us to be able cope with 'peak oil' without severe disruptions. Another study (Marchetti 1977) showed that it would take several decades to replace one primary energy source with another, and that it would take a hundred years for a new energy source to reach 50 per cent market share. What lies ahead is nothing short of a revolution.

Given the challenges we face in terms of both climate change and 'peak oil', two components would form the basis of a successful energy transition:

- radical improvements in energy efficiency, especially in end use;
- massive development of renewable energies and advanced energy systems with CCS (Carbon Capture and Storage) for both fossil fuels and biomass.

As so often in human history, we have responded far too late to the risks of major disruptions in the energy market. If the investment in renewable alternatives had begun in earnest twenty or thirty years ago, the energy transition would have been far easier. Instead, we are now in a situation that demands massive investment in the coming decades, both in efficiency and new energy technologies. Even if this happens, we do not know if we will manage the transition in an orderly fashion.

We know in theory how climate change can be effectively addressed. Most studies give us a respite of five to ten years. Thereafter, total greenhouse gas emissions must begin to decline by 5 to 10 per cent annually. As for 'peak oil' and the conditions to meet such a situation without inflicting a deep crisis in the global economy, the uncertainty is much greater. If the extraction of crude oil begins to decline within the next few years, there is a high risk of serious disruption in the global economy, mainly because we will not have developed the alternatives sufficiently to facilitate a transition.

Today, renewable energy sources represent only a small percentage of the world's energy mix, although they are currently expanding by 20 per cent a year or more. Fossil fuels account for more than 80 per cent, large-scale hydro and nuclear power for about 6 per cent each. The challenge is to go from 2 to 3 per cent renewable energy today to more than 80 per cent during this century (in this calculation the use of traditional biomass in developing countries is not included). Alternatively, expansion of nuclear power could be accelerated, but the consequences, both in terms of cost and from a safety perspective, seem to us to be highly questionable. (It is important to note that while the cost of all renewable energy has been significantly reduced in recent years, the cost of new nuclear is increasing.) The experience gained after Fukushima, furthermore, points to further cost increases as a consequence of new security requirements.

Even in scenarios of rapid expansion of renewable energy, fossil fuels will continue to dominate energy markets for a long time to come. There appear to be two options for curbing carbon emissions: joint use of biomass and fossil fuels – so called co-production – at the same facilities, and deployment of Carbon Capture and Storage (CCS).

CCS is considered by most energy experts to be a key abatement option. It accounts for 18 per cent of emissions savings in the 450 Scenario by IEA in World Energy Outlook 2011. The importance of CCS as a bridging technology is also stressed by the Global Energy Assessment (GEA 2012). Expanding CCS, however, will require reducing its costs, supporting scale-up, assuring carbon storage integrity and environmental compatibility, and securing approval of storage sites.

While agreeing with the importance of CCS, we still have doubts about the future role the technology will play. To make a difference, very large volumes of CO_2 have to be stored. So far very few pilot projects have been established. A key problem is that there is still no agreement about putting a price on carbon emissions, which clearly means that there is very little incentive to develop the technology. Government intervention is crucial, but even so the future of CCS is highly uncertain.

Factor 5 is already here

The decisive factor in the energy transition will be energy efficiency. If it can be substantially enhanced, the task of replacing fossil energy will be much easier. The German scientist Ernst Ulrich von Weizsäcker, in his acclaimed book *Factor 5*, has shown that the the technology is already on the market, across all the key sectors, to reduce energy consumption to one-fifth of today's level (von Weizsacker *et al.* 2010). The transition will take time to implement, but the technologies exist.

Residential and commercial buildings are a particularly interesting area because they consume nearly 40 per cent of today's energy. But passive houses and buildings that can supply energy back to the grid are also being developed. To build in wood, replacing concrete, is another interesting option. The really big challenge is how to make all existing buildings and houses more efficient. Even for existing buildings a lot can be done. One prominent example is the Empire State Building on Manhattan. Through retrofitting, more than 40 per cent of the energy consumption was saved, with a payback time in three years.

Another strong proponent of energy efficiency is Amory Lovins. Amory has revolutionized thinking in many industries in terms of energy use. In a recently published book from his organization, the Rocky Mountain Institute, *Reinventing Fire*, he determines that 'a US economy that has grown by 158 per cent by 2050 could need no oil, no coal, no nuclear energy, and one-third less natural gas – and cost 5 trillion dollars less than business as usual, ignoring all hidden costs'. The main component of this strategy is a more efficient use of energy.

However, there is one catch with regard to energy efficiency measures: the rebound effect, implying that some or most of the savings made will be eaten up over time. Weizsäcker would counteract this by gradually raising taxes on energy so that relative prices remain the same. This latter proposal would certainly be less popular among the general public, but there are few other ways to deal with the fact that increased productivity in both energy and resource use most often leads to an increased demand over time.

Can we deploy the alternatives in time?

In July 2010 the IEA announced an action plan for the world with the goal of both increasing energy security and reduce greenhouse gas emissions (*Energy Technology Perspectives*). The aim of the study was to reduce CO_2 emissions worldwide by 2050 by 50 per cent, compared to 2005. (As already noted, this reduction is not enough to be on the safe side in terms of dangerous climate change.). The 50 per cent reduction target would require a very large investment in new energy technologies and energy efficiency.

The IEA study assumes that investment in the energy sector, for both new production and utilization, would have to increase by nearly a billion dollars a year from today. If this happens, and with the assumptions set out by the IEA, renewable energy would account for 50 per cent of the world's energy production in 2050 compared to 18 per cent today (when including biomass in poor countries). In addition to the rapid expansion of renewable energy, the IEA's action plan requires an equally rapid expansion of nuclear power and the technologies related to the capture and sequestration of CO_2 (CCS), primarily from coal-fired power plants.

Similar studies agree with the IEA study on the need for investment in the energy sector. However, there are differing opinions on the role of nuclear energy. Green Peace International and the European Renewable Energy Council (EREC) presented a study in 2010 in which fossil fuels are replaced entirely by renewable energy by the end of the century. In an acclaimed study from 2009, *Wind, Water and Solar Power for the World*, researchers Mark Jacobson and Mark Delucchi made the assessment that renewable energy, with emphasis on wind, solar and hydropower, could completely replace fossil energy within twenty years (Jacobson and Delucchi 2009). In their study a total of nearly 4 million wind turbines would be erected, with an average output of 5 MW each. This can be seen as a very large number, but we must not forget that more than 70 million cars are produced annually in the world. So technically it would not be difficult to build 4 million wind turbines in 20 years.

Nuclear: a choice, not a requirement

The most recent major energy study, the Global Energy Assessment (GEA), shares many of the same conclusions as the IEA. It analyses a large number of different energy pathways and concludes that the energy transition is possible and can take on many forms. GEA underlines that:

> major changes in energy systems are not likely to occur naturally or automatically due to institutional inertia and the inability of existing organizations to respond effectively to changing conditions. Thus, clear and consistent policy signals are needed to initiate and sustain the transformative changes required to meet the sustainability challenges of the 21st century.

Nuclear expansion is an important component in some of the GEA pathways. However, unlike IEA, GEA sees nuclear as a choice but not a requirement for the necessary energy transition.

In order to meet the 2 degree target, investments in the energy sector must increase by between US$400 and 900 billion per year compared to today. Out of this total, between US$300 and 500 billion must be allocated in support of demand side investment, i.e. energy efficiency. For scenarios with maximum renewable penetration, and where low priority is given to nuclear and CCS, global investment in renewables must increase from $160 billion in 2010 to an average of $800 billion per year. This represents a more than fourfold increase and will require strong incentives from governments, such as feed-in tariffs.

EU Roadmap 2050

If we look at the specific ability of Europe to transform its energy system, we can rely upon a number of independent studies. The European Climate Foundation (ECF), with the help of the international consulting firm McKenzie, conducted a study that also extends to 2050. The report, called *Roadmap 2050*, was presented in 2010 and attracted a lot of attention. The starting point was to reduce CO_2 emissions in the EU by between 80 and 95 per cent by 2050. The study's conclusion asserts that a CO_2 reduction of that magnitude is quite feasible to implement. The chief recommendation is that renewable energy should account for at least 80 per cent of electricity production by 2050. A prerequisite for the goal to be reached is that energy efficiency is given high priority. Also important will be putting the right price on CO_2 emissions. The cost of the new technology, as in the IEA study, may be perceived as high, but this is to forget the bonus effect in terms of much lower operating costs over time. Thus for any country deciding upon such a strategy, there would be at least three advantages: it would have much lower emissions of both CO_2 and other pollutants; it would become less dependent on fossil fuels; and it would also have a significantly lower energy bill in the long run.

The good news about all these studies is that they demonstrate beyond any doubt that pursuing an energy transition based on renewable energy and energy efficiency is fully feasible. In addition, they show convincingly that the total cost of energy supply over time would be significantly lower than would be the case with a continued reliance on fossil fuels. Since a strategy based on massive investment in renewable energy and energy efficiency would also provide significant bonus effects in the form of new jobs, it should not be a difficult choice for governments to make.

A phase-out of fossil fuel subsidies

One important requirement for the energy transition to succeed would be the removal of fossil fuel subsidies. In the words of Fatih Birol, chief economist of IEA, when presenting a new IEA study in January 2012:

> Energy markets can be thought of as suffering from appendicitis due to fossil fuel subsidies. They need to be removed for a healthy energy economy. Energy is significantly underpriced in many parts of the world, leading to wasteful consumption, price volatility and fuel smuggling. It's also undermining the competitiveness of renewables.

According to IEA research, in 2010, 37 governments spent $409 billion on artificially lowering the price of fossil fuels. Critics say the subsidies significantly boost oil and gas consumption and disadvantage renewable energy technologies, which received only 66 billion dollars of subsidies in the same year. Fossil fuel subsidies are often claimed to benefit the poor segments of the populations. This argument, however, is refuted in the IEA study. According to IEA, on average only about 15 to 20 per cent of the subsidies actually benefit poor households.

Birol and the IEA said that a phase-out would cut 750m tonnes of CO_2 a year by 2015, potentially rising to 2.6 gigatonnes by 2035. Birol claimed such cuts could provide up to half the emissions reductions needed over the next decade to reach a trajectory that would limit global warming to 2 degrees. 'Fossil fuel subsidies are a hand brake as we drive along the road to a sustainable energy future,' Birol said. We could not agree more.

8 The forgotten issue

> Overpopulation and overconsumption are both central to resolving the planet's environmental problems.
>
> Joseph Chamie

The 1990s marked the decade of major UN conferences: Rio de Janeiro in 1992 on development and environment; Cairo in 1994 on population issues; Copenhagen in 1995 on social development; and Beijing in 1995 on women's issues. These meetings were intended to lay the groundwork for a closer co-operation between the governments of the world on environmental, climate, health, gender and social issues.

The conferences took place at a time when world politics was undergoing considerable changes, with the fall of the Berlin Wall, the collapse of the Soviet Union, financial market deregulation and the establishment of the World Trade Organization. Over a short period these events laid the foundation for the increasingly intertwined global economy that has since evolved.

The UN conferences attracted great interest. Extensive preparations paved the way for a number of policies that had one primary purpose: to give social and environmental values and objectives a stronger position in economic development. Looking back, we can conclude that the results of these efforts have been mixed, or, as the *Human Development Report 2010* puts it:

> The past 20 years have seen significant progress in many areas of human development. Most people today are healthier, live longer, have higher education and better access to goods and services. Even in countries with unfavourable economic conditions, health and education has improved significantly. Progress has also been made in increasing the people's power to select leaders, influence public policy and exchange knowledge. But all is not positive. During these years, gaps have widened – both within and between countries. Our production and consumption has also, increasingly, proved to be unsustainable. Progress has also

varied and the people in some regions such as southern Africa and the former Soviet Union, have experienced periods of decline, particularly as regards health. (UNDP 2010)

The Cairo conference

Of all the major conferences in the 1990s Cairo has ended up as the most ignored and least referred to. Yet the motives and background of the conference were of great importance.

The very rapid population growth during the 1900s, from 2 billion in 1928 to 5.7 billion in 1994, had made it increasingly difficult for many poor countries to improve domestic living standards. When the population of a country increases by 3 to 4 per cent a year, it becomes extremely difficult to cope with expanding services in the form of schools, healthcare and infrastructure. Many regions were further characterized by the growing shortage of both fresh water and arable land. Many experts expressed concern over how natural resources and services from the living ecosystems would suffice in the future.

In the preparations leading up to Cairo, health issues were given special priority. The glaring deficiencies in maternal and child health in many developing countries were highlighted. It was estimated that more than half a million women died annually in pregnancy, almost half of them as a consequence of unsafe abortion. Infant mortality was alarmingly high in many countries.

The Population Conference in Cairo resulted in a broad Action Plan, whose main purpose was to radically improve the situation of women and thereby reduce birth rates. The conference noted that the measures to reduce population growth, reduce poverty, improve welfare and reduce environmental degradation were closely linked and mutually reinforcing. The Action Plan confirmed the strong inverse correlation that exists in a country between birth rates and living standards. The lower the quality of life, the higher the birth rates.

The areas of work that were to be given priority were measures to improve maternal health, increased access to family planning, reducing child mortality and increasing school attendance for girls. These issues were later to become the most central objectives of the UN Millennium Development Goals.

Progress from Cairo

A follow-up to the Cairo Action Plan shows that significant progress has been made. Mortality among young children in developing countries (percentage of children who die before the age of five) has been reduced from more than 10 per cent to 8 per cent. At the same time, birth rates have declined significantly in a relatively large number of countries. Over the years birth rates in the world have declined from an average of almost 5 children per woman in the mid-1950s to 2.6 in 2010. The exceptions are mainly in Africa south of the Sahara and parts of the Arab world. The rapid reduction in birth rates is an important step forward for improving welfare and wellbeing globally. But one should not forget that many of the poorest countries are still lagging far behind, and thus world population will continue to increase for many decades to come.

At present, the growth rate is around 80 million people per year, all of whom should be entitled to good development and decent welfare. Hence, one of the greatest challenges ahead will be not only to provide access to energy and resources to help raise the living standards for the more than three billion people living in abject poverty today, but also to provide for the two to three billion new citizens that will be born during the next forty years. (Think of it as adding the needs of two Chinas!)

More than seventy countries around the world today have a lower birth rate than two children per woman, meaning that their population is expected to decline over time. These include Canada, Australia, Japan and many European countries, but also countries such as Singapore, Hong Kong, South Korea, Russia and Uruguay. China, with its strict policy of no more than one child per family, also belongs to this category. In China, however, the population will continue to increase for decades because of today's very large number of women of childbearing age.

For the world as a whole, a stable or even declining population in the long term is undoubtedly positive, seen from the perspective of lower demand for energy and raw materials and reduced emissions of greenhouse gases. But we should not underestimate the difficulties certain countries will face – and some face already – with an increasingly skewed distribution between the proportion of working-age people and those already retired.

Continuing high fertility rates

In spite of the progress made in many countries on the Cairo Action Plan. there are significant exceptions. Both national governments and donors have been slow to live up to their promises to improve maternal and child health services, expand family planning and improve access to education among young girls. An estimated half a million women, worldwide, still die during childbirth. Hundreds of millions of couples lack access to contraception, a situation that the Catholic Church, in particular, has helped to cement. Although many more children are attending school today than ten years ago, a large gap still remains between boys and girls. In countries such as India, Nepal, Togo, Yemen and Turkey, there are 20 per cent more boys than girls in school. In the poor rural districts in Pakistan, the proportion of girls is less than a quarter.

In most countries in Africa, as well as countries such as Afghanistan, Yemen, Saudi Arabia, Pakistan, East Timor, Papua New Guinea, Guatemala and Bolivia, the number of births per woman is still between four and eight.

The primary cause is poverty, but the general status of women in society plays a major role, and discrimination against women is still a huge problem.

The Human Development Report celebrated its twentieth anniversary in 2010. A recurring theme in the report has been that poverty is not just a matter of low income. Increased per capita income is but one of several important factors when it comes to lifting people out of poverty. Efforts to improve health and education are crucial, as are measures to support entrepreneurship and job creation – such as access to modern energy. Sri Lanka, Cuba, and Kerala in India have given priority to health and education and greatly improved the living conditions of the poorest parts of the population. As a consequence, both the birth rates and mortality among young children have sharply declined. Experience bears out that increased schooling for girls worldwide is the single most important measure to reduce both birth rates and child mortality in poor countries.

Make population part of climate policy

If we consider the size of the world population in the light of climate change, resource constraints and the increasing pressure on our most important ecosystems, it becomes clear that measures to reduce the number of births should be given high priority. Whatever issue we choose – greenhouse gas emissions, the lack of fresh water and energy, or the loss of biodiversity – the larger the population, the more difficult the problems will be to tackle.

Already in the 1980s, Paul Ehrlich introduced a formula to calculate environmental impact: I = P x A x T (Impact = Population x Affluence x Technology). The environmental impact depends on the size of the population, its purchasing power and the technologies that are used. Later, more sophisticated formulas were developed to specifically calculate a given population's impact on climate change. This also takes into account the energy intensity and the share of fossil energy in a country's energy mix.

Thus long-term biophysical sustainability requires both improved technology, offering greater resource efficiency and reduced resource-consumption by the rich, *and* stable or reduced populations. Smaller populations can sustainably consume more resources per person than larger ones, while remaining within the biophysical limits of a finite planet. Indefinite growth being physically impossible, it is certain that population growth will end in any case at some point. This can only happen, either sooner by fewer births or later by increased mortality.

Some people claim that the size of the world population has no importance for sustainability because of the low resource and carbon footprints of the poor. While such an argument may be valid in the short-term perspective – global consumers have until now accounted for by far the greatest amount of pollution and resource depletion – it totally misses the point in the longer term. All people born on this planet have the right to decent living conditions. That is what governments ought to prioritize. From such a perspective it is obvious that the prerequisites for achieving sustainability will be more favourable the sooner the world population stabilizes.

The UN now projects the population for 2050 as between 8.1 and 10.6 billion – a range of 2.5 billion, or the Earth's entire population in 1950. Clearly, sustainable development will be far easier to achieve if the population stabilizes as close to 8.1 billion as possible. The solution comes down to setting priorities and determining the distribution of resources, first and foremost in active strategies for poverty reduction. But it will also depend on how countries that continue to experience high population growth give priority to measures that can help lower fertility rates.

The Cairo Action Plan puts forth many good arguments for empowering women. The most important, of course, is that a reduced birth rate will improve the lives of both women and children – a great value in itself. Despite this, efforts to reduce birth rates have remained very sluggish in many countries. One reason is that donor support for family planning services has decreased significantly in recent years. For example, EU aid for family planning represents only 0.4 per cent of total EU development co-operation. There are currently an estimated 215 million women (and rising) without access to family planning. The cost of meeting this unmet need, an estimated $6–7 billion dollars, is less than the US spends yearly on celebrating Halloween. It seems to us that the Cairo Action Plan needs a fresh start.

There is a unique opportunity to highlight the issue of population growth in the climate negotiations. Countries where the population is still growing rapidly can make valuable contributions to climate change by developing proactive strategies to reduce birth rates and thus achieve lower CO_2 emissions in the long term. There are ample examples of how this can be done. Expansion of reproductive health, including family planning, and increased school attendance among girls would be the two most important steps. Equally important would be to improve access to modern energy, mainly the availability of electricity and the replacement of inefficient stoves. The relationship between access to modern energy and lower birth rates is unequivocal. When people are forced to make do with firewood and animal dung, poverty – and high birth rates – become entrenched. In virtually all countries with high birth rates there are very large gaps in the energy supply.

Under the Climate Convention, it has already been decided to allocate funds to support strategies for adaptation and low carbon technologies in low-income countries. It should not be difficult to extend funding to include measures aimed at reducing population growth and thus the total emissions over time. Simple maths shows that reducing the number of births would result in a significant reduction of greenhouse gas emissions in the future. Emissions per capita vary widely across countries today, but in the long term, it is reasonable to assume that every newly born person accounts for between one and two tonnes of CO_2 per year.

Ashok Khosla, president of Development Alternatives and the Club of Rome, together with his son Karen Khosla, produced an interesting review of the conditions connecting the issue of population growth to climate negotiations. The cost for expanding schooling among young girls is estimated at $2,000 per child. The costs of increasing access to electricity and replacing inefficient stoves can also be estimated at about $2,000 per household (when connected to the central grid; the cost will be significantly lower in decentralized solutions at village level).

If the population of the world were to reach eight billion people by 2050, instead of ten billion, it would mean a reduction in CO_2 emissions per year of two to four billion tonnes, according to the assumption made regarding the quantity of emissions per capita. This would avoid the emission of tens of billions of tonnes of CO_2 by 2050. And for each year thereafter, the total global emissions would be two to four billion tonnes lower. If we estimate the cost of each tonne of CO_2 at thirty dollars tonne – a low figure – the avoided cost would amount to between sixty and a hundred and twenty billion US dollars per year. Compared to the cost of increased school attendance and/or access to modern energy carriers, the benefits would be many times larger.

But cost-benefit calculations such as these are not the most important. The biggest gains from significantly lower birth rates would be the combination of a better quality of life for both women and children and a greater potential for stabilizing the climate. To describe these benefits in monetary terms can never give a fair picture of the importance of a lower population in the long term.

9 The weapon of doubt

> We should refrain from asserting that the planet has warmed or cooled in any given period without immediately pointing out that such theories are based upon data that critics have called into question.
>
> Bill Sammon, managing editor of Fox News, in an internal staff email, December 2009.

One of the reasons for writing this book has been to respond to attacks levelled against climate science. Both the IPCC and individual climate scientists have been challenged on numerous occasions in an unscientific and often aggressive manner. Too often the criticisms have gone unchallenged, putting the public in a difficult situation. Who can you trust? The vast majority of people lack the knowledge to understand the details of climate science. Therefore there is a great need for dependable scientific evidence. When allegations of serious errors are aimed at the IPCC, there is a great risk that confidence in scientists will be shaken.

The attacks on climate science

Criticism of climate science intensified sharply in November 2009, one month before the conference in Copenhagen, in connection with the theft of a large number of emails from East Anglia University in England. The emails, which were posted on the Internet, contained statements that could be interpreted as revealing how climate scientists at the university had tried to cover up and manipulate data within their area of research.

The incident at East Anglia, combined with a couple of faulty wordings in the IPCC report of 2007, led to a veritable barrage of criticism of climate science in various media, primarily in the US and Europe. The criticism became even stronger after the unsuccessful climate conference in Copenhagen in 2009. 'Conspiracy', 'rush job', 'alarmism', 'manipulation' – the criticism was often merciless. It was as if certain media deliberately allowed stories critical of climate research to be published in a misguided desire to 'balance' the debate. The reasoning seemed to be that the IPCC and all those who support the climate panel's findings had had their fair share of attention in the years before Copenhagen. 'Now it was the deniers' turn.' We know from personal experience that when we attempted to respond to the attacks, it was virtually impossible to get media coverage.

Could the same situation have occurred in any other area of scientific research? Can you imagine organizations and individuals without medical expertise being given media exposure to violently attack cancer or brain research, accusing the scientists in these fields of manipulation and deliberate mistakes? But that is exactly what happened in climate science. The vast majority of attacks on the IPCC and climate research have lacked all sense and proportion. Of course the workings of the IPCC should be further developed and improved, and this work is ongoing. But the knowledge base that has been built up is robust. Occasional errors or exaggerations in the reports do not change this.

The demands on science are unreasonable

The attacks on climate research have been depressingly effective in country after country, especially in the US, where critics of climate science have been particularly vocal. The US Senator James Inhofe once famously claimed that 'the threat of catastrophic global warming is the greatest hoax ever perpetrated on the American people'. What is truly worrying today is that the Republican Party at its very core appears to agree with him.

The percentage of the public who perceive climate change as a threat has noticeably diminished in recent years. A contributary factor has been the notion that once research has been presented, any uncertainty in the matter has been dispelled. Thus when a certain research is questioned, it is interpreted by many to mean that the entire core knowledge is uncertain. In this view, scientific research is much like a house of cards. If one detail is questioned, the whole body of knowledge is questionable. But that is not the way scientific research works. The appropriate metaphor for climate change is not a house of cards but a large puzzle. That individual pieces are missing or in doubt is a minor matter. The overall picture still comes together.

All scientific research contains a significant element of questioning and always strives to break new ground. When questioning is taken out of context, not least by those forces that deliberately try to create doubt, the result can be devastating.

A principal strategy used by many climate deniers is to create the impression that scientists are divided. One way to do this is to address issues where there is uncertainty. But such efforts set unreasonably high standards for accuracy in a scientific process where there will always be uncertainty. It is the totality of the evaluation that is important, not the individual parts.

The crucial role of the media

Why haven't scientists been far more active in the debate, responding to all the accusations? This is of course an important question. With a few exceptions, such as Jim Hansen, the late Stephen Schneider, John Schellnhuber, Stefan Ramsdorf, Tim Flannery and Katherine Richardson, most climate scientists have chosen to keep a low profile in the face of criticism. One important reason is that most scientists are not accustomed to the role of communicator. They simply do not consider the dissemination of research findings through the media as their primary task. Today's research is more of a team effort and individual researchers are reluctant to speak out on their own.

Moreover, it is difficult to enter into the infected discussion that has surrounded climate research. It's one thing to be an expert in a scientific field, and quite another to be part of a polemic that is full of invective and harsh attacks, and which the scientists often perceive as both inappropriate and often highly political. Scientists are also reluctant to speak through the media simply because time is too limited for well-reasoned arguments on complex issues, which would include climate research It does not lend itself to one-liners. No wonder many scientists remain silent or keep a low profile.

'Balanced and fair'

The media's contention that 'both sides' in the climate debate needed a hearing is based, wilfully or not, on a fatal misconception. It presupposes the involvement of two equal actors, where 'for the sake of balance' the media is required to give the same airtime to both sides.

Climate change is about science and facts, not ideology. Yet it is seen in some circles, especially in the US, as an ideological issue. But for most people in other parts of the world this is clearly not the way they regard it. Taking a stand on climate change is something completely different from taking a position on tax rates, defence spending or the degree of privatization in education or healthcare. On such issues, in which ideology dominates, it is obvious that the media's role is to provide appropriate room for different opinions. However, regarding issues such as climate change, the media's role is different and far more demanding. Their responsibility is to seek out the facts, interviewing various scientists, trying to establish where the majority of scientists stand, and then reflect all this in their reporting. If this was how journalism was conducted, more than 95 per cent of the reporting on climate change would describe the issue in much the same way as the IPCC. Deniers would receive mention in a footnote, no more. This would reflect the overwhelming support for the central message of the UN climate panel to be found among the preponderance of the world's climate scientists.

A scientific study presented in PNAS (Proceedings of the National Academy of Sciences) in June 2010 confirms the overwhelmingly strong support for the IPCC among climate scientists. The study examined a total of 1,372 climate scientists and their published research. The conclusion is that 97 to 98 per cent of the most active and most cited scientists stand behind the IPCC's principal message of humanity's impact on climate. In spite of this kind of evidence, climate deniers have been given great visibility in the media, particularly after the climate summit in Copenhagen. Most regrettably, the media have helped to reinforce doubts among the public about both climate science and the seriousness of the climate threat.

No one is perfect

Not everything the IPCC produces is perfect. Its reports are extensive – several thousand pages long – and are based on contributions from a large number of sources. During work on the most recent report, the *IPCC Fourth Assessment Report*, published in 2007, more than 90,000 comments were contributed. All of these needed to be reviewed and the facts examined before the report was ready for publication. It would be remarkable if one or two errors or exaggerated claims had not crept into the report.

Criticism of the IPCC is not new. For many years climate sceptics have had their opinions on how the IPCC organizes its work. Criticism has been levelled against the IPCC for not being sufficiently independent and claims have been made that the panel is controlled by governments. This latter criticism is way off target. Governments are certainly involved in the review process, but not in ways that compromise the results. The main part of the work is conducted by three different groups among the scientists. The working groups are independently responsible for their reports. The 'Summary for Decision-makers', produced in conjunction with each new assessment and drawn from the three main reports, is determined in consultation between the scientists and government representatives. One can of course discuss this approach, but the benefits are indisputable. By engaging government representatives in the process, it is far easier to spread the message into the corridors of power. Otherwise the obvious risk, as with many other important scientific reports, is that the message will not get through. Politicians work with an abundance of information. It is therefore imperative to ensure the dissemination of important knowledge.

The only risk of undue influence ascertained so far is that governments such as Saudi Arabia who strive to downplay the threat of climate change for political reasons could have a major influence on the margins of error and safety. If the report for policy-makers were biased in any direction, it would be by erring on the side of caution about potential risks and threats, not vice versa. But that is not how climate sceptics perceive the IPCC. Their criticism has been exactly the opposite.

Responding to deniers

When criticism is made of the IPCC and climate research the scientific community tends not to respond. Many climate scientists believe that the attacks on the research are so poorly informed that they are not worth a response, or that the arguments have already been dismissed in previous reports. This attitude may be understandable, but it is untenable. Climate change is complicated, and therefore it is easy for simplifications – or blatant errors – to become entrenched among the public. Calling the IPCC into question has at times spread like wildfire in blogs and letters to the editor. Who will put out the fire if not the scientists themselves? Who else has the credibility?

We therefore believe that it is absolutely vital to confront the repeated arguments raised by climate sceptics. The criticism is there and it lives its own life, not least on the Internet. It must be countered. And this is what we are going to do here. The task is by no means easy. The arguments of those who deny or downplay the threat of climate change are far from consistent. On the contrary, the arguments put forward by deniers basically fall into the following five different categories.

Conspiracy theory

Climate scientists are accused of participating in a massive plot in which temperature data and other research data are being manipulated. The aim is said to be to force supranational regulations upon the world that will control everyone's lifestyle and consumption habits. A variation on this argument, primarily in the US, is that environmental and climate organizations are, heart and soul, socialists, 'They are like watermelons – green on the outside and red inside.' Another motive is said to be that scientists want to milk the governments for hefty funding in support of climate research.

These allegations are wildly extravagant. How could anyone successfully corral thousands of climate scientists from around the world into such a conspiracy? As climate scientist Ken Caldeira put it: 'The mere thought that individual scientists would act fraudulently – and consciously assert things they know are false – runs counter to how each scientist acts, if they want to succeed in their work.'

Dubious experts

Climate deniers constantly refer to a slew of scientists who reject the conclusion in the IPCC's work that human emissions of greenhouse gases affect the climate. Closer analysis shows that 97 to 98 per cent of climate scientists stand behind the IPCC. The vast majority of scientists to whom climate deniers refer may be experts in many important areas – but not in climate.

'Cherry picking'

It is a common tactic among deniers to pick out a detail from climate research, question it and then give the impression that the entire scientific foundation rests on shifting sands. It is both dishonest and factually wrong to imply that the entirety of climate science stands or falls with isolated details.

The demands made upon science are unreasonable

The uncertainty that naturally comes with different assertions from climate research, particularly in climate models, is used as an argument against the research. But scientific research always works with uncertainty, regardless of the area of inquiry. Many deniers know this but still use uncertainty as a main argument against climate science and the IPCC.

Inconsistency

Some deniers claim that the climate has not become warmer at all. Still others accept global warming but believe that it is due to natural variations.

Our task here is to analyse and comment on the key arguments made by 'climate deniers'. We are aware that the term 'climate denier' is not appreciated by most of those who have criticized the IPCC. But we cannot find a better comprehensive term. Climate deniers are not a monolithic group. On the contrary. Bit by bit, the differences in opinion are split apart, often leading to a confusing debate.

The cast of players

In our view, there are currently six main categories of actors who make their voices heard on issues related to climate change. They move between two extremes, from the view that we have already caused too much impact and that it is too late to solve problems, to the position that we simply do not have a climate problem.

In the first category there are the scientists and commentators who argue that it is already too late and that it is hubris to believe that humans can turn the clock back and 'save' the planet. These scientists and commentators argue that we have already triggered feedbacks in the planet's biophysical systems that will inevitably mean that the climate will be increasingly unstable by its own amplifying forces. The most famous spokesman of this pessimistic view is James Lovelock, who developed the Gaia theory. Lovelock's ideas have been followed up by a new movement, 'Dark Mountain', which brings together environmentalists, scientists and commentators who argue that we must now adapt to the inevitable catastrophic change in living conditions on Earth.

The next category consists of the scientists and commentators representing a more integrated approach to climate change, known as Earth System

Science and Global Sustainability Research. Here the issue of climate is put into the larger perspective of the environment, with over-exploitation of many ecosystems as a key issue, and how the various problems interact is the focus of study. This group has paid particular attention to the risk of threshold effects and are critical of mainstream climate science for underestimating these risks. This category includes scientists such as Jim Hansen, John Schellnhuber, Will Steffen and Tim Flannery.

The third category is what we call 'the IPCC mainstream'. Here we find the largest number of scholars, commentators, politicians and even many business leaders. Their position is supported by the world's scientific academies and many large companies, as well as by a majority of the world's governments and heads of state. They accept the IPCC's conclusions that climate sensitivity is on average around three degrees of warming for a doubling of the concentration of greenhouse gases. They argue further that we still know too little about how the numerous amplifying feedbacks interact with the planet's other systems to be able to weigh these risks.

The fourth category consists of so-called climate sceptics, people who constructively criticize various elements in climate research. This science-based criticism is essential and a normal part of all research. Different possible explanations are weighed against each other and then objective scientific methodology is allowed to determine what 'truth' is passed on to the next trials. Characteristically, sceptics are open to factual arguments and prepared to accept them.

Then there is a group that we want to call 'the social climate under-estimators'. They are seldom scientists, but rather social commentators of various sorts. They do not have any real objections to the IPCC's position that human emissions of greenhouse gases lead to a change of climate. But they argue that humans have more pressing matters to take care of first. The climate may be changed by humans, but issues such as poverty, water shortages and health problems such as HIV/AIDS and malaria are more important to tackle. In their view, it makes no economic sense to invest in emission reductions. The poster boy for the climate under-estimators has long been Bjørn Lomborg, a Danish statistician and author of *The Skeptical Environmentalist: Measuring the Real State of the World.* Lomborg has recently modified his stance, but it is unclear where he stands on the need for decisive action against greenhouse gas emissions.

Finally, in the last category we find the climate deniers. Here we have the group whose ideas are not based on science; commentators, people and institutions that create uncertainty by unfounded criticism of scientific research. Their specific arguments are examined in detail in a later chapter. It is paradoxical that a limited number of deniers receive such high visibility in the media – and indeed even fill two chapters in this book. The reason is simply that they have been extremely successful in disproportionately influencing the debate in general. In the US their activities undoubtedly contributed to the climate and energy package being stalled in the Senate.

In the process they managed to turn the overwhelming majority of the Republican Party into climate change deniers. It is therefore extremely important to examine the deniers' motives, funding and specific claims. Only by exposing their activities, and the hollowness of their arguments, can we hope for a more objective discussion. Our objective is to demonstrate convincingly that the risk of an increasingly unstable climate is real and requires decisive action – and that the arguments of those who attack and question climate science do not stand up to critical scrutiny.

What drives the deniers?

Before we go into the deniers' arguments in detail, it is important to try to understand what lies behind their often harsh and unforgiving campaign against climate science. Are we dealing with people who are strongly convinced of their cause, burning with the conviction that the truth as they see it must be told? Or are there other, more sinister motives behind their efforts?

The situation is not black or white. It would be wrong to try to judge all the critics from a single template. Taking a sceptical approach to expert opinion in various fields of inquiry is not wrong. The task of research is in large part precisely to question already established truths. Among the whole group of those who hesitate to acknowledge climate change, and humanity's role in it, are many individuals whose attitude is characterized precisely by that of the sceptics. You can reason with them. They listen to arguments. Often they point out areas where there is a need for in-depth knowledge to strengthen the confidence in making decisions. But it is not people with a healthy scepticism who dominate the debate. Instead, there are organizations and groups of individuals who seem to have a single purpose: to discredit the ongoing scientific research. When they are confronted, they normally avoid getting into the substance itself; instead they stubbornly continue to describe the research statements as false, exaggerated or part of a great conspiracy.

In a country like Sweden, knowledge about climate deniers and what drives them is limited. No special research exists, nor do we know of any books on the subject. The only attempt at a survey that we know of was published in the climate magazine *Effekt* in June 2010. The story was interesting but it only managed to scratch the surface. Interviews were conducted with senior representatives of the Stockholm Initiative – a self-proclaimed island of sanity in a climate world gone mad. What seems to unite them is an almost total rejection of climate science, a negative view of the entire environmental movement, an obsession with carbon dioxide and its role in climate change, a belief that the IPCC greatly exaggerates the role of carbon dioxide, and an overall scepticism of supranational institutions and decision-making.

In North America there have been several studies on the activities of the deniers. Many books have been published in recent years. Some prominent examples are *Merchants of Doubt* by Naomi Oreskes and Erik M. Conway (2010); *The Climate War: True Believers, Power Brokers and the Fight to Save the Earth* by Eric Pooley (2010); and *Climate Cover-Up* by James Hoggan (2009). All three books are impressive overviews of the leading climate deniers, who they are, their motives and how they are financed. Pooley's book describes in detail the struggle to get energy and climate legislation through the US Congress, a struggle that has so far been won by those who do not want to take any action; Oreskes, Conway and Hoggan analyse those forces outside the political system that work most actively to discredit climate science and the IPCC's work.

An interesting pattern unfolds. As in other complex issues where science played a central role, such as tobacco and cancer, and acid rain and ozone depletion, the primary objective of climate deniers in the United States has been to discredit climate science in any way they can and give the impression that the scientists as a group are divided. The main strategy is to delay or block policy initiatives on the issue.

Tobacco companies showed the way

This tactic was initiated by the tobacco industry in the 1950s and proved to be highly effective. Although scientists at the beginning of the decade could demonstrate clear links between smoking, lung cancer and a number of other diseases, the industry's tactics managed to prevent action on a political level for several decades.

As early as the autumn 1953 scientists at Sloan-Kettering Institute in New York had published research that showed that rats exposed to tar cigarettes developed severe tumours. The report received considerable media attention and created panic in the tobacco industry. The leaders of the four largest tobacco companies came together and decided to implement a comprehensive propaganda effort in America. The aim would be to question the scientific basis of the relationship between tobacco and cancer. One of America's most successful advertising company, Hill & Knowlton, was hired and a long-term strategy was developed.

As part of the campaign it was decided to engage leading scientists to achieve greater credibility. A special agency was set up, the 'Tobacco Industry Research Committee', charged with supporting research on other risk factors associated with cancer in order to tone down the role of tobacco as a serious health risk. Externally the argument was that companies wanted to make their contribution to the solution of a number of serious health problems in society. Internally the focus was quite different: to try in different ways to hide or water down the knowledge that existed about tobacco's health risks. This would primarily be done by creating uncertainty around health research and its results. As written in a memorandum in 1969 from one of the heads of the tobacco industry, 'Doubt is our product'.

The campaign's success is beyond question. Apart from a decision in the 1960s about restrictions on the advertising of tobacco products, it was not until the year 2000 that Congress seriously addressed the health risks of smoking. A host of lawsuits against tobacco companies was initiated, but without success. One important reason was that companies constantly pumped out information, claiming to be scientifically-based, which stated that there could be numerous causes for cancer, including bad genes, and that it was therefore wrong to single out smoking. Many judges were influenced by this propaganda. It would take until 2006 for an important ruling to be handed down on the issue (US vs. Philip Morris *et al.*) and massive penalties levied against the tobacco industry for concealing the harmful effects of tobacco for decades.

Leading scientists are part of the misinformation

A person who played a central role in the tobacco companies' campaign, and has since done the same in the case of climate science, was Professor Frederick Seitz. Seitz had a long career as a physicist and scientist. He had been deeply involved in the Manhattan Project (the US nuclear weapons programme) and held various senior positions in academia, including as chairman of the US Academy of Sciences.

Towards the end of his career Seitz was asked by tobacco giant R.J. Reynolds Tobacco to set up and lead a research programme totalling 45 million dollars. The aim was to 'defend the product' at a time when research had for many years convincingly shown tobacco's adverse health effects. The programme would seek to identify the factors other than smoking that could potentially have a negative effect on your health, such as genetics, dietary habits, exposure to various air pollutants, the presence of asbestos in the local environment and the individual's own psychological state. In Naomi Oreskes' words, the aim was 'like a magician waving his right hand in order to hide what he is doing with the left'.

A key question is why Seitz accepted the offer from Reynolds. The programme he was appointed to lead was controversial by any standard. Seitz's own explanation was 'that he felt gratitude to Reynolds for the support the company gave during his time as president of Rockefeller University', one of the leading biomedical institutions in the United States. But the most important reason was probably that Seitz had long felt that the research had become increasingly 'irrational' and under left-wing influence. This in turn meant that the scientific community, according to Seitz, did not sufficiently promote traditional American values.

Seitz was already on a collision course with many colleagues by supporting the US war in Vietnam to the very end. Even on matters of defence policy in general, opinions were divided. A majority of the scientists in the United States supported the limitation of armaments by international agreement; Seitz was against this. Instead, he advocated that the United States should strengthen its position of power in the world by developing even more 'superior weapons'. Seitz was a fierce anti-communist, and this was manifested in his unreserved support for virtually everything private industry sought to undertake. Anything that to him smelled of socialism – including a proposal to regulate aspects of industry's activities – was anathema to Seitz.

Seitz early on saw environmentalists as adversaries. He looked upon environmental advocates as 'Luddites', people who distrust progress and want to halt it. Seitz claimed that much of the health damage allegedly caused by industrial activity could be explained instead by the victims having bad genes. All this background shows why it was probably not a problem at all for Seitz to accept the presidency of Reynolds Tobacco's sponsored research programme.

Star Wars then the environment

The reason we specifically discuss Seitz's role is because he became the dean of a small group of highly trusted American scientists who from 1970 onwards were to play a crucial role in forming public opinion in the United States on issues ranging from tobacco's health risks, acidification of forest land and ozone depletion to climate change. In all these matters Seitz and his colleagues acted with great force to defend narrow corporate interests. Whether it was the harmful effects of tobacco, acid rain damage to the forest floor or the adverse impact of fluorocarbons on the ozone layer, Seitz and his colleagues had the same answer: the scientific basis is too weak. In an effort to prevent legislation, they did everything they could to portray the research as fragmented and unreliable. The tactic was, as we have seen, extremely successful when it came to tobacco. The same applied to efforts to delay the legislation against acid rain. Since the 1990s the same tactic has – again with success – been used to delay or block action against greenhouse gas emissions.

At the end of the Cold War, Seitz became a founding member of the George C. Marshall Institute, whose aim was primarily to support President Reagan's initiative to develop a comprehensive defence against missiles: the Strategic Defense Initiative (SDI), or Star Wars as it became known. SDI had met with stiff resistance from many American scientists, and Seitz and a group around him wanted to organize a defence of Star Wars through the Marshall Institute. The group included two other leading physicists, William Nierenberg and Robert Jastrow. Nierenberg had been head of the Scripps Institution of Oceanography and Jastrow was a renowned space scientist. What united Seitz, Jastrow and Nierenberg was that they had all been heavily influenced by the Cold War and were fanatical anti-communists and outspoken hawks on defence. The Marshall Institute was funded by a handful of conservative think tanks, and in the latter part of the 1980s its focus was on Star Wars and the arms race. Jastrow, Seitz and Nierenberg participated extensively in the debate. The most prominent argument was that the Soviet Union sought military superiority in every way and that SDI was therefore essential.

The whole argument behind Star Wars fell apart a few years later when the Berlin Wall came down and the Soviet Union dissolved. Although the Soviet threat was gone and the US 'won' the Cold War, the Marshall Institute continued its activities. The new enemy became the environmental movement.

Climate resistance: a question of ideology

The Marshall Institute is just one of many organizations in the US which are actively working to deceive and confuse both the public and decision makers on climate change. Another important player is the Heartland Institute, which – just like Seitz – had long played a central role in the campaign to hide the harmful effects of tobacco. Other key players include the American Enterprise Institute, the Competitive Enterprise Institute, the Americans for Prosperity Foundation, the Mercatus Foundation, the Heritage Foundation and the Cato Institute. These institutions are in turn financed by a number of businesses and foundations. What unites these organizations are above all two things. First, they are strong advocates of free enterprise and free markets. Community development and public interest are assumed to be served best by giving self-interest the widest possible scope. And secondly, they actively oppose the IPCC and mainstream climate science findings and refuse to accept the conclusion that human emissions of greenhouse gases could have an impact on the climate.

The more one penetrates the arguments of these organizations, the clearer the picture becomes. The pattern that emerges is of an ideological struggle in which the conservative think tanks see any interference with the activities of companies in the form of taxes, regulations and standards as a fundamental attack on free enterprise and freedom. It considers the whole concept of 'sustainable development' as an attempt to put the brakes on progress and thus as a threat to the rights and freedoms of citizens. They continually talk about market solutions. They abhor economic instruments like taxes and fees – or subsidies – and insist on as little political interference as possible. Their motto is thus 'The minimum possible disruption to the economy for the best possible outcomes for the society and its citizens.'

The ideological resistance is often strongly linked to narrow business interests. Energy-intensive businesses annually pump in huge sums to lobby members of Congress. At the same time they also give broad support to various conservative think tanks for their efforts against action on climate change. In 2009 there were more than 2,300 lobbyists registered in the US Congress who had climate change as their principal issue. Often, ideological opposition and specific business interests coincide, as in avoiding CO_2 taxes or emissions trading. But the strongest force among climate deniers has ideological overtones: a fervent belief in limited government. Here is where the climate debate differs between the US and Europe. Even in Europe there is considerable opposition to climate policies, but it is essentially rooted in the concerns of many companies about increased costs and loss of competitiveness.

The ideological struggle on the climate issue has also received strong support from the senior physicist Fred Singer, who was one of the driving forces behind the development of satellites to observe the Earth's surface for environmental and security reasons. Singer was initially involved in environmental issues in a positive way. He wrote articles and books on global environmental issues as early as the 1970s. In a contribution to a report in 1970 on the theme of *Global Effects of Environmental Pollution*, published by the American Association for the Advancement of Science (AAAS), Singer wrote that 'man is now capable of changing the important natural processes on earth and . . . a number of developing problems, such as acidification, the effects of DDT and global warming, show this.'

However, Singer changed sides and has for decades touted environmental measures as too costly and therefore detrimental to business. For the past decade he has been one of the most active among the climate deniers. He has initiated many different efforts, including the so-called Oregon Petition, signed by more than 17,000 academics and researchers, that argued that climate change was wildly exaggerated and based on poor research. (It should be noted that only a few of the scientists who signed the petition had any connection with climate research.)

Big money backs the deniers

Millions of dollars annually is pumped into lobbying the US Congress to oppose legislation on energy and climate change. Individual members of Congress also receive large contributions from the fossil fuel industries. Support for various conservative think tanks is also extensive. To our knowledge, there is no reliable figure of the total monetary support given to climate deniers and their activities in the US. A conservative estimate, however, points to annual contributions of the order of several hundred million dollars.

In March 2010, Greenpeace released a report showing that a relatively anonymous business group, Koch Industries, owned by brothers Charles and David Koch, is by far the largest contributor among the organizations supporting the campaign to discredit climate science. The Koch brothers belong to the billionaires club in the US and have, not surprisingly, large interests in the oil industry. While managing to keep an extremely low profile over the years, their considerable influence is becoming increasingly apparent.

Between 2005 and 2008 alone it has been reported that Koch Industries donated close to 25 million dollars to organizations engaged in campaigns against climate science. By comparison, Exxon Mobile's contribution during the same years, for similar purposes, was approximately 9 million dollars. That the Koch brothers are also major contributors to (some would claim the initiators of) the so-called Tea Party movement confirms the picture of two individuals who are trying in any way possible to strengthen the very political forces in the US that are working against responsible legislation on energy and climate change.

In many ways this makes a mockery of the democratic process upon which America was founded.

10 The greenhouse effect

Climate has undergone major changes in Earth's history. Some of these changes have been sudden and overwhelming, as with the cooling that occurred more than 60 million years ago, leading to the extinction of the great reptiles. The probable cause was that Earth was hit by an asteroid that stirred up large amounts of dust and blocked the sunlight. Major volcanic eruptions have been among the other causes of sudden changes in climate.

The Earth was warmest immediately after the birth of the planet. The atmosphere then contained large amounts of carbon, which meant that some of the energy radiated into the Earth was trapped as heat – what is called the greenhouse effect. As green vegetation evolved and began to use the carbon dioxide (CO_2) as a building material, the greenhouse effect was reduced.

Changes in climate over long periods of time, especially when the Earth oscillates between glacial and temperate conditions, depend on several factors: the movement of continental plates, changes in the Earth's orbit or the tilt of the Earth's axis towards the sun, as well as variations in the strength of radiated energy from the sun. Various feedback mechanisms in nature, such as changes in the distribution of ice and snow on the planet, also have a great impact on changes in climate. Climate is a complex system where many factors are continuously interacting.

The past two to three million years of Earth's history have been characterized by fluctuations between ice ages and warmer periods. The difference between a glacial and temperate condition is like night and day. An ice sheet several kilometres thick covered parts of the northern hemisphere as recently as ten thousand years ago. The prospects for human societies in those latitudes were then nil. Still, the average temperature on Earth was only 4-5 °C lower than today, reflecting the high sensitivity of the climate system: just a few degrees variation in temperature leads to large differences in climatic conditions.

Alteration between ice ages and warmer periods has gone in cycles that last many tens of thousands of years. Driving these cycles above all are the previously mentioned variations in Earth's orbit and axis toward the sun. These are caused in turn by the sun's gravitational pull on the Earth, Venus, Jupiter and the moon. Over time these forces effect large-scale changes in climate, but they also provide an explanation for why we have four seasons. In winter, Sweden and the northern hemisphere generally lean away from the sun and we get a colder climate.

Since the last ice age the Earth has been in an unusually stable period, the Holocene. The average temperature has, in a geological perspective, changed very little during those ten thousand years, thus creating favourable conditions for the development of our societies. During previous large swings in climate – in and out of ice ages – planet Earth could not have supported the large number of people we have today.

Given that the Holocene has provided almost ideal conditions for human societies, the extent to which the growing influence of human beings, both on the climate and ecosystems, will drastically impair the prerequisites for societal development in the long term therefore becomes a key question.

The natural greenhouse effect

As we have noted, climate conditions are controlled, by a number of factors. The all-important one is, of course, solar radiation. The average amount of solar energy that reaches a cross-section of Earth, at the top of the atmosphere, is about 1400 watts per square metre, the so-called solar constant. Some of this radiation will bounce directly back into space, but about 1000 watts per square metre passes through the atmosphere and reaches the part of the land that is currently lit by the sun. Since the sun hits the Earth's surface at different angles at different latitudes – and only half the earth is illuminated at any given time – the average solar energy per unit area is about a quarter of the total, roughly 240 watts per square metre. However, when measuring the heat emitting from the ground after it has been warmed up, it is an average of about 390 watts per square metre – more than 50 per cent larger than the solar energy influx. The explanation is that about 150 watts per square metre of the heat remains in the atmosphere, near the Earth's surface, trapped by greenhouse gases which absorb and re-release the heat. Without the greenhouse effect the present conditions for life on Earth would be lost. The average temperature would be -18 °C, which is about 33 degrees lower than today. The presence of greenhouse gases makes the atmosphere work like a sophisticated greenhouse by retaining a substantial portion of the heat that would otherwise have radiated back into space (an ordinary greenhouse prevents heat loss by closing in the air, while greenhouse gases absorb the energy radiated by Earth and then return it to Earth).

The gases in the atmosphere primarily contributing to the greenhouse effect are water vapour, carbon dioxide, methane, nitrous oxide and chlorofluorocarbons. Water vapour dominates, followed by the next most important, carbon dioxide. Several of the greenhouse gases overlap. For example, water vapour and carbon dioxide to some extent cover the same spectrum of thermal radiation (i.e. take up the same wavelengths or parts of the heat flow), in what is called the electromagnetic spectrum. To calculate the exact contribution of each individual gas to the greenhouse effect is therefore complicated. The answer that scientists normally give is that the specific contribution of CO_2 to the natural greenhouse effect is between 9 and 26 per cent. The contribution of water vapour, in combination with clouds, is estimated at between 66 and 85 per cent (Kiehl and Trenberth 1997; Ramanathan and Coakley 1978).

The conclusion we draw from these studies is that the specific contribution of CO_2 to the natural greenhouse effect can be estimated at around 14 per cent (Clough and Iacono 1995). If we try to translate this figure in terms of its contribution to the heat balance of the Earth's surface, it would represent roughly 20 watts per square metre (14 per cent of 150 watts).

With this in mind, one thing is established beyond any doubt: carbon dioxide contributes substantially to the natural greenhouse effect.

11 What climate deniers do not want to know

We have already noted that climate deniers put forth a long series of arguments against climate research. Many of these are contradictory: for example, 'there is no warming' and 'warming is happening, but it is not caused by man but by natural variations'. In what follows we shall consider a number of the most frequent arguments against climate science and against the understanding that human emissions of greenhouse gases are an essential part of the climate.

Global warming doesn't exist

Let's start with the argument that the climate has become warmer. Here we are basically faced with two claims repeatedly put forward by climate deniers.

Rising temperatures, if they ever existed, stopped in 1998

Our response: The statement is wrong.

2005 and 2010 were the warmest years to date since temperature measurements began. 2007 was the second warmest. Global temperatures in 2011 were the tenth highest on record and higher than any previous year with a La Niná event, which has a relatively cooling effect. Added to this is the fact that 1998 was a so-called El Niño year, a year when the temperature of the Earth was warmer than normal due to exceptional weather conditions in the Pacific. Therefore, to take 1998 as the starting year for comparison is highly questionable. But, as we have shown, even in comparison with 1998 the temperature measurements show that the temperature continued to rise.

An absolutely key question is *how* changes in temperature should be measured. Focusing only on temperature measurements on land or in the atmosphere ignores the accumulating warming of the whole planet. The oceans absorb more than 90 per cent of all the extra warming. A specific issue in connection with the measurement of ocean temperature is that measurements are difficult to make, especially at great depths. The necessary measurement equipment is not in place. However, new research

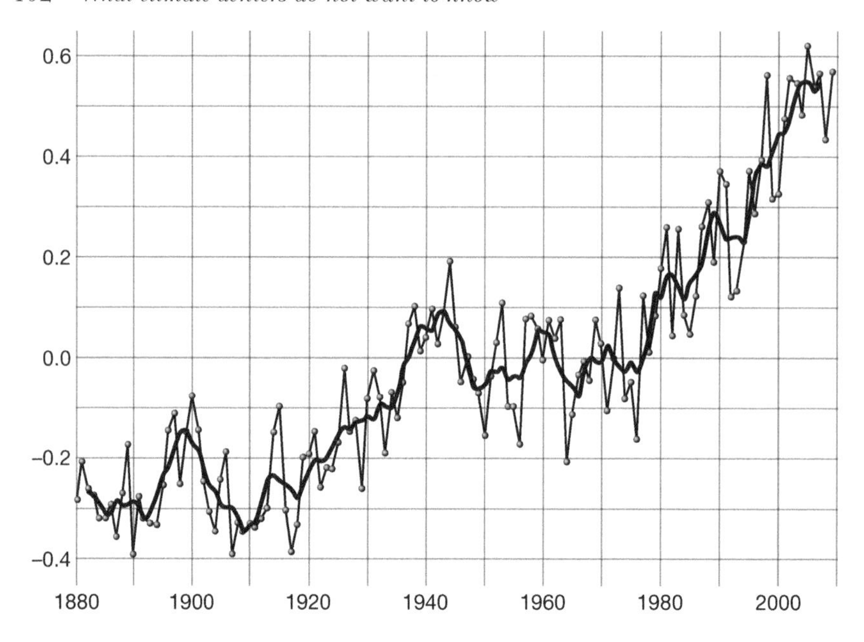

Figure 11.1 Changes in average global temperature (°C) since 1880
Global average temperatures from 1880 to today. Note the extremely warm year in 1998, which was a so-called El Niño year. Global temperature increased even after 1998, with record warm years in 2005 and 2010. The global trend line during this period is evident, with a global average warming of over 0.8 degrees since before the Industrial Revolution.

has cleared up the issue. Sarah Purkey from the University of Washington and Gregory Johnson at the National Oceanic and Atmospheric Administration (NOAA) have compared the temperatures over time at great depths in a number of different parts of the world's oceans. The results of their research show that the temperature in the southernmost parts of the oceans presents a very clear warming trend. This heat build-up corresponds to the amount of heat that would be generated if every person on Earth was equipped with five hairdryers at 1400 watts each and kept them on continuously for twenty years.

A special debate arose in the winter of 2009-10. Northern Europe experienced the coldest and, for many parts, snowiest winter in several decades. Many climate change deniers used this for their own benefit, claiming that global warming or climate change was a 'scam'. Such reasoning is completely wrong for several reasons:

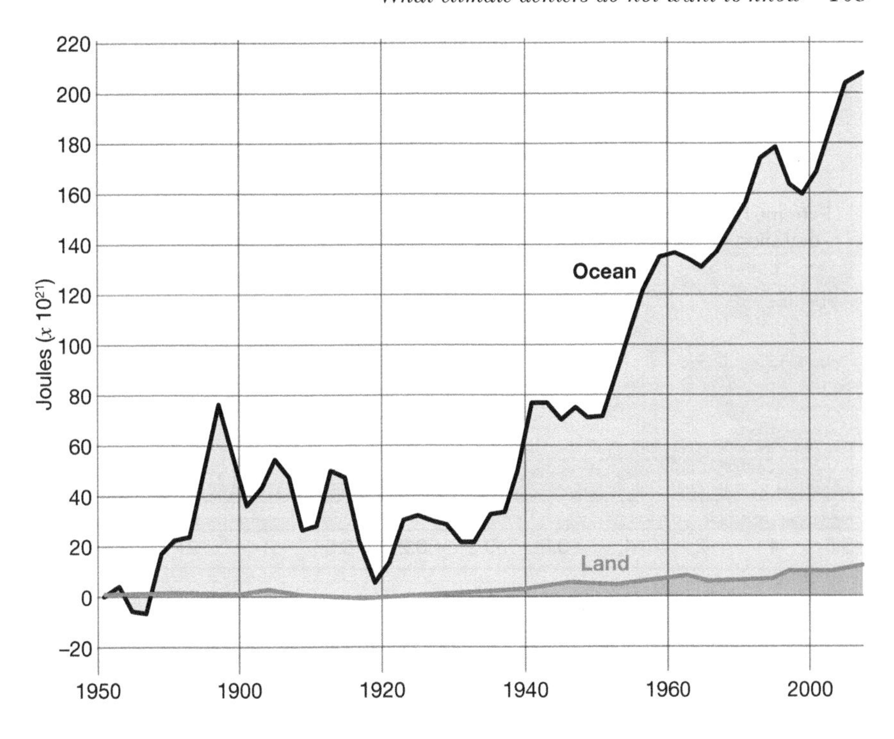

Figure 11.2 Oceans absorb a large portion of the warming
Variations in the Earth's total heat content since 1950 (Murphy et al. 2009). The figures for the sea come from Domingues et al. 2008. The figures of land surfaces and atmosphere include the heat needed to melt the ice. The unit of scale to the left is in joules (x 10^{21}).

- One must distinguish between climate and weather. Climate research has not suggested that cold winters would disappear, even as the average temperature on Earth rises.
- Climate change is first and foremost a question of an increasingly unstable climate. The warming that is occurring causes different effects in different parts of the world, though with a common pattern: greater variability, particularly in the form of more extreme weather. Various feedback mechanisms – such as the melting Arctic ice absorbing more solar energy – enhance warming.
- If we comment at all on the weather conditions on Earth, we cannot select individual regions. It is true that Scandinavia, Russia and the eastern United States experienced a colder than normal winter in 2010, but the winter was warmer than normal in all other regions. In the Arctic and central and north-eastern Canada, the temperature in January 2010 was more than 4 degrees warmer than normal.

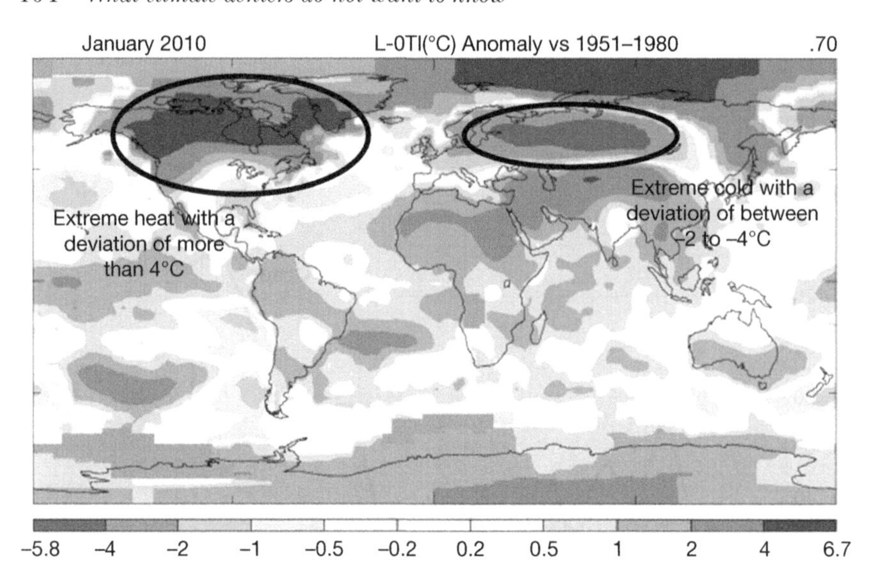

Figure 11.3 Satellite observations from NASA showing the temperature deviation during January 2010 compared with average temperatures from 1951 to 1980. Sweden, and parts of northern Europe and Russia, were in the grip of an extreme 'cold spell' while the rest of the world experienced one of the warmest January months of the last decade. Note especially the extreme conditions in the Arctic and the warmth of North America- where among other issues the Winter Olympics in Vancouver had a problem with thawing snow and ice.

It has not become warmer. The alleged warming is due to the manipulation of temperature data by scientists, including their tampering with the monitoring stations.

Our answer: Completely unreasonable accusations. The idea that a large number of scientists around the world would participate in a deliberate falsification of temperature data is absurd – and wrong.

Yet the argument is repeated, again and again, that the temperature measurements used as the basis for calculating the average temperature on Earth are knowingly false. One stated reason is that too many weather stations are located in urban environments, which would cause the global temperature increase to be overestimated.

Let us begin by reiterating that a very large part of the heat is absorbed by the oceans and the temperature there has increased. As to those measuring stations in the cities, it has been known for a long time that these may show higher temperatures than surrounding stations. A methodology has been developed that makes it possible to compensate for this when the average temperature of the world is calculated. Extensive study has also shown that the temperature trend in urban environments is equivalent to the trend in rural areas. NASA's Goddard Institute for Space Studies (GISS), which is one of several institutions responsible for temperature measurements, has generally determined that the phenomenon of urban warming is limited. It even found that 42 per cent of the measurements made showed that the urban environment has relatively lower temperatures than surrounding rural areas, possibly due to the placement of measurement stations in cities, which are often located in parks where the temperature is usually slightly lower.

Another study worth noting in this context was made by David Parker. He wanted to compare the temperature in cities during windy and calm conditions. The phenomenon of urban warming is mainly associated with days when the wind is low. Parker, however, found no difference in temperature trends between windy and calm days. He was thus able to dismiss the claim that the measured temperature increase on Earth would be the result of an imbalance in the measurements brought about by urban environments.

Climate deniers further claim that the temperature measurements are under the control of a few government-controlled institutions in the world. This is incorrect. Four institutions in the world measure the current global temperature trends, using different methods (NASA, NOAA, the Hadley Centre and the University of East Anglia). The climate scientists at East Anglia, especially its director, Phil Jones, landed squarely in the spotlight in connection with the theft of their emails in late 2009. After this, their operational activities have been subject to rigorous review. These audits have since exonerated both Jones and his colleagues from the allegations of conscious error and manipulation. Criticism was, however, directed against Jones for lack of openness with research data.

Natural warming

Other climate deniers accept that there has been a warming, but that this is entirely due to natural variations or the sun.

The climate has always changed. Today's warming is just an effect of natural variability.

Our answer: Only human emissions can explain the exceptionally rapid temperature rise that occurred during the 1900s.

If we go back in history, we know that the climate has undergone enormous changes. One question that is often asked in the climate debate by those who doubt is whether the temperature increase we have experienced during the 1900s, particularly in the last fifty years, isn't simply a consequence of the natural variability in climate.

Let us begin by noting that the temperature increase we have had during the last 150 years has been exceptionally fast: the temperature has risen by about 0.8 °C. In a statement in March this year the World Meteorological Organization (WMO) reported that the global temperature has increased by an estimated rate of 0.16 degrees per decade since 1971. If we compare this to the warming that occurred after the last ice age, a total of 4 to 5 degrees, that process lasted more than five thousand years and is considered fast from a geological perspective. This corresponds to a warming of about 0.1 degree per century. Today's warming, which has occurred over the past fifty years, is thus more than ten times as fast as at the time of the last ice age. The actual rate of change of temperature therefore gives cause for serious concern.

Climate scientists have carefully considered whether only natural variations could be the explanation. The unequivocal conclusion is that they are not. Temperature effects that are the result of changes in the Earth's axis and orbit around the sun take many thousands of years. Moreover, changes in the sun's strength that could explain the warming have not been observed. On the contrary, the sun's strength has been lower in recent decades, which should lead to a drop in temperature. Nor have major volcanic eruptions played a role. This all adds up to the only explanation that exists for the very rapid increase in average temperature during the 1900s: our rapidly increasing emissions of greenhouse gases.

That does not mean that everything is 100 per cent clear about climate and its variations. On the contrary. There is still uncertainty, particularly around issues of land use, how different types of feedbacks come into play and how large the cooling effect is due to air pollution (aerosols). But that human emissions play a crucial role in the warming we have experienced so far, there is no scientific doubt. Exactly how much impact humans make is, however, the subject of further research.

It's the sun that caused the temperature increase on Earth

Our answer: That's not what the research tells us. For example, if the sun were the cause, the stratosphere, the upper part of the atmosphere, would also be warmer. But the relationship is the opposite. The stratosphere has become colder.

The climate deniers who accept that the Earth has become warmer often use the argument that the sun is the cause. According to this theory, it is variations in the flow of solar energy that lie behind the warmer climate, not human emissions of greenhouse gases. Those who make this claim cite in particular the statements from some solar researchers, that refer to the sun cycles of eleven years, where the outflow of energy varies in step with the so-called sunspots, implying that climate models underestimate these effects. Other researchers point out that the sun's effect also varies over time and that a so-called 'grand minimum' – with a greater temperature reduction – may be imminent. Finally, Danish solar scientists, led by Henrik Svensmark, have argued that eruptions on the surface of the sun impact the Earth's atmosphere and thus cloud formation and climate.

Let us examine these arguments. The first thing to be noted is that if the sun were causing the warming, the top of the atmosphere, the stratosphere, should also have got warmer. But it has not. The stratosphere, as we have already stated, has become colder. Further, the warming should be faster during the day than at night. But it is just the opposite, which therefore supports the view that there is an enhanced greenhouse effect behind global warming.

In a detailed analysis, scientist Judith Lean has shown that it is certainly true that climate models do not fully reproduce the eleven-year cycle that the sun exhibits, but that the variations in the radiation are so small that the effects on climate are marginal (Lean 2010). Similarly, two other scientists recently showed that even if a 'grand minimum' in solar activity were to occur it would only lead to about a 0.1 degree drop in temperature. Moreover, such a minimum would only be a temporary effect (Feulner and Rahmstorf 2010).

When it comes to Svensmark's theories about changes in the Earth's magnetic field, which in turn could alter cloud formation and hence climate, we can only point out that the causal chain is long and complex (Svensmark *et al.* 2009). Other research groups have found no evidence to support Svensmark's claims. The only possible conclusion to draw is that with today's knowledge it is not possible to claim that eruptions on the sun would provide an alternative explanation for the warming during the 1900s.

The importance of CO_2

Another type of argument has to do with the importance of CO_2.

Increased CO_2 emissions have no effect on climate

Our answer: A doubling of CO_2 concentration would lead to serious risks for the continued development of human societies.

A decisive issue in the climate debate is how a continued increase in atmospheric concentrations of greenhouse gases in the atmosphere, primarily CO_2, will affect the heat balance and thus climate in the future. Intuitively, you would think that the relationship between CO_2 concentration and temperature would be simple and linear. In line with the reasoning in the section on the natural greenhouse effect in the previous chapter, doubling the concentration of CO_2 could then be expected to boost the heat balance on the Earth's surface by an additional 20 watts per square metre. But this is not the case. The atmosphere gradually becomes saturated, which means that the contribution to the greenhouse effect from a particular gas decreases with higher levels of concentration.

How this works has been ascertained through extensive experiments, the results of which have been taken into account in the calculation models made for possible changes in climate in the future. The claim that further releases of CO_2 would not matter is contradicted by these calculation models. But even more important than the evidence of the models is that this assertion is also contradicted by the measurements made from satellites. Such measurements provide clear evidence that the increase of carbon dioxide affects both the heat radiating out (Harries *et al.* 2001) and the amount of heat that bounces back to Earth (Wang and Liang 2009). There is incontrovertible evidence that a continued increase in carbon dioxide indeed alters the heat balance and helps to strengthen the greenhouse effect.

Summarizing the current state of knowledge, the IPCC makes the assessment that a doubling of the amount of CO_2, from the level before the Industrial Revolution, would be expected to make an additional contribution to the heat balance of about 3.7 watts (± 0.4) per square metre (Hansen *et al.* 2005). This may not sound like much, but look at it this way: in Sweden the extra carbon dioxide would produce an amount of heat equivalent to that produced by more than 600 large nuclear reactors spread out across the country. For the entire Earth this would add up to more than half a million reactors.

The crucial question, then, is how this increased amount of energy on Earth's surface affects the temperature and hence climate. To this question there is no exact answer. The temperature change depends not only on the concentration of greenhouse gases in the atmosphere, but also on various feedback mechanisms on Earth, that is to say, how the biophysical systems of the Earth – the global water cycle, the oceans, terrestrial ecosystems, the troposphere, stratosphere and cryosphere (the permanent ice on Earth) – respond to and interact with each other. The assessment of climate research is that climate sensitivity with a doubling of the CO_2 concentration (meaning that the heat balance will increase by about 3.7 watts per square metre) would result in the average temperature on Earth increasing by 3 °C (± 1.5 degree) (Jensen *et al.* 2007). This scientific assessment is however associated with considerable uncertainty (1.5 to 4.5 degrees).

Is this an uncertainty that allows the whole of climate research to be questioned? The answer is no. The science is unambiguous and clear in its assessment that an increase in the average temperature of just 2 degrees would result in very serious consequences and can be designated as 'dangerous'. The scientific uncertainty thus varies between a dangerous risk (2 degrees) and a catastrophic risk (4.5 degrees) for humanity as a whole. After the Copenhagen summit, most countries agreed that 2 degrees should be regarded as the limit for dangerous warming. At the Cancun and Durban meetings this view was reinforced, based on the latest research that the 2 degrees limit is not cautious enough and that the upper limit of temperature should be set at a maximum rise of 1.5 degrees.

The latest report by the IPCC was submitted in early 2007. Since then, new research has been presented that suggests that the sensitivity of the climate system may be larger. The report did not include, for example, 'slow feedbacks' such as reduced albedo as ice caps and glaciers shrink (when the white surfaces turn dark and thus absorb, not reflect, most of the incoming solar radiation) or the risk of increased leakage of methane from the tundra in Siberia and Alaska. If these factors are included, you cannot rule out a temperature increase of up to 6 degrees (± 2) (Hansen *et al.* 2008). This is a dramatic conclusion. Uncertainty is therefore significant in terms of the consequences of a doubling in the concentration of greenhouse gases – a range between 1.5 degrees and 8 degrees. Moreover, at the beginning of 2011, a study was published that indicates that emissions of methane from the Siberian tundra are significantly larger than previously assumed (Shakova *et al.* 2010).

The genuine uncertainty about climate sensitivity is obviously a major problem and a source of extensive debate within the scientific community. Overall, our assessment is that most climate scientists are very worried that climate sensitivity may well be greater than the 3 degrees that the IPCC assumes. It is in this light that the many recommendations from leading climate scientists to stabilize greenhouse gas concentrations at a much lower level – 350 ppm CO_2 – should be interpreted. Thus there is a significant risk that climate sensitivity could be greater than the IPCC assessment. But it cannot be excluded that the increase may also be lower, on the order of 1.5 degrees. If this were so, the consequences of climate change would be less severe. But even an increase of 1.5 degrees would cause considerable changes for societies, significant challenges for adaptation, severe droughts in some areas and more floods in others. The marine environment would change dramatically, not least with oceans becoming more acidic. Many inland glaciers would melt away.

So no matter how large climate sensitivity may be, we can assert that a further increase in the concentration of CO_2 will lead to significant risks – from very severe to catastrophic – with climate in the future, and therefore for our societies.

Emissions of CO_2 do not increase temperature, rather the opposite

Our answer: CO_2 and temperature reinforce each other.

Viewed over time, there is a good correlation between the concentration of greenhouse gases in the atmosphere and the temperature of the Earth. Ice cores drilled from glacial ice, which provide evidence of both climate variability and atmospheric composition over many hundreds of thousands of years, have clearly shown this. The relationship, however, is far from simple. Analyses of the ice cores show, for example, that the increase in temperature after the ice age about 240,000 years ago occurred about 800 years *before* the increase of CO_2 in the atmosphere (Callion et al. 2003). Other periods of warming show similar shifts. This phenomenon lies behind the oft-repeated claim from the climate deniers that 'anthropogenic emissions have nothing to do with global warming'.

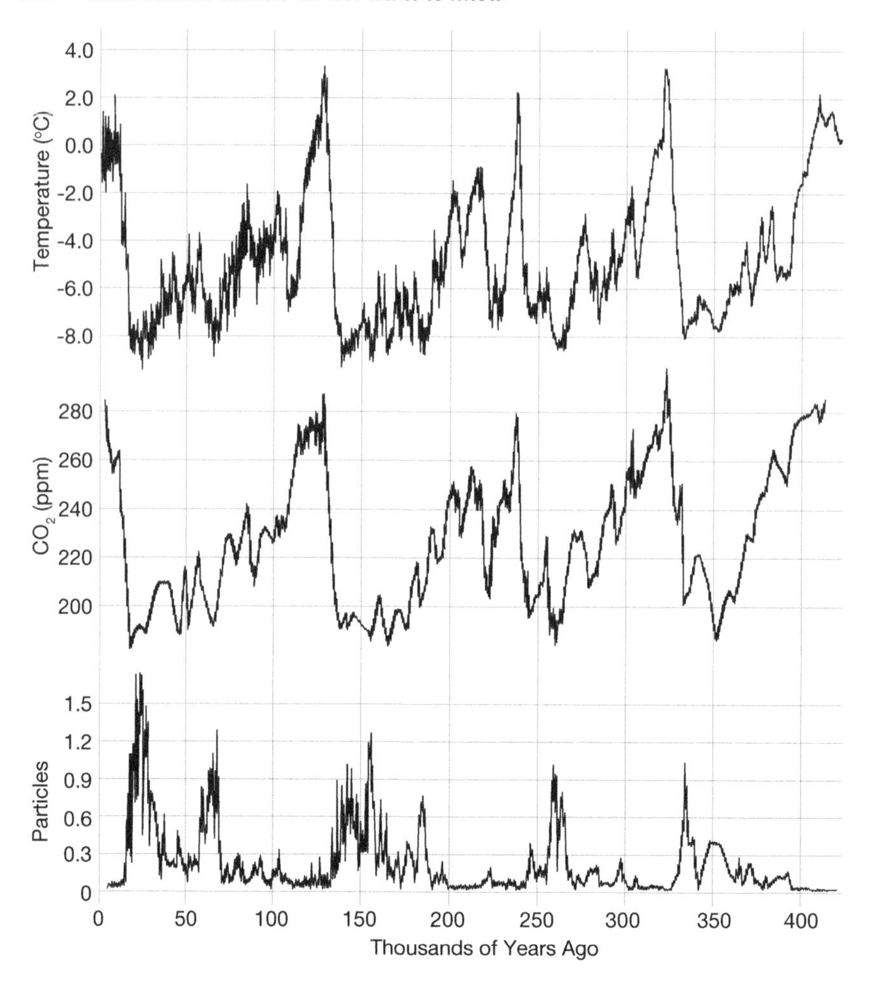

Figure 11.4 Correlation of temperature and CO_2 concentration
Three curves from Antarctica that show, from the top, temperature, carbon dioxide content and the amount of particles in the atmosphere. From Petit et al. 1999, Nature 399: 429-36.

This entire problem area has been the subject of extensive debate among climate scientists for several decades. It is not a question of 'new, sensational knowledge' from climate deniers. Jim Hansen and several colleagues had already addressed the issue in a report in 1990 that stated that the transition from the last ice age was initiated by changes in the Earth's axis and its orbit around the sun, according to the Milanković theory ('Orbital Forcing'). As a result, the temperature began to rise. Then two things happened. The ice retreated step by step, which caused the Earth to absorb more heat than before. At the same time the biological activity increased and so also the exchange of both CO_2 and methane from terrestrial ecosystems, in oceans and atmosphere. This then increased the concentration of greenhouse gases in the atmosphere, reinforcing the warming. What we are experiencing now is that every year human beings pump out tens of billions of tonnes of CO_2 into the atmosphere. Logic tells us that this increase results in the same kind of feedback from the planet as occurred at the end of the last ice age.

The phenomenon that Hansen and others describe is in fact a good illustration of one of the most central issues in climate research: What feedbacks are there on Earth? When the climate balance is disrupted for any reason – whether by increased solar radiation, changes in the Earth's axis toward the sun, or increased CO_2 concentrations in the atmosphere – we know that various feedback mechanisms come into play. The great scientific challenge is not only to identify these feedbacks but also to estimate the cumulative effect. Based on today's knowledge, we can conclude that a relatively modest change in the heat balance results in the mean temperature being increased further by various feedbacks (IPCC 2007).

Yet another type of opposition to climate science and the IPCC has to do with the descriptions of what has happened on Earth as a consequence of the warmer climate.

The reported reduction of summer sea ice in the Arctic has not occurred.

Our response: This is not true. Both the extent of ice cover and ice thickness have been reduced considerably in recent decades.

Few issues occupy as much interest among those who claim that there is no ongoing global warming as the ice in the Arctic. Many research reports have shown that in recent years summer sea ice covers a much smaller area than before. Meanwhile, ice thickness has decreased significantly. Both of these conditions are challenged by many climate deniers.

The extent of the decline in sea ice in 2007 was a record for several reasons: higher temperatures in the Arctic; special wind conditions; and an unusual amount of sunshine. In subsequent years the summer ice covered a slightly larger area, only to approach the 2007 record low level again in 2010 and 2011, and a new record low level in 2012. Since 1979, the extent of Arctic sea ice in September has declined by 12 per cent per decade. Sea ice reflects sunlight, keeping the Arctic region cool and moderating global climate.

Measuring the thickness of the ice is just as important as following the surface ice distribution in the summer. Recent data on the age of sea ice shows that the youngest, thinnest ice, which has survived only one or two melt seasons, now makes up 80 per cent of the ice cover. As NSIDC scientist Julienne Stroeve said in an interview in October 2011, 'The oldest and thickest ice in the Arctic continues to decline, especially in the Beaufort Sea and the Canada Basin. This appears to be an important driver for the low sea ice conditions over the past few summers.'

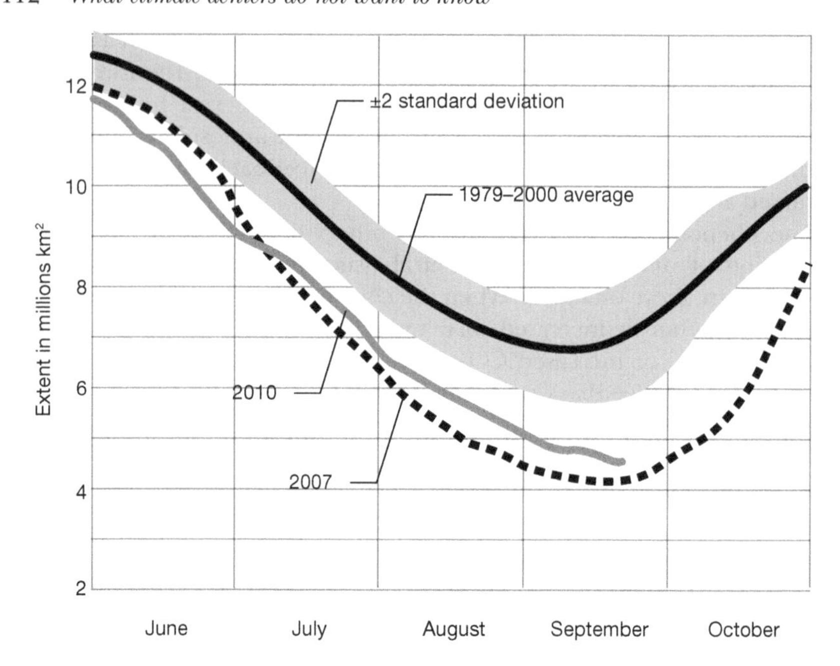

Figure 11.5 The extent of summer sea-ice in the Arctic

Glaciers are not melting down.

Our response: Even this research shows conclusively that the vast majority of glaciers in different parts of the world reveal a declining trend.

Glacial development has been one of many contentious issues between climate deniers and climate research. The debate turned dramatic when it was discovered that the United Nations scientific panel had exaggerated the risks of melting Himalayan glaciers in its report in 2007. A single statement in a report of more than 3,000 pages alleged that the glaciers could disappear as early as 2035. The assertion proved to be a significant exaggeration, for which the IPCC received considerable criticism.

The glaciers in the Himalayas are exposed to influences from both a warmer climate and a special form of air pollution, black soot (black carbon) from partial combustion. The research is clear: most of the glaciers studied in the Himalayas are decreasing in volume and size. But the pace is not as fast as the IPCC report stated. According to Lonnie Thompson, a glacier expert at Ohio State University, about 800 glaciers in the Himalayas are included in a scientific study to assess the rate of melting. So far the results show that 95 per cent of glaciers are decreasing in size. These represent only a small percentage of the total number of glaciers in the area, so much research remains to be done, especially at high altitudes. If you look at the totality of the world's glaciers, the trend is clear, and the figures below show how the total volume of ice has evolved over the last fifty years.

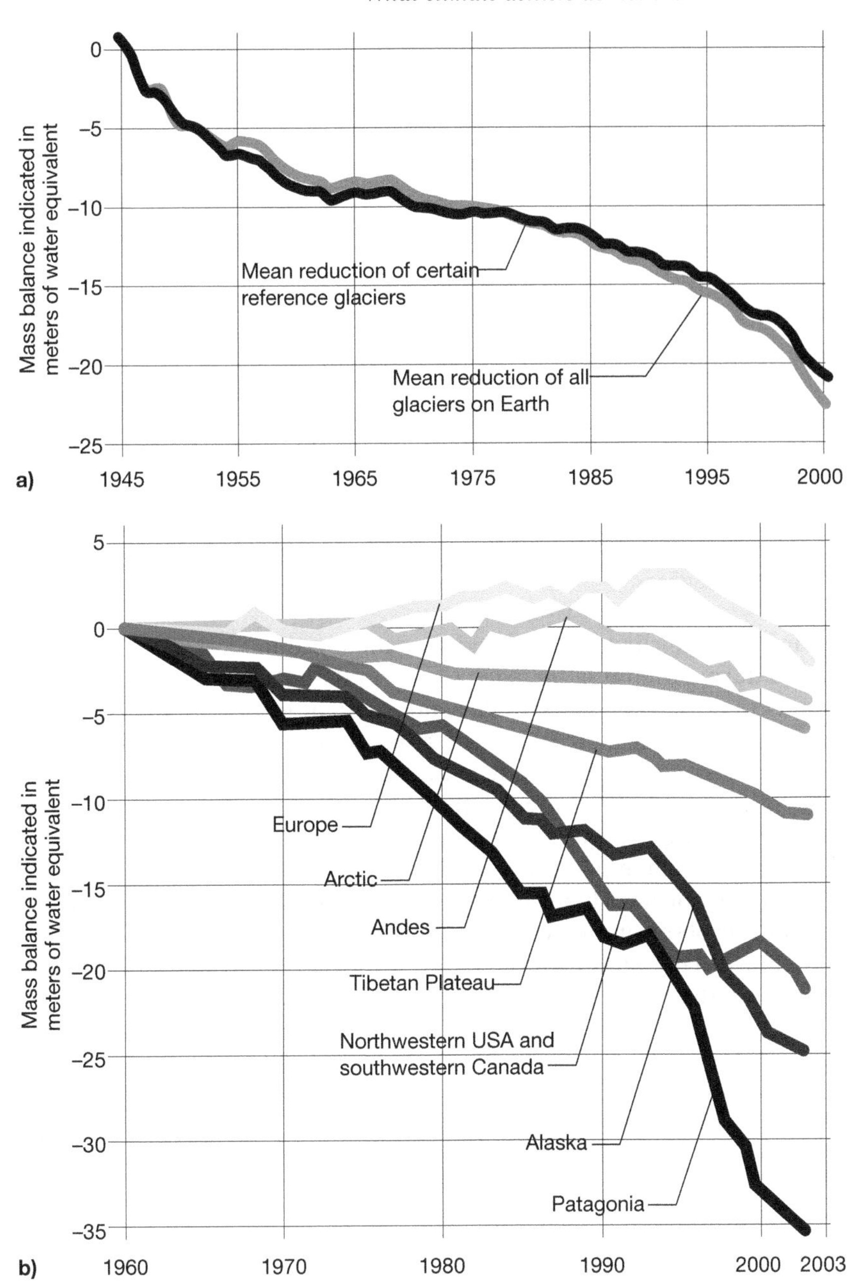

Figure 11.6a and b Changes in glacial ice volume

That glaciers are growing in some areas is not difficult to understand. A warmer world leads to precipitation increases. When this happens in high altitude areas, where the temperature is usually well below zero, then the consequence is, of course, that the glaciers grow. But for the vast majority of glaciers in the world, the combination of a warmer climate and large amounts of black soot points to a decrease in both extent and volume.

Natural variations are the cause of warming, not human emissions of greenhouse gases

Climate deniers claim that the Little Ice Age, when Swedish King Charles X went with his whole army in 1658 across the frozen Little and Great Belt straits to Denmark, and the Medieval Warm Period, when grapes are thought to have been grown in Greenland, provide evidence of significant global climate changes over the last thousand years – greater than the warming we have experienced since the industrial revolution. This would prove that natural variations are the cause of warming, not human emissions of greenhouse gases.

Our answer: The climate has varied over the last thousand years, but even the cold during the Little Ice Age (LIA) and the heat during the Medieval Warm Period (MWP) represent deviations in temperature that are smaller in both size and speed than the warming we are experiencing now. Moreover, it is unclear whether these two extreme periods are representative of the Earth as a whole or whether they were actually regional phenomena.

The following figure shows ten different scientifically published reconstructions of temperature over the past 1,000 years (most of them with data from the northern hemisphere). The black line shows the instrumental temperature observations, while the others are indirect estimates of the temperature (compiled by R.A. Rohde, www.globalwarmingart.com). For comparison, the observed temperature increase in 2004 is displayed. These data are not directly comparable, because the warming of 2004 is a global average (which is lower than in northern latitudes) and because it is only one year compared with five-year averages for the other curves in the figure. Despite the fact that there are large uncertainties in the historical determinations of the global mean temperature (before observations began to be more common in the mid-1800s), these data series nevertheless still show a clear trend in climate variability during the past 1,000 years that is still less than the rapid warming we have observed over the past 150 years.

These data series have been subject to sharp attacks from climate deniers, but scientific investigations have repeatedly shown that the analysis is scientifically robust.

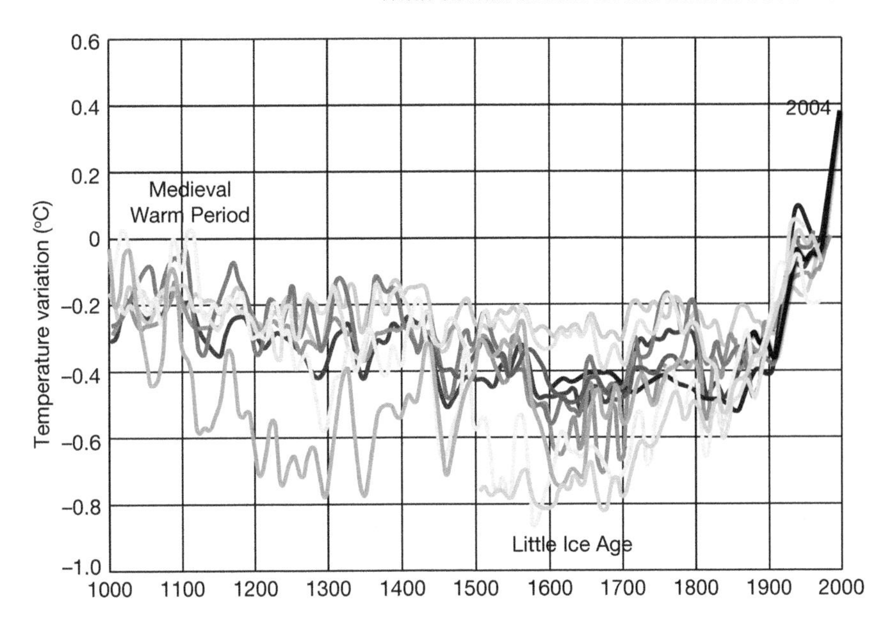

Figure 11.7 Temperature variations for the past 1000 years
A reconstruction of temperature over the last 1000 years, based on ten scientifically published calculations and observations. The famous periods of the 'Little Ice Age' and 'Medieval Warm Period' are marked in the figure, and show, especially for the Medieval Warm Period, that it was most probably 'colder' than the warming we have experienced since the Industrial Revolution.

12 The Arctic: the canary in the mine

The Arctic hosts unique social cultures and ecological systems. The Inuit communities have mastered the extreme living conditions in the Arctic for millennia, establishing sustainable social–ecological practices for ecosystem use. The Arctic environment is now changing at a record pace, and as a result acts like a canary in a coal mine, warning of the danger of abrupt environmental change on a global scale.

If Earth could communicate its state of affairs to humanity, the Arctic would have the loudest voice of all. It functions as an amplifier and the end of the pipeline for many of the environmental changes generated by human beings. Ocean waters from the Pacific and the Atlantic flow into and through the Arctic, bringing heat and depositing nutrients and pollutants. This is part of the remarkable global conveyor belt that is driven by the heat and salt gradients in the oceans, continuously pumping ocean water around the planet. Atmospheric currents congregate in the Arctic, pulling in air from neighbouring land and water masses and concentrating soot, nitrates, sulphates and other chemical pollutants into the Arctic. These in turn accumulate in high predators such as polar bears and humans. The position of the Poles in relation to the sun, and their close range to the stratospheric shield against solar radiation – the protective ozone layer – further amplifies warming. The Arctic has therefore warmed at least twice as fast as the average warming on Earth.

In 2007, a dramatic global watershed moment provided us with the sharpest rationale so far for global action on climate change. Abruptly, in just a couple of months, the Arctic lost 30 per cent of its summer sea ice cover. An incredible 42 per cent of the multi-year sea ice was lost over a period of 5 years (2004-8). This took science by surprise. Even in the worst-case scenario of unabated global warming, no one had imagined that such a degree of melting would occur so fast. Now, an unpredictable and abrupt change was occurring on a massive scale, rapidly changing an entire biome on the planet, with consequences for the entire Earth system, and thus the world.

The developments in the Arctic region are a serious cause of concern on many levels. It is a unique social–ecological system. It is also a planetary regulator of living conditions for every society in the world. The Arctic cools

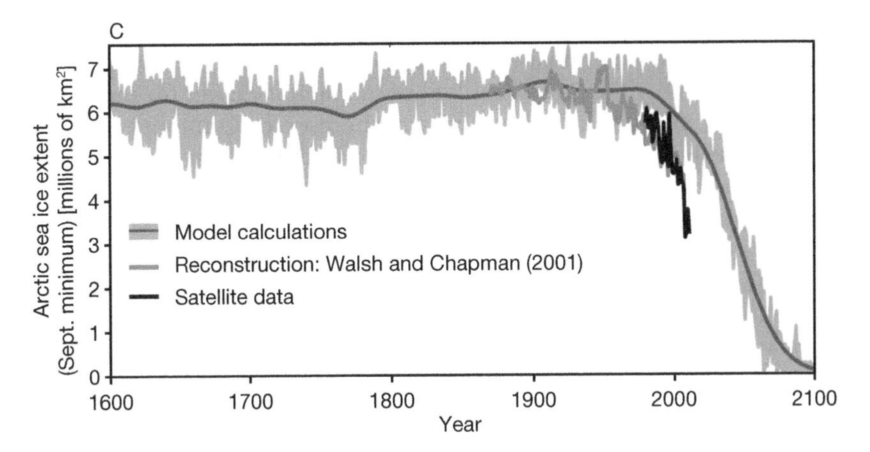

Figure 12.1 Abrupt loss of sea-ice extent in the Arctic.
Reality surpasses simulations of the worst case melting trends (adapted from WBGU 2011)

the planet by reflecting incoming solar radiation and buffering pulses of changing temperatures, as well as absorbing energy when things get warmer by melting ice – which is an energy consuming process. The status of the Arctic and Antarctica, should therefore be a global concern and responsibility for all the economies in the world. The changing environment around the Poles is the result of activities in other parts of the world. Rapidly changing conditions in the polar regions will generate consequences for other parts of the world. We exist in a symbiotic relationship, not only in social and economic terms, but also in terms of safeguarding stability and resilience.

Abrupt and unprecedented change is one thing. The feedback mechanisms that cause the Arctic to self-accelerate change are well known. When ice melts it changes colour from white to a dark land or water surface. It shifts from reflecting incoming radiation, keeping it cool, to absorbing radiation, which amplifies warming. The albedo (degree of reflection) changes dramatically, from an ice surface where around 85 per cent of incoming radiation bounces back into space, to surfaces that instead absorb 85 per cent. This is probably the most important climate feedback on Earth. When surfaces change colour from light to dark, more energy is injected into the biosphere, reinforcing the energy imbalance on Earth and speeding up change. Due to the albedo feedback, we cannot exclude the possibility that the entire Arctic will cross a tipping point, shifting from a cold, ice-covered and stable state to an ice-free warm state. Today, the Arctic is in flux, with nobody knowing whether it could bounce back to its cold Holocene state or tip over to a permanent warm state. There are signs, however, that the Arctic may have entered what Mark Serreze, Director of the National Snow and Ice Data Center, called in 2010 a 'Death spiral'.

The reason why the Arctic is changing extraordinarily fast, in unpredictable and non-linear ways, is the result of many interacting factors (Moran *et al.* 2006). The Arctic has had permanent ice cover for the past 13 million years, and now we are in a phase where we can no longer exclude the possibility that the Arctic may be ice-free within less than a century. This is a shocking reminder of the current pace of change, with no plausible explanation other than human influence.

Recent satellite data, together with sonar measurements from Arctic-going submarines, record a rapid decline in ice thickness; this, combined with reduced ice surface, shows that the entire Arctic ice volume is reducing rapidly. We are at the lowest Arctic ice volume since measurements started in the early 1970s, and can no longer exclude the rapid loss of multi-year ice even at the North Pole; old multi-year ice from Siberia was spotted in the Barrow Strait off Resolute Bay in the Canadian Arctic Archipelago in July 2011. The changes in the Arctic have shifted from a long period of gradual change to a phase of abrupt change. The Arctic is melting, freshening, acidifying, emitting methane from thawing permafrost, shifting food webs and ecosystems, and affecting regional climate. Many of these abrupt changes are not well understood. But the knowledge we do have shows that the system is complex, that the clock is ticking, and that we are dangerously late out of the gate.

It is not only changes in air temperature and albedo effect that drive abrupt warming and subsequent melting of the ice. The Arctic is also intrinsically connected to the Pacific and Atlantic Oceans that flow into the Arctic, warming the system from below. Melting of ice reduces the salinity levels in the Arctic Ocean, shifting fish stocks and food webs. Permafrost is thawing faster than predicted, emitting large volumes of methane, an aggressive greenhouse gas. Ocean and ecosystem fronts are on the move, non-indigenous species are invading, and hypoxia (oxygen depletion) is on the increase. Importantly, all these physical and biological changes interact with chemical changes in the ocean. Ocean acidification – driven by human carbon emissions – is hitting the Arctic Ocean particularly hard. More acid conditions change the carbonate balance in the oceans, creating a deficit of calcium carbonate, which is the building block for all shell and coral forming marine organisms. When oceans gets too acidic they may become corrosive to calcium carbonate (CaCO3). No ocean in the world had previously reached this dire state, until, that is, scientists showed in 2008 that the Arctic Ocean had tipped over and become corrosive to aragonite (the most sensitive form of $CaCO_3$), a shocking non-linear shift in the balance of Arctic marine life.

Recent developments in the Arctic are cause for serious concern. There is probably no scientific data in the realm of climate change as alarming as those that explain the rate of change in the Arctic. It is imperative that policy-makers all over the world devote sufficient time to learn about the changes in the Arctic and draw the right conclusions. If ever the term 'Crash Programme' was warranted, it is now.

The canary in the coal mine is choking.

13 Is Sweden a world champion in climate policy?

For decades environmental policy was primarily focused on point source emissions, such as manufacturing and power production. In recent years the focus has increasingly been directed towards 'diffuse pollution' or consumption and lifestyle. The reason is obvious. The production phase of a product accounts for only part of the environmental impact, often a minor part. For many goods, like cars, the major impact occurs when they are in use.

The Natural Step, cancer physician Karl-Henrik Robert's network for research and advocacy on sustainable development, has formulated the problem of the consumerist society as follows: 'Nothing disappears. Everything spreads.' The point emphasizes that matter is indestructible, that it is constantly exposed to impact and change, and sooner or later ends up as molecular waste. Petrol, in the form of heat and exhaust fumes, is a good example. Rusting metal is another.

The important role of consumption and lifestyle is very obvious in the case of climate change. Point source emissions from both electricity production and the manufacture of various consumer goods have a significant impact. But another equally important and growing part relates to the use of the various products and services connected with transport and travel, tourism, housing and the consumption of everything from food to vehicles, computers and household appliances.

Official statistics reflect only part of reality

The official accounting of Sweden´s climate impact captures only part of the picture. The statistics are based on domestic greenhouse gas emissions in a particular country, and do not account for embedded emissions in imported products. Sweden's method of reporting its carbon footprint is no different from that of other countries. Accounting is linked to the physical emissions in each country, in part because it is much more difficult to calculate the CO_2 content of the consumption of goods and services. While it is easy to calculate how much CO_2 is generated in the course of processing a tonne of steel or a kilogram of plastic, it is far more difficult to calculate the amount of CO_2 that results from the production of complex products such as cars, refrigerators and computers. Research is ongoing in many areas, including the CO_2 data for a growing number of products. But official statistics will most probably continue to be based on domestic emissions from industry, energy production, agricultural production, transport, waste management, land use and so on for a considerable period of time to come.

The fact that official accounting has focused on the domestic emissions in a given country should not be an excuse to ignore the impact of imports. On the contrary. Officially, a country like Sweden reports about six tonnes of CO_2 emissions per person per year. But if we take into account trade flows, the Swedish footprint goes up by several tonnes per person.

The amount of CO_2 in imports is rising fast

Sweden in fact belongs to a small group of countries where imports are particularly CO_2-intensive. In some wealthy countries more than 30 per cent of the CO_2 that is 'embedded' in consumption comes from imported goods (Davis and Caldeira 2010). For other countries such as China, the situation is the reverse. Estimates show that between 25 and 30 per cent of China's emissions are attributable to the export of goods, primarily to the US and the EU. In Sweden's case, the climate impact that stems from imported goods has grown particularly fast. A report from the Nordic Council (November 2010) estimates that the CO_2 content from imports to Sweden in 2004 amounted to more than 90 per cent of domestic emissions. Imports from Asia are rising fast, with more than 23 per cent per year from China, for instance. The fastest growing groups of imports include cars, electronic products, meat and clothing.

Now that a rapidly growing share of consumption in many countries such as Sweden occurs through imports, it should obviously be taken into account when discussing climate impact. Instead, it would seem that the vast majority of politicians and governments have chosen to avoid the issue. Sweden is no exception. Consumption and lifestyle are rarely touched upon by political parties and are obviously seen as politically sensitive.

As an example, suppose that Sweden ceased all production of meat and instead bought the meat it needed from Denmark. Such a move would significantly reduce our emissions of CO_2 and methane. The official reporting to the UN would announce a reduction in domestic emissions. But the carbon content of our consumption of meat products would be the same. And it would be awkward, to say the least, if we stopped feeling responsibility for these emissions just because the meat was produced in Denmark.

China, the world's 'new factory'

The entire discussion on consumption and lifestyle must proceed from an international perspective. The economy is increasingly globalized. The responsibility for climate impact cannot therefore be limited by national borders. Today, developing countries produce an increasing share of goods in the world; China is often referred to as the world's 'new factory'. Social and environmental conditions in these newly producing nations must of course be part of our responsibility.

The growing importance not least of China as a producer of an increasing part of our consumer goods has at least two consequences. First, carbon emissions occur outside the industrialized countries. Second, much lower production costs in China lead to substantially lower commodity prices in the EU and the US. The result is that people in industrialized countries can buy even more products from China. Alternatively, the 'surplus' can be used for other types of consumption or travel. But the end result is that consumption goes up, along with CO_2 emissions.

Earlier on in history, when world population was less and economic output was a fraction of what it is today, there was less need to analyse the impact of global trade. The overall footprint of industrialized countries was small. But this is no longer the case. While most forms of pollution in a country like Sweden are far more limited today than fifty years ago, our contribution to the global environmental burden is large and growing. The impact on climate is one example, our share of overfishing and deforestation in tropical countries is another. The increased imports from countries like China and India – and the resulting environmental damage and impact on climate change – must also be taken into account. Calculations show that if all the world's citizens had the same consumption patterns as the average Swede or American, we would, in the long run, need three to five planets to satisfy the needs and to manage and absorb all the waste products. The conclusion is that we must radically change course to get the economy and ecology to work together in synch.

The relationship persists

Back to climate change. Sweden's climate impact became a major issue ahead of the climate conference in Copenhagen in 2009. Both Prime Minister Reinfeldt and Environment Minister Carlgren travelled around the world in advance of the meeting, as part of the Swedish Presidency of the EU, and presented Sweden as something of a world champion in climate policy. The message in 2009 was that since 1990 Sweden had increased its economic growth by nearly 50 per cent and simultaneously reduced greenhouse gas emissions by more than 9 per cent.This point was made above all to demonstrate that it is possible to combine fast economic growth with reduced environmental impact. If all the CO_2 that is 'embedded' in goods imported into Sweden had been taken into account, the image would of course have been different. The 9 per cent reduction in carbon emissions, compared to the 1990 base year in the climate convention, would instead have turned out to be an increase of more than 10 per cent, according to estimates by the Stockholm Environment Institute.

A fresh report by the Swedish EPA in March 2012 noted that carbon emissions abroad – through Swedish imports – increased by 30 per cent between 2000 and 2008. At the same time domestic carbon emissions decreased by 13 per cent. In total this means that Swedish carbon emissions, as measured through consumption, actually increased by 9 per cent during this period – in volume an increase from 90 million tonnes to 98 million tonnes. Comparable analyses, including those done for Britain, come to the same conclusion. Carbon emissions have in fact increased over time if imports of goods from other countries are included.

It is natural for us to examine Swedish policies and performance in particular. The Swedish government obviously knows about the limitations of the official accounting of greenhouse gas emissions, but there has still been a conscious effort to present Sweden in as positive a light as possible. The message has been conveyed that rapid economic growth can be reconciled with a reduction in carbon emissions. But the reality is not that simple. That many people, both in Sweden and abroad, took this message to heart, has not improved matters. Fostering such public opinion can only serve to mislead and confuse. If we are to be serious in all our talk about reducing our carbon footprint, then we must also account for the import of goods and propose measures to reduce the impact in this area as well.

This being said, we do not want to belittle the importance of the constructive measures taken by Sweden in order to reduce domestic CO_2 emissions. The tax imposed on CO_2 in 1991 has had a major influence, particularly in the housing sector, where fossil fuels have gradually been phased out and replaced by biomass. Housing currently accounts for only about 5 per cent of the total CO_2 emissions. The corresponding figure on the European continent is between 30 and 40 per cent. But despite various national measures, the fact remains that the total carbon footprint of Sweden since 1990 has increased – not decreased, as the official accounting claims.

Worth noting in this context is that domestic carbon emissions in Sweden, which declined during the years leading up to Copenhagen, showed more than a 5 per cent increase in 2010. All this demonstrates the difficulties encountered when trying to delink economic growth from climate impact. It reinforces our view that sustainable development can only be achieved if it is based on a thorough review of the economic model so far entertained.

14 Getting the economy right

> The idea is essentially repulsive, of a society held together only by the relations and feelings arising out of pecuniary interest.
>
> John Stuart Mill

The world finds itself in a triple crisis: the global financial crisis; the economic crisis of nations – with large budget deficits, high unemployment and high public debt; and the crisis of the economy of nature. This situation inevitably leads to the conclusion that our conventional economic model is not fulfilling its role. In this chapter we shall consider the criticism of the regulatory frameworks of the economy primarily in terms of sustainable development. Our focus will be on the way the economy deals with climate, environment and resource issues.

What is the real purpose of the economy?

The way the conventional economy operates with regards to climate, environmental issues and sustainability is increasingly debated. The 'Stiglitz-Sen-Fitoussi-report', commissioned by French President Sarkozy, the TEEB Report by UNEP and the report *Prosperity Without Growth* by the UK Sustainable Development Commission are some of the most salient examples. New research initiatives have been launched, such as the Great Transition Initiative by nef, the New Economics Foundation, and the Institute for New Economic Thinking by Georg Soros.

The Nobel Laureate Symposium on Global Sustainability, held in Stockholm in May 2011, stressed in their statement the need to rethink the conventional model of economic development:

> Tinkering with the economic system that generated the global crises is not enough. Markets and entrepreneurship will be prime drivers of decision making and economic change, but must be complemented by policy frameworks that promote a new industrial metabolism and resource use.

The Symposium statement makes a few suggestions with regard to policy measures needed to move away from today's unsustainable systems of production and consumption and pave the way for a 'new industrial metabolism and resource use'. But the wider question, i.e. the specifics of the economic model required, was not addressed.

Several international organizations are also rethinking economics. OECD is developing a green-growth strategy; and UNEP recently launched its report *Towards a Green Economy*, presenting different pathways to sustainable development and poverty reduction. 'Green economy in the context of sustainable development and poverty eradication' was the theme chosen for Rio +20, the UN conference on sustainable development in June this year. The launching of the UNEP report was the result of a growing awareness that achieving sustainability will primarily depend on getting the economy right. The report states that 'there is no trade-off between environmental sustainability and economic progress' (UNEP 2011b). On the contrary, a sustainable green economy is projected to grow faster over time than a brown economy. The brown economy will, according to UNEP, be constrained by pollution and an increasing scarcity of energy and natural resources.

The UNEP report does not dwell specifically on the concept of economic growth. Instead, the notion of 'economic progress' is consistently used. There is no elaboration of the wider implications of this position for policy-making. The UNEP report emphasizes that 'greening the economy is not a *luxury* only wealthy countries can afford'. On the contrary, the point is made that a green economy is absolutely central to the alleviation of poverty. The livelihoods of poor people are directly dependent on healthy and productive ecosystem services. Furthermore, poor people are generally far more vulnerable to the adverse effects of climate change.

Strangely enough, the concept of a 'green economy' does not yet have a clear-cut definition, although there is obviously a need to try to clarify its wider meaning. What do we mean by a 'green economy' and how does it differ from the current economic model? A key question will be: Can the challenges of sustainability be met by minor changes in the conventional economic model – 'by tinkering with the current economic system' – or does it require more fundamental changes?

The primary purpose of this book is to clarify the relationship between the economic system and nature. Everything is connected and needs to be discussed as a whole, something the conventional economy has by and large failed to do. The responsibility is also shared by politics, not least in its reluctance to apply the principle of 'polluter pays', i.e. to let market prices reflect the social costs of production and consumption. The need for reform in the economy is great, whether we describe the problems as market failures (as did Lord Stern's report on climate) or, more generally, as inadequacies in economic theory.

Theories from the 1700s control today's economy

The present economic model is based on assumptions that go back to the infancy of industrialization. The theory is based on the writings of the British philosopher and economist Adam Smith. Smith wrote his most important works in the middle 1750s and naturally his theories were anchored in the historical context of their time.

World population during Smith's lifetime was less than one billion. The world's total GDP was barely $200 billion. Under these circumstances it was perfectly reasonable to consider nature and its resources as infinitely large, although farmland was certainly a limiting factor, mainly because of the low productivity of agriculture. While there were numerous examples of negative environmental impacts in the form of devastated forests, eroded land and severe contamination of air or water, the problems were mostly local and largely ignored.

We are facing a different reality. The population is seven times greater and is expected to increase by at least two billion people by 2050. Concurrently, various long-term economic forecasts predict that the world economy will continue to grow rapidly, to as much as fifteen to twenty times larger in 2100 than today. But planet Earth is not growing. The total amount of resources is essentially a given. Measured in biophysical terms, the planet is actually 'shrinking' as fish-stocks in the oceans are depleted, tropical forests disappear, farmland erodes, groundwater levels decline and biodiversity is becoming extinct. The only resource that continuously gives us more is the sun, which warms the Earth and which, in combination with photosynthesis, can stimulate the growth of the renewable resource base.

The rapid erosion of the resource base seems to have escaped the attention of most economists. There is no other way to interpret the fact that the vast majority of economists shun these critical issues and discussions. Still today, nature seems to be perceived as 'the constant and stable background for economic activity,' as related in the article 'Homo Economus as a keystone species' (O'Neill and Khan 2001). Partha Dasgupta, one of Britain's most respected economists, put it in a similar way: 'Nature is insulated from current economic thinking. Even in cases where economists make an effort to include nature, it is treated like any other part of the capital stock whose purpose is to be exploited for humanity's interest.' The problem of an economy that grows at the expense of its own resource base can hardly be described more clearly.

Conventional economists lying low

How can such lack of interest by economists best be explained? One answer definitely involves lack of knowledge. The core curriculum of economics devotes limited time both to climate and environmental issues and to an understanding of the fundamental importance of the role that natural systems play in the functioning of an economy. Thus when questions such as the risk of shortages of some natural resources or the overuse of certain ecosystems are brought up, the answer is usually that the solution is a combination of growth, substitution and new technology.

The basis for such reasoning is the notion that various natural resources are interchangeable. Even more important is the conviction held by most economists that environmental impact in a country is somehow automatically reduced as the economy grows. This relationship is usually described as the reversed Kuznet's curve. Granted, certain local environmental problems such as polluted air or water usually are reduced when material conditions in a country improve. But many other forms of environmental impact increase, such as emissions of CO_2, the amount of waste and residues and the loss of biodiversity. This is usually expressed as the increase of a country's ecological footprint. Rich countries have large footprints; and, as a rule, the greater the purchasing power, the greater the footprint will be. Consumption and lifestyles are crucial.

Not all economists subscribe to the simplified picture that an increase in economic growth will solve environmental problems, or that a variety of resources from nature can be easily substituted. There are exceptions, particularly among the group of ecological economists that includes Herman Daly, Robert Constanza, Manfred Max-Neef and Charles Hall. They all regard the conventional economic model as an oversimplification of reality. Their goal is an economy that is firmly grounded in science, not separated from it. Notable exceptions also include a number of leading economists of the more conventional kind, such as Joseph Stiglitz, Lord Stern, Partha Dasgupta, Amartya Sen, Frank Ackerman and Paul Collier. In Sweden there are economists who have taken strong positions in the environment and climate change debate, such as Thomas Sterner, Peter Söderbaum, Karl-Göran Mäler and Klas Eklund.

The two cultures

The tension between natural scientists and economists is not new. In the 1950s British physicist and author C.P. Snow was already known for his attempts to bridge the gap. Snow criticized the British educational system for giving too much space to the humanities and social sciences, at the expense of the natural sciences. In a widely publicized speech in New York in 1959 on the theme 'The two cultures,' Snow said that he often heard bitter comments among humanists and social scientists about the lack of understanding of culture and literature among those in the natural sciences. 'I usually then routinely ask the audience how many know the principles of thermodynamics. The response tends to be zero, often belligerently negative. Yet, the question is at least as central as asking someone if he or she has read his Shakespeare' (Snow 1959).

Thermodynamic principles are constantly evident in everyday life. They have a great bearing on what happens in the economy. Each energy conversion results in waste products and/or excessive heat. The use of different types of materials leads to deterioration in quality, such as wear and corrosion and entropy, or disorder, increases. Thermodynamics thus imposes a limit on the effectiveness of various industrial processes and machines. Knowing these principles, according to Snow, is of fundamental importance for anyone who wants to understand the deeper meaning of energy and material usage in our societies.

There is widespread ignorance of the limits that thermodynamics sets upon the effectiveness of energy conversion. This is in all probability the reason for the overconfidence in innovation and technological solutions, not least among economists. The central importance of thermodynamics was evident to Albert Einstein, who claimed that it was 'the only theory of physics of general significance which I am convinced will never be overturned.'

Thermodynamic principles are central starting points for the growing criticism of conventional or neoclassical economics that has developed in recent decades. This criticism has resulted in the emergence of two new disciplines in economics, ecological economics and biophysical economics. The latter discipline is particularly interesting because its aim is to describe the energy and resource flows behind different economic activities in both physical and monetary terms. Both the ecological and biophysical economists have produced extremely valuable contributions to the discussion of a more sustainable society. Unfortunately, their influence on mainstream economic thinking, and the training of economists, is so far limited.

GDP: a poor measure of human welfare

American economist Herman Daly has for decades been a leading critic of conventional economics for its unwillingness to properly evaluate the economy's total dependence on the living ecosystems and natural resources on Earth. According to Daly, 'the world today is more and more full', in that the pressure on natural systems has reached a limit. One result is that continued conventional growth risks becoming 'uneconomic', in that the negative consequences exceed the benefits. Our current way of measuring the welfare and progress of society can make this difficult to perceive. GDP statistics make no distinction between activities that are positive or negative. In addition, many of the negative consequences of GDP growth do not occur in our immediate environment but in other parts of the world, and therefore beyond our grasp.

The limitations of GDP

National accounts, reported in terms of GDP, are poor instruments for measuring changes in human welfare and wellbeing. GDP measures only the sum of all economic transactions of a country, regardless of quality and consequence. One manifestation of this is that pollution and damage to vital ecosystems do not count as negative entries. Furthermore, GDP statistics do not take into account how natural capital develops. A country can deplete their stocks of fish or clear-cut their forests and still show a positive trend in terms of GDP. The essential services that ecosystems perform for us for free, such as sequestration of carbon, pollination of plants, filtration of fresh water or the creation of new topsoil, are never accounted for.

When the political discourse continually focuses on changes in GDP, which only tells us about the transactions in the economy, reality is obscured. What in reality is a loss is presented as a credit on the balance sheet. All consumption of goods and services is based on contributions from nature, which in fact constitute a huge subsidy. Economists claim that there is no such thing as a free lunch in the economy. But what is this extraction of natural capital, if not a 'free lunch'? Not only natural capital is omitted from the accounts. Various activities such as work in the home and volunteer work, performed for the benefit of society are also left out. Such shortcomings in the GDP accounts are not obvious to members of the public, especially since the mantra of 'growth' is constantly repeated. Most people probably believe the notion that society gets better the more the GDP grows.

Growth in conventional terms, where the demand for energy and natural resources increases almost linearly, is obviously needed in poor countries, and there it mostly yields great benefits. Further material growth in the wealthy part of the world is a different matter. It is no longer self-evident that the welfare of society as a whole will automatically increase with growth. We should instead be giving priority to strengthening the ecological and resource base in order to secure the welfare of our children and grandchildren and to allow for the necessary growth and poverty reduction in developing countries.

The argument that rich countries should limit their material growth in order to leave room for a rising standard of living in poor nations usually faces strong opposition from most economists. Their contention is that growth in rich countries is essential in order to help developing countries raise their standards through increased demand and trade. According to the book *Growth is Failing the Poor*, the only problem is that in today's global economy less than 1 per cent of a growth increase goes to raising living standards among the poorest (UNDESA 2006). If anything, this demonstrates the fallacy in the argument that even the most prosperous people on Earth must have it better in order to fight poverty.

We do not underestimate the difficulties in changing course. As the economy is organized today, there is a strong push from developing countries to increase trade and for industrialized countries to buy higher volumes of commodities. But the current course is not sustainable. And the transition to a more sustainable economic system will prove difficult, particularly because of tensions between industrialized and developing countries. Transition must be green, but fair as well. This will be a major challenge.

Natural capital is not enough

This whole issue of confronting the conventional economic mindset contains an explosive force. Today we live in an economic system based on a host of complex relationships and mechanisms. Drastically implementing changes in the framework conditions is impossible. One country alone cannot begin to work against this tide without immediate risk to both its prosperity and its competitiveness. One issue seriously complicating the picture is the financial markets' rapid expansion and increasingly independent position. These markets work to boost growth in the economy, a prerequisite for all borrowers to meet their debt service, which in turn leads to greater pressures on nature.

Although it is a difficult issue, it must be discussed. There is simply not enough natural capital to sustain the policies of conventional growth. And priority must be given to allowing the world's poorest populations to grow materially. Such a priority implies that people in rich countries will have to constrain their demand for energy and resources. And therefore a key prerequisite is development towards far more efficient use of both energy and other natural resources.

Although all the answers to the dilemma of growth do not yet exist, the questions about access to resources must be raised at both national and international level. Unless we start using resources more efficiently and equitably, we will face the consequences: constraints on resources leading to tensions and armed conflicts; and the death of several billion people from starvation.

Alternative measures to GDP

The conclusion that GDP is not an adequate measure of welfare means that we must look for other ways to measure how society develops. Many attempts have been made in recent decades, but so far with limited impact. The United Nations Development Program, UNDP, has developed the Human Development Index (HDI), as a complement to the GDP concept. HDI takes into account not only income and changes in purchasing power in a country, but also life expectancy and educational attainment. It is an excellent complement, especially as it highlights the extent to which poor countries are successful in their investments in education and health care. But the index has its limits and leaves out the environmental quality in a country.

Manfred Max-Neef, Chilean economist and recipient of the Right Livelihood Award in 1982, has developed a model in which a total of nine core human needs are given priority. Among these are purely material needs, but also the functions of, and need for, protection, freedom, identity, understanding, participation, creativity and affection. To only measure human welfare and wellbeing in material terms, by purchasing power, means, according to Max-Neef, that we are omitting basic needs that are not material and not automatically met simply by a rising GDP.

Max-Neef's contribution to the discussion about welfare and wellbeing is fundamental and should form a key element in any discussion of society's long-term development.

Another alternative to GDP as a yardstick for development was formulated by Herman Daly and John Cobb in their book *For the Common Good* (Daly and Cobb 1989). They created an Index for Sustainable Economic Welfare (ISEW) in an attempt to correct the most glaring shortcomings of the GDP concept. Activities that are directly adverse to development, such as pollution and a degraded environment, are subtracted from the GDP figure. Activities that are positive for the economy, but not included in GDP, are added. The interesting thing about Daly and Cobb's work is that studies of several countries, including Sweden, reveal a distinct pattern. Up to a certain level, increases in GDP equate with an increased quality of welfare. But above this level the analysis shows human welfare levelling off – or decreasing. This is what Daly means by his concept of 'uneconomic growth'. Research led by Professor Karl-Goran Mäler at the Stockholm School of Economics further shows that most countries' net domestic product (NDP) figures would develop in a negative direction if changes in natural capital were included.

In recent years numerous studies, such as the Happy Planet Index, have been conducted on the theme of 'happiness'. Citizens of diverse countries have been interviewed in depth about their lives and their experiences of happiness and wellbeing. The same pattern emerges here as in the ISEW measurements: above a certain level of material living standard, happiness and well-being will not automatically increase with growing purchasing power. Quite the contrary.

Several countries have recently decided to establish metrics to capture how people's quality of life and wellbeing develop over time. In the United Kingdom a first national report was planned for the summer of 2012. The Prime Minister David Cameron endured a fair share of criticism when the decision was announced.. But he was not left at a loss for words: 'To those who say that all this sounds like a distraction from the serious business of government, I would say, that finding out what will really improve lives and acting on it is actually the serious business of government.' Bhutan has taken a somewhat different path. It has established a Gross National Happiness Index (GNH) with the aim of highlighting both the material and environmental aspects, as well as people's cultural, spiritual and emotional needs. The GNH has given rise to a far-reaching debate, both in Bhutan and abroad.

The various initiatives to develop alternative ways of measuring welfare and wellbeing are intriguing, because they show that some governments have realized the shortcomings of using GDP as a measure of a country's development. Methodological work will need to be further developed and fine-tuned, but it's probably not a bad guess to say that within five to ten years robust indicators of welfare and wellbeing will have complemented, if not replaced, GNP as the primary indicator for development.

Weaknesses in the economic model

The current economic model is in need of re-evaluation. The current system has at least six key weaknesses:

- *It is untenable from the standpoint of climate, environment and resources.* While true market failures can be handled within the current framework, it does not at present give a fair valuation of natural capital. The same applies to phenomena such as the threshold effects of non-linear systems. According to IUCN, we have already lost 75 per cent of genetic diversity in agriculture. At the same time it is estimated that up to 70 per cent of plants and animals face extinction.
- *It is untenable from the standpoint of fairness.* Income gaps are increasing rapidly, within countries and between countries. In the US, 80 per cent of the increase in wealth between 1980 and 2005 went to the percentage of citizens with the highest incomes, leading to frequent claims that 'the middle class is disappearing'. Ariana Huffington's latest book, *Third World America,* is subtitled 'How our politicians are abandoning the middle class and betraying the American dream' (Huffington 2010).' Even more tenuous is the situation for the citizen at the very bottom of the income ladder,
- *It is unstable.* The crisis in the financial system demonstrates this. Financial bubbles are a serious problem, with ordinary taxpayers being the real losers. The financial market is also less able to pursue its primary objective, which is to offer credit for long-term and sustainable investment.
- *It is not capable of creating the necessary jobs.* Especially serious are unemployment figures among young people. The present economic system is not able to provide jobs and decent living standards for a growing share of world citizens.
- *It underperforms in the provision of public goods.*
- *It does not increase wellbeing.* A large body of studies from a number of developed countries shows that once a certain material standard is achieved, the degree of wellbeing does not automatically increase with increased growth.

In an attempt to redress the situation we propose some of the most important and central changes we feel need to be implemented

Stop using growth in GDP as a target for development

GDP is a measure of the level of economic activity, but it says nothing specific about the development of human welfare and wellbeing. A superior alternative for a government would be to set up a number of clear human welfare goals, including expanded labour opportunities, good health services, good opportunities for education, fair income distribution, ecology in balance and a stable climate, and then focus policies towards these goals.

Recognize the importance of high quality energy

An adequate supply of reasonably priced energy is vital for all economic activity. We have cheap oil to thank for the rapid rise in the standard of living that has occurred over the last hundred years. If access to high quality energy were to be constrained – which is a likely consequence of peak oil – it would immediately impact economic development. The economic system has given no advanced warning. We are very poorly prepared for peak oil, not least because of the long time it takes to develop an alternative to society's enormous dependence on fossil fuels. Energy prices would go up rapidly, and its share of GDP would rise. We cannot say exactly when the kind of economy we have created will cross its pain threshold, least of all in the transport sector, which is totally dependent on cheap oil. Analyses within the Pentagon, the German Defence Ministry and the IMF suggest that the world economy is extremely vulnerable both to disruptions in energy supply and permanently higher prices for energy. The conclusion is that both efforts to expand alternatives to fossil fuels and energy efficiency measures must be intensified.

Give natural capital a value

Natural capital has no specified value in the current economic model, other than as raw materials in production processes. Energy and raw materials from nature are transformed into products and services, thereby increasing the financial assets in the economy. No attempt is made to evaluate how the supply of natural capital is affected. When different types of industrial capital such as machinery and equipment are subject to wear and tear, a deduction is made both in national accounts, when GDP is converted to NDP, and in business bookkeeping. With few exceptions, no corresponding depreciation loss is accounted for when natural capital – fossil energy, minerals, fish stocks, farmland, forests or ground water – is over-exploited and exhausted. The current world economy operates without a proper balance sheet.

Currently, growth and wellbeing are being subsidized by the planet's natural capital at a rate that clearly reduces the capacity to create prosperity for future generations. The many services from ecosystems – purification of air and water, decomposition of wastes and residues, the creation of new resources, pollination of plants, the regulation of both climate and water cycle, and a natural landscape's ability to create optimal water flow – are not reflected in the traditional economic model. These natural services are taken for granted. It is only when one of them fails that we recognize their value.

Substitution has its limits

Different types of resources from nature are assumed to be completely interchangeable. While this does happen – wood can be replaced by plastic, labour can be replaced by machines, and so on – it is obviously not always the case. Some resources or components of the biosphere do not have easy substitutes. The same is true for the important ecosystems services such as vegetation functioning as a carbon sink, the purification of air and water, pollination of plants and the creation of new topsoil. Without access to these resources and functions, the development of society would come to a halt. This aspect is fundamental when considering a reform of the economy. The task is to distinguish different types of capital – industrial capital, financial capital, human capital and natural capital. This has long been a topic of debate between economists of different schools of thought – between 'soft substitutability' and 'hard substitutability'. For us it is clear that it is 'hard sustainability' that applies.

Apply 'the law on diminishing returns' on the Earth system as well

Within the micro-economy there is the assumption of 'diminishing marginal utility' in different activities. This means that at some point in a production process it is assumed that the cost of an activity outweighs the benefits. However, that a similar relationship could be true of planet Earth as a system is nowhere to be found within the conventional framing of the world's economy.

Rethink the discounting of future values

Cost-benefit analysis is a well established tool in neoclassical economics. Normally a positive discount rate applies, which means that both future revenues and costs are given a lower value in the present. At its root lies the assumption that future generations will be richer than today and therefore can better afford to take on the various added costs. The higher the discount rate chosen, the weaker the motivation is to take action today against, for example, greenhouse gas emissions, which explains why many leading economists express strong doubts about putting an ambitious climate policy into place today. They argue that it would be both easier and cheaper in the future. As Harvard economist Martin Weizman points out, this is extremely dubious reasoning. Both ecosystems and the climate system are nonlinear in nature, which means that threshold effects – and thus abrupt changes – cannot be excluded. The implications of these threshold effects could be disastrous for our societies. To postpone action into the future would therefore be extremely irresponsible. The conclusion is that the discount rate should be low, near zero or zero, in the context of climate policy strategies. As economist Partha Dasgupta stressed, even a negative discount rate may be justified when there is a risk of unacceptable threshold effects such as a destabilization of the Greenland ice sheet or extensive releases of methane from the Siberia tundra. The costs of adapting the economy to such a catastrophic development, even if possible, would far outweigh the costs of preventing such a catastrophe.

Develop efficient markets for ecosystem services

Efficient markets work well for a wide range of products and services. But we lack well-functioning markets to conserve fresh water and marine resources, protect the atmosphere from greenhouse gases, protect biodiversity, including tropical forests, and refrain from building on fertile farmland. These issues, characteristic of the 'public good', have thus far received low priority in economic research. This presents an enormous challenge for economists.

Rethink the concept of 'externalities'

The negative impacts on the environment and nature by economic activities have traditionally been termed 'externalities'. The very term suggests that the effect is marginal. This was the case during industrialization's infancy, but today it is just the opposite. Externalities, in the form of negative impact on the climate and environment, have rapidly become a growing problem in many countries – not to mention the global impacts on the great commons of the world's forests, oceans and atmosphere. A logical measure in a new economic framework would be to abandon the concept of externality. All environmental effects have repercussions in the real economy and cannot reasonably be regarded as an effect outside the economic model.

Rethink the organization of the economy

One obvious way of overcoming the unsustainable use of both finite and renewable resources, and unsustainable levels of pollution, would be to move towards circular material flows by radically increasing activities like reuse, recycling and reconditioning. The aim would be both to extend the worth of products and the materials used by increasing their longevity – and to move towards closed material loops.

A very attractive way of both increasing the longevity of products and encouraging circular material flows would be to shift from simply selling products to offering services instead, by leasing products and offering upgrades when available. In practice, such a shift would not generally constitute a significant difference for the consumer. The customer would be provided with the products needed but the producing company would still own the products and be in control of the materials involved. Companies would have strong incentives to earn revenue as long as possible from what is already produced and optimize material flows. One obvious consequence and co-benefit would be the many more jobs offered in the local economy to cater for the services and maintenance operations needed.

In order for solutions like these to emerge, the right economic incentives need to be in place. A variety of policy options could be considered, such as binding resource efficiency targets for certain materials, mandatory rules for circular material flows for parts of the economy, as well as a tax shift from labour to resource use.

The list goes on. But these examples illustrate the need for new thinking in economic science. The economy does not grow in a vacuum. It grows within the ecological web, by constantly consuming non-renewable and renewable resources and, in the process, generating residues and wastes, Thus, step by step, the money economy eats its way into nature, destabilizing a wealth of important ecosystems and even, now, the climate of the planet. The conventional economy's responses to these and more difficult problems are negligible. Economists are not the only ones at fault. Politicians must bear their share of responsibility. Many of the market failures we experience today could have been a relatively simple matter for the politicians to solve, through regulation , taxes, tariffs or subsidies. The solutions must be sought both in a renewal of economic theories and in regulatory frameworks.

The economy's regulatory framework must be fundamentally changed if humanity is to have a fighting chance. We, the authors of this book, are amateurs when it comes to economic theory. We approach the economy from the vantage point of many natural scientists and their understanding of the risks that humanity faces because of our unsustainable use of ecosystems and natural resources. While we do not challenge the market economy's strengths when it comes to organizing the exchanges of goods and services and stimulating innovation and efficiency in the economy, we strongly question the current regulatory shortcomings in relation to nature and natural capital and hence, over time, living standards.

We hope that this book can help to initiate a broad discussion among leading economists. The prevailing economic framework is in need of critical examination, in order to deal effectively with the problems of an increasingly unstable climate, biodiversity loss, degraded ecosystems, 'peak oil' and the supply of high quality energy and food in the future.

The necessity of a new mind-set

Many people will probably ask themselves how everyday life can go on as usual when the threats to the climate, ecosystems and energy supply are so severe. The answer is quite simple. Let's use a metaphor. A family that sells a vital capital asset such as a house can live well for several years on the payment they receive. But when the money is spent, the family has nowhere to live and nothing to live off. The same holds true for nature's capital, and to some extent with the climate balance. We can live for several years on more than the annual yield of the natural systems. We can increase the level of greenhouse gases without overly serious repercussions in the short term. But sooner or later we come to a point where the natural systems no longer yield the returns we expect and the climate becomes increasingly unstable.

The collapse of fisheries off Newfoundland in the early 1990s is a clear example, as are the devastated forests in the Philippines and many African countries The large population movements taking place in Africa as a result of extreme drought and unsustainable land management, over-extraction of fresh water in a growing number of regions and the increasing erosion of valuable agricultural land worldwide are other examples.

An important lesson is that once a crisis strikes it is often too late to take action. This applies to the management of marine resources as well as to greenhouse gas emissions or the extraction of fresh water. For each of these problems, we know that development has gone too far. It may be impossible to turn back the clock. All of this indicates that we must build an economy that alerts us to situations of scarcity of essential resources, or environmental space, and helps to steer us away from behaviours that threaten the common welfare. Given the problems we face today in terms of the tension between the economic and natural systems, these issues should be priority number one for economist everywhere. But they are not.

The lack of commitment to environmental, climate and resource issues by conventional economists is undoubtedly grounded in a lack of understanding of how nature works and its fundamental importance for all economic activity – coupled with a general, and exaggerated, optimism for new technology. The fact is that, with a few exceptions, most economists have little interest in the study of energy, biology and ecology. Understanding how nature works is simply not part of their curriculum. The question we, the authors, keep asking ourselves is how serious do the environmental and climate crises have to become in order to force conventional economists to rethink?

15 The financial sector: ignoring the risks

> I am a most unhappy man. I have unwittingly ruined my country. A great industrial nation is controlled by its system of credit. Our system of credit is concentrated. The growth of the nation, therefore, and all our activities are in the hands of a few men. We have come to be one of the worst ruled, one of the most completely controlled and dominated Governments in the civilized world; no longer a Government by free opinion, no longer a Government by conviction and the vote of the majority, but a Government by the opinion and duress of a small group of dominant men.
>
> Woodrow Wilson, after signing the Federal Reserve into existence

The crisis for both the Euro and the US economy has a complex and multifaceted background. In the US, the causes include costly wars, large and unfunded tax cuts, a sudden increase in mortgages to households with a weak ability to repay and an increasingly polarized Congress. An analysis by Alan Stoga, an American communications consultant, shows that the political will between congressional parties to co-operate and compromise is lower than at any time since the Civil War in the 1860s.

The crisis in Europe is more complicated. As in the United States, rapidly increasing deficits in many Member States constitute a major problem. But added to this are the problems of the euro itself, the single currency. The EU has developed a close political co-operation on a range of areas such as the internal market, environmental and energy issues and the operations of police and customs. But fiscal policy continues to be the sole responsibility of Member States. Many experts have long warned that sooner or later the eurozone would face high risks if fiscal policy co-operation was not strengthened. Today's deep crisis with the euro demonstrates how right they were.

But political shortcomings are not the only cause of the economic crisis. It is equally important to highlight the role of the financial markets. Excessive risk-taking developed into a crisis that was close to bringing the whole financial system to a halt. When the bubble burst many governments were forced to step in with broad support programmes.

Let there be no doubt: governments were intimately involved in all of this. There are many examples of serious malpractice within the financial sector. But had it not been for the systematic deregulation of the banks by governments, in order to stimulate economic growth by issuing more debt, the situation would have been different.

Dissecting how the financial sector works is not the primary purpose of this book. However, some aspects of financial markets are of particular relevance to the issues with which we deal. There are practices within the financial sector that seem to totally disregard the impact they have on people and the planet. We are particularly concerned about short-termism, the process of interest on interest – imposing exponential growth on the economy – the failure to account for long-term climate and environment risks and the devaluation of social capital.

The way credit manages and portfolio managers are compensated is part of the problem. They are normally rewarded on the basis of results from the previous three months or on the level of stock prices. In such an environment it is hardly surprising that issues of long-term risk are neglected, especially those relating to the environment and climate.

A key question is how the financial market relates to the real economy. In the words of Otto Scharmer of MIT in his book *The Blind Spot of Economic Thought* (Scharmer 2009):

> Imagine an economy based on Wall Street but no Main Street. It would be worth nothing. Now imagine the reverse: Main Street without Wall Street. Then you would see an economy where people still produce and consume goods and services, but they lack the connective tissue that money provides ... Money is to the real economy what the circulatory system is to the human body. It keeps the parts of the system connected and alive. That means that the institutions that guide the circulation of money must do so in the same spirit: serving the whole system rather than extracting from it and exploiting it. Mindlessly pumping money into a system that leads to a 30-40 trillion US dollar bubble does not serve the real economy. Extracting profits from the real economy, that rise from 10% to 41% of US domestic corporate profits, does not serve the real economy. It is obscene. All these behaviors do the opposite of serving the economy; they are looting it.

Scharmer concludes that 'we have a system that accumulates oversupply of money in areas that produce high financial and low environmental and social returns, while at the same time an undersupply of money in areas that serve important societal investment needs.' To us the obvious conclusion is that there is an almost desperate need to redesign the system so that it better serves society as a whole. Scharmer´s comments relate first and foremost to the situation in the US. There may be differences between the US and the EU, but the basic logic and the financial instruments are the same. We ask ourselves: When will political leaders start to seriously challenge the many questionable practices within the financial community? The action taken so far is far from convincing.

The large gaps in knowledge of how financial markets work

One reason why the financial system has gone astray is that very few people outside the financial markets – including political decision-makers – know how the sector works. At a conference in late 2011 organized by Positive Money (a British NGO working for fundamental financial sector reforms) Steve Baker, a young Conservative member of the British Parliament, said that in his experience there are only a handful of members of the British Parliament who understand how the financial system works. This poor level of understanding among elected representatives underscores the need to scrutinize the financial sector. Our belief is that if the public had a better understanding of how the sector works, the demand for fundamental reforms of the financial system would quickly grow.

The vast majority of people live securely with the notion that new money is created by the central bank in the country where you live. While central banks play an important role in the financial system, they generate only a small percentage of the money flow in our economies. Most of the newly created money is the result of debts issued by commercial banks. The banks determine who gets to borrow money and for what purpose. They want the loans to be as safe as possible and normally favour loans for secure assets such as real estate. Loans for investment in new production are often perceived as being more risky and are thus harder to obtain. In many developing countries, for example, the possibilities for small and medium-sized enterprises to borrow money are very limited. As the loans are paid back the money supply is reduced. Hence there is a strong interest among banks to continuously increase lending. That is how they earn revenue. Moreover, it is only through increased lending that already granted loans – and the interest on those loans – can be paid back. The whole system sounds not unlike a pyramid scheme.

Historically banks built their businesses by providing loans secured by pledged assets that were deemed to be the best possible. But conditions have changed. A number of new credit instruments have been created that lead to increased risk-taking. The collateral value held by many banks, as we have seen, is far from stable. The housing bubble in the US in 2008 showed how fast property values can fall. The recent financial crisis revealed that it is not uncommon for the same security to be used several times over – so-called re-hypothecation. Many consumer loans often lack any collateral at all.

The financial crisis put the spotlight on several important issues ranging from the ratio between banks' reserves and their loans to the question of where the line should be drawn on what the banks and financial companies should be doing in the first place. Professor Harald Sverdrup from Lund University has expressed it this way: 'We must distinguish between "banking" and "gambling".' He considers many of the new financial instruments that have evolved over the past two decades to be 'gambling'. These instruments were introduced as a way to manage and diversify risk, but have come to be used in exactly the opposite manner – to take bigger risks.

Our purpose is not to question the issuance of credit. Without access to credit both to start and run businesses and make long-term investments, as well as allocate consumption expenditure over time, our modern economy would not function. But the business of banking as currently conducted raises a number of critical issues.

Criticism of the financial system grows

The financial system has had its critics, but the general lack of knowledge in society about how the system actually works has most probably held back a motivated debate. Since the financial crisis of 2008-9, however, the behaviour of banks has come under increased scrutiny. The more or less unrestricted right to provide new loans – and the risks that accrued – was a significant reason behind the highly-inflated real estate values that almost led to the collapse of the financial markets. This raises many questions.

First, the role of banks in the creation of new money, by increasing debt. Under the current system there is plenty of money during periods of prosperity. As the economy weakens, banks are less willing to grant loans and the money supply is reduced. Central banks can certainly affect the money supply by intervening in the market, for example by buying bonds. But the system is extremely susceptible to cyclical influences. An alternative could be that the money supply is solely the responsibility of the central banks.

Second – and closely linked – the consequences of a rapid expansion of the volume of credit. Economists of the so-called Austrian school, for example, believe that new loans should only be provided relative to deposits on hand, that is, the savings in the banks. A rapid rise in borrowing increases the risk of both inflation and unsound speculation. Credit volume in the world has gone up on average by 7.5 per cent annually between 2000 and 2009 (World Economic Forum 2010), far more than the rise in economic growth. In some parts of the world such as Ireland, Greece and Spain and in the housing market in the US, the credit volume grew even faster, with disastrous consequences. Cheap mortgages helped drive up property values to almost astronomical levels. When the credit bubble finally burst, it was followed by a deep crisis that forced millions of people out of their homes.

An additional aspect has to do with environmental and climate impacts. A rapid increase in credit volume leads to an acceleration of both investment and consumption. The pressure on already scarce natural resources accelerates – trees are felled, waterways polluted, wetlands drained, there is greater exploitation of oil, gas, coal and materials such as cement and rare metals, as well as higher greenhouse gas emissions.

Third, the type of lending that financial institutions preferred and how employees are compensated. The patterns that stand out are deeply worrying. A significant proportion of common lending practices have centred on speculation in higher property values and various derivatives. The highest possible return in the short term has been the goal. Whether money is lent to businesses based on fossil fuels or renewable energy has been irrelevant. The important thing was the short-term return, and in that situation fossil energy gains the advantage almost as a rule, especially in a period of rising oil prices. At the same time, it has been difficult to arrange financing for investment in sustainable infrastructure and energy, for which the yield is deemed to be lower and the pay-back time longer.

Basel III

The only formal restriction on making loans today is that banks must maintain certain reserves relative to their total lending. After the financial crisis, efforts have been made in the OECD countries to tighten capital requirements through the so-called Basel process, an international regulatory framework for banks. The requirement of capital adequacy has increased with the decision on Basel III, but according to many experts it is still set too low – in the order of 7 per cent of outstanding loans. The new rules will be fully implemented at the end of 2019, thus leaving the problem of reckless lending largely unresolved.

Living on credit

The vast majority of people in the industrialized world look back on the post-war period as a golden age in which economies grew fast and the standard of living shot up in an almost spectacular fashion. For a long time it was a matter of meeting people's more basic needs in terms of secure jobs, security in sickness and old age, along with good education and good housing. But over time the demand for more grew, in terms both of income and purchasing power, and leisure time. One solution was to borrow. As we have already noted, the possibility of getting a loan greatly expanded, especially loans for housing and consumption. The increasingly more generous consumer credits actually mean that people are given the opportunity today to consume tomorrow's resources. The system is based on the premise that economies must continue to expand as before.

Consumption has become a part of life. As the German philosopher Zygmunt Bauman said in an interview in Stockholm in August 2011:

> When I was a young man, people went to the contemporary counterpart to the malls to buy new clothes when the old ones could no longer be used. It was to replace anything worn out with the new. Today, we are seeking confirmation and identity through shopping.

Who could have foreseen such a development? 'Man is certainly satisfied,' says Bauman, 'but lonelier, more anxious and more insecure than ever.'

The rapid increase in credit volume in many countries has masked growing income inequality. Even households that have lagged behind in the income tables have been able to keep up their consumption. The more liberal rules for borrowing money in the US – especially in the housing market – were a way for people with lower incomes to balance an increasingly skewed income distribution. When home values suddenly started to decline, the situation quickly became untenable. More than four million households in the US have been forced to leave their homes since 2008.

Financing is an indispensable part of the economy. But when the credit volume expands faster than the economy in general, and when the loans are based on short-term, often speculative, returns rather than long-term sustainability, it means that values are inflated and risks start building up. Sooner or later this will lead to great, and sometimes irreparable, damage to the economy in general as well as to individuals, the climate and ecosystems. It does not improve matters that the incentives for many who work in the financial sector put a premium on this type of lending.

The downside of growth

Rapid material growth, in all its aspects, has a downside. Consequences such as climate change, over-exploitation of important ecosystems and a gradual depletion of important finite resources are becoming more serious. In addition, growth has often come about through a harsh and unfair exploitation of poor people in other parts of the world. For a long time energy and raw materials were delivered to industrialized countries at abnormally low prices. Now, when the most readily available resources are dwindling, and as energy becomes more expensive, the vast majority of poor countries face a tough uphill struggle to get development started among the broad masses of people.

The debt that's been built up in nature is not as easy to calculate as the liabilities in the monetary economy. We lack a proper balance sheet that regularly accounts for the changes in natural capital. Revenues from the sale of record harvests of fish, for example, are reported as a positive item in the GDP. There is, however, no corresponding record of the depletion of the fish stocks that occurs – and that leads to smaller harvests in the long run. We are not able to distinguish between stocks and flows of different resources. A private company could never manage their accounts in such a manner.

Short-termism in the system

In the chapter on energy supply (Chapter 7), we highlighted the problems that most economies are facing because of the trend-breaking cost of energy and many of the most important raw materials. After more than a hundred years of falling real prices, costs are now on the rise as a result of rapid economic growth in countries such as China, India and Brazil, combined with the increasing scarcity of certain commodities, such as crude oil. Unfortunately, there is limited understanding of what these rising prices will mean for economic growth in the long run, and thus for the ability to pay off the growing debt in many parts of the world. The debate among both politicians and economists is carried out as if everything is only a question of money. But growth requires energy and raw materials, and the higher prices will inevitably lead to a reduction in growth.

The lack of understanding of the impact of significantly higher energy and commodity prices on the economy's long-term development is just one example of the deficiencies in the financial sector's long-term risk analysis. An equally important question is the significance given to the risks of climate and the environment. Here the picture is, by and large, bleak. There is little interest and understanding of these issues among the vast majority of actors in the financial market.

However, there are bright spots. For a number of years the United Nations Environmental Program (UNEP) has established a network of financial companies and worked with them on 'Principles for Responsible Investment' (PRI). By 2011 nearly one thousand financial institutions had endorsed the principles, which require that various investment decisions must take into account the social and environmental aspects. The PRI initiative is welcome. The weakness is that the principles applied are not very stringent.

Parallel to UNEP's work, several similar initiatives have emerged in the financial sector. One example is the so-called Equator Principles, which is supported by, among others, the World Bank, regional development banks and a relatively large number of commercial banks, particularly in Europe. The requirements are reasonably tough in terms of environmental and climate concerns, but so far the monitoring is weak.

Also worth highlighting is the American economist Hazel Henderson, who for decades has spearheaded an effort to make financial firms more aware of the social and environmental aspects of their management. Henderson produces a television series on the theme of 'Ethical Markets' and has garnered many adherents in the United States. A recent initiative by Ethical Markets – the Green Transition Scorecard (GTS) (Ethical Markets 2012) – is worth special attention. The GTS is a time-based, global tracking of all sectors of the private financial system investing in green markets. The most recent report, in February 2012, reported investments worldwide of more than 3.3 trillion US dollars in the green economy since 2007. While this is encouraging news, we still have a long way to go for the necessary transition in the economy to take place. The unique thing about the GTS is the database it has developed and the overview gained.

In spite of these initiatives, the banking and financial sectors lag significantly behind in work for sustainable development. One might have expected it to be the opposite, since one of the financial sector's main tasks is precisely its risk management. The institutions responsible for public pension assets, not to mention the retirement savers themselves, should be especially careful. Instead, there is a startling lack of both awareness and responsibility. Ethical Markets has proposed that pension funds allocate at least 10 per cent of their capital to green sectors of the economy. In a recent report the insurance company Mercer did suggest that pension funds ought to allocate at least 40 per cent of their funds to the green economy – half to hedge against climate and environmental risks and half to capitalize opportunities in green sectors. Given that the total assets controlled worldwide by pension funds is in the range of 130 trillion US dollars, we are only in the very beginning of a green transition. Far too many pension funds continue to allocate most of their funds to the brown economy.

There are many reasons for the deficiencies in the way financial markets work. Deregulation in the 1980s led to rapidly burgeoning credit volumes. New credit instruments were developed, some positive, others of more dubious character. The development of computer technology was of great importance. Right now there is an important ongoing discussion about so-called robot trading. Securities change hands in a fraction of a second. 'Making money on money' has become more and more an important part of business.

Companies listed on the stock market are increasingly valued according to short-term parameters, such as quarterly financial statements and expected 'cash flows' for the next few years. Future risks are discounted to present values and thus become less and less relevant in an investment the higher the interest rate. Incentive programmes in financial firms are also decidedly short-term: an account manager's performance is as a rule based on the previous three months. As a result of all of this, responsibility and long-term risk analysis take a back seat.

High risk exposure

Banks and financial institutions willingly lend out large sums to, or invest in, companies whose risk exposure is significant when energy, climate and other environmental issues are taken into account. This needs to change, both to reduce the risks for individual depositors, and also to reduce the flow of capital invested in activities that pollute the atmosphere and destroy natural capital, instead to support new investments in sustainable technologies.

In these circumstances, it is a major problem not to have in place a global price on CO_2 emissions. Having no price on greenhouse gas emissions does not mean, of course, that the risks associated with investment in the extraction of oil, coal and gas or businesses that use a lot of fossil energy, would be equal to nil. Any investment that threatens the climate or results in environmentally destructive activity is taking a risk. Political governance at global level is certainly anything but efficient, but most indications are that regulations will be tightened, as has already occurred in the EU. The decisions at the climate conference in Durban confirm this.

The EU system of emissions trading has significant shortcomings, and the price of carbon is currently (March 2012) at too low a level, but the trend is clear. The decisions taken by the EU mean that emissions trading will continue, no matter what happens with the international climate negotiations. The EU's decision means that the volume of emission allowances will be reduced by 1.7 per cent annually. Businesses that produce greenhouse gases – mainly CO_2 – will have to pay more and more in the future.

The financial sector can no longer ignore these issues. The best thing that could happen would be for the industry to propose its own rules for how risks should be managed, such as a shadow price for CO_2 emissions of at least €40 per tonne (according to numerous studies, a price exceeding €40 per tonne would be a strong enough incentive for investments in low-carbon technology and energy efficiency to take off).

Irresponsible valuation of fossil companies

A new organization, Carbon Tracker , has recently been established in the UK. Its aim is to closely monitor the holdings of financial investors and the valuation of companies in the stock market engaged in the extraction of oil, gas and coal. The purpose is twofold:

- to analyse the extent to which climate risks are considered – if at all;
- and to serve as a kind of wake-up call to avoid financial bubbles such as the crash of IT companies in 2000 and the housing market in 2008.

The starting point for the organization is that world governments have agreed to avoid dangerous climate change. The goal that has been set, most recently at the climate conference in Durban, requires measures to be taken to avoid an increase of the average temperature on Earth of more than 2 degrees compared to the pre-industrial temperature. There is no binding agreement yet that forces governments to take such actions, but it would be both irresponsible and immoral to assume from this that governments are not serious. We must believe that resolute action against fossil fuel emissions will be decided in 2015, in accordance with the decisions made in Durban. In the meantime, a series of actions are already being carried out in many individual countries, with the purpose of gradually transforming the energy system and reducing dependence on fossil fuels. Climate change is a major reason for such actions, but the risks of 'peak oil' and soaring oil prices also play a part.

Carbon Tracker has tried to estimate how much CO_2 the world can generate for the rest of this century without putting the 2 degree target at risk. They draw here upon a study conducted by the Potsdam Institute for Climate Studies (PIK) (Meinshausen *et al.* 2009).

In PIK's analysis the atmosphere should not be exposed to more than an additional 565 billion tonnes of CO_2 in the form of emissions from human activities. We also know that the total reported reserves of coal, oil and gas in the world corresponds to potential emissions of close to 3,000 billion tonnes of CO_2. Carbon Tracker shows that the 200 largest oil, gas and coal companies listed on the world's stock markets reported reserves equivalent to an emission volume of 745 billion tonnes of CO_2 – almost 40 per cent above the carbon budget set by PIK. Since this volume represents only about a quarter of the total estimated fossil fuel reserves, most of which are held by various state-owned companies, it is completely unreasonable to imagine that more than a small portion could be used. Otherwise, the consequences in the form of runaway climate change would be disastrous. Yet the valuation that the market makes of these companies is directly proportional to the reserves they have reported. The market thus appears to consider that all of these fossil fuel reserves will be used. One can hardly imagine clearer evidence of the discrepancy between the market and politics, to say nothing of the market and science.

An alternative interpretation – at least in theory – could be that the market expects that CCS technology – technology to capture and store CO_2 – will develop quickly and thereby neutralize emissions. But the technology is highly uncertain today, both in terms of cost and the ability to transport and store the huge volumes of CO_2 in question; over the long term we are talking about billions of tonnes of CO_2 per year.

In a January 2012 letter to the Bank of England by a coalition of researchers, investors and NGOs in the UK, attention was directed to the financial market's high exposure to investment in companies with a major involvement in oil, coal and gas, or in highly environmentally destructive activities. The letter warns of the consequences. In due course, it argues, climate and energy policy will gradually be tightened and future breakthroughs in new and cleaner technologies will emerge. The letter asked the Bank of England to analyse carefully the risk exposure as a consequence of the financial sector's support for environmentally destructive industries, and to make suggestions for guidance on how such risks can be both reported and, eventually, minimized. One of the signatories was David Nussbaum, Executive Director of WWF-United Kingdom. In the context of the letter he said:

> There are significant long term financial and environmental risks associated with high carbon investments, and policymakers and regulators need a thorough appreciation of these. It's clear that we cannot burn all the fossil fuels currently listed as assets on the world's financial markets without seriously impacting the value of other listed assets – which would affect the future pensions on which we'll all depend. Taking the high carbon risks seriously should also assist us in the transition towards low carbon investments, like renewables.

A few weeks after the British initiative, former Vice President Al Gore commented upon the same questions in Bloomberg's online magazine.

> Investors in oil and gas now repeat similar mistakes made by those mortgages that have caused the financial crisis in 2008. The costs of

greenhouse gas emissions are ignored and investments are made based on the idea that emissions are problem-free. Such 'absurd' assumptions may well lead to the energy companies' shares collapsing over the next decade.

The conclusion, in our opinion, must be that the valuation of the vast majority of fossil fuel companies rests on very shaky ground. Either the market is making a cold calculation that governments will fail in their attempts to limit carbon emissions – or they assume that CCS will be developed in time. However, if CCS is to have a chance to meet these expectations, then large private investment should be taking place to develop the technology, and this is definitely not the case. Several major development projects have been shut down in the past year and the future of CCS is highly uncertain. We ask therefore: How many financial institutions in general have actually made an assessment of fossil energy companies and their reserves from the perspective of a responsible climate policy?

Reform of the financial sector

Although it is tempting to offer suggestions for a thorough reform of the financial system, this is not our purpose. Our focus is instead on those changes that will make the financial sector a constructive force in overall efforts directed towards a more sustainable society. The absence of long-term responsibility that currently characterizes much of the financial markets must be reversed. It is doubly irresponsible to ignore the risks caused by investment in activities that are heavily dependent on fossil fuels or unsustainable use of the biosphere. It accelerates climate change and undermines future economic development. It also puts millions of individual savings at risk, not least those savings in pension funds.

But the nonchalance and ignorance go much further than that. Credits or loans to businesses that lead to a further depletion of many important ecosystems such as rain forests, wetlands, agricultural land and marine resources, or large-scale exploitation of scarce freshwater reserves, are examples of activities that ultimately undermine the very basis of human welfare. If banks and financial firms took account of more of this type of risk they would be making a positive contribution towards achieving sustainable development. Today, their contributions are often quite the opposite.

There are several opportunities for the financial sector to become a positive force in working for a sustainable society:

- A shadow price minimum of €40 per tonne of CO_2 could be applied to the assessment of all loans to, or investments in, businesses that rely heavily on fossil fuels. This price is higher than the current price of carbon in the EU emissions trading system, which is far too low. On the other hand, the higher price is less than half of the CO_2 tax that

Sweden has charged for more than 20 years. The level of €40 per tonne is consistent with what many analysts believe is needed to create sufficient incentives for the rapid deployment of renewable energy and energy efficiency.

- Another important step towards greater sustainability within the financial sector would be to introduce mandatory reporting by all major companies on how their activities affect important environmental and resource issues.
- In parallel, the system of quarterly reporting should stop – a step recently taken by Unilever. Reporting every three months inevitably heightens corporate short-term focus at the expense of long-term responsibility.
- Another important step would be the development of compensation systems that reward long-term value and not, as today, short-term capital appreciation.
- Finally, it would be of great value if a code of education for sustainability existed for those working in banks and finance companies.

16 Growth's dilemma

> Those who believe that economic growth can go on forever are either mentally deranged or they are economists.
>
> Kenneth Boulding

Everyone talks about economic growth. In the 2010 Swedish election campaign even culture could be adapted to growth, with slogans such as 'Cultural policies for growth'. One question that few talk about is how long the conventional kind of growth can last. If you believe the parties represented in the Swedish Parliament, with the possible exception of the Green Party, the answer is for ever. The situation is more or less the same in parliaments all over the world.

With the current growth rate, the world economy will grow to twice its present size in less than twenty years. If the trend continues, the economy will be between fifteen and twenty times greater in 2100 than today. But what would such a growth rate do to the foundation upon which the whole economy ultimately rests, namely the living ecosystems and natural resource base?This very issue has preoccupied the American economist Herman Daly since the late 1960s. As described in a previous chapter, Daly believes that today's economy is already too large for the ecological base and that the situation is rapidly getting worse, year by year. Daly is certainly controversial, but we have so far not met any economist who has convincingly disproved Daly.

What then are the most important tensions between conventional economic growth and the problematics concerning the environment and natural resources? Without prejudicing the analysis, we can say now that we are in strong agreement with Daly. Continuing with conventional growth policies will lead to an ever worsening collision with ecosystems, biodiversity, a stable climate and the availability of several critical finite resources such as crude oil, phosphorus and croplands.

Ironically, the problem that seems to be the easiest to manage is climate change. A massive expansion of renewable energy in various forms, coupled with investments in energy efficiency, would no doubt be able to cope with long-term energy needs on Earth. That would eliminate more than two-thirds of greenhouse gas emissions. The big question is whether we have enough time to deploy such energy systems before 'peak oil' strongly impacts supply or, for that matter, before the adverse effects of climate change are too serious. Current rates of investments in renewables are far from sufficient.

The real challenge is the pressure on the natural resource base as a whole. Simply put: How will ecosystems provide ample food for a population of nine billion people or more in 2050? What will be required in any case is that we make far more effective use of nature.

If GDP increases, so does demand

Historically, the relationship between economic growth and the use of energy and raw materials has remained largely linear. In plain language this means that economic growth has been entirely dependent on a corresponding increase in the supply of energy and raw materials. During certain periods of development, in conjunction with major infrastructural expansion, the demand for both energy and raw materials increased even faster than economic growth.

A slight decline in energy demand relative to economic growth can be discerned over time in developed countries, including Sweden. Energy efficiency is one explanation. But some of the gains are gradually eaten up by increased growth in the economy (the rebound effect), to which we shall return later in this chapter. Another important explanation for the relative decline is that we have moved from less efficient forms of energy to a greater demand for electricity. Primary energy consumption is then generally much lower.

Regarding the impact of economic growth on climate, biodiversity and our most important ecosystems, there is an abundance of research showing we are already exceeding the planet's sustainable limits. The IPCC, for example, reported on this, as did the previously cited article in *Nature* on 'Planetary Boundaries' and the Millennium Ecosystem Assessment (MEA), which estimated that two-thirds of the most important ecosystems are exploited beyond their capacity. This global 'health check-up' of the world's ecosystems has recently been followed up by an attempt to calculate the economic value of sustainable management of ecosystems and biodiversity. The Economics of Ecosystem Services and Biodiversity (TEEB), led by economist Pavan Sukdhev from Deutsche Bank in India, clearly shows the necessity of including a valuation of all the important ecosystem functions (from plant pollination to purification of air and water and preservation of the climate balance) in every strategy for greater prosperity (TEEB 2010). If a fair valuation of ecosystems is left out of the equation, we risk being blinded by the potential for rapid growth in the short term by the overuse of different ecosystems, and at the same time forced to recognise that growth in the longer term will deteriorate as the productive capacity of ecosystems are eroded. A clear example of this occurs when mangroves are felled to make way for the cultivation of prawns.

Another way to describe this condition is by the size of a society's ecological footprint. This concept was launched at the beginning of the 1990s as an attempt to illustrate the rapidly increasing pressure on the environment from the growing economy and an increasing population. The ecological footprint refers to the land area needed to supply a country's population with food, housing, transport and energy and to take care of the wastes and emissions generated. If we took into account the size of the world population and the total productive biological surface of the Earth, every person would be entitled to a footprint equivalent to 1.8 hectares. The average in the world today is substantially above this, around 2.7 hectares per capita, which is not sustainable. This concept gives us a good indicator, especially for the overall situation, but also for individual countries. But the ecological footprint is not complete as an indicator, because it does not include the use of chemicals nor the impact on biodiversity. In addition, no account is taken of the fact that ecosystems are dynamic and living, not static. They change character all the time due to climate variability, water availability, and so on.

The United Nations Development Programme (UNDP) has made a comparison of the Human Development Index (HDI) and the ecological footprint. The calculation shows a relatively strong correlation between footprint size and the material standard of living of a country. For example, the ecological footprint per capita of the US is about 8 hectares; Sweden is about six hectares per capita; and most African countries are significantly below that level, at 1.8 hectares per capita.

UNDP calculations sweep aside the myth of the inverted Kuznet's curve, which implies that higher growth per se will automatically provide more sustainable communities. There are no simple relationships here. The environmental impacts made by the poorest countries are generally small. The big problem is archaic farming practices that often depletes the earth and an increasing pressure on forests in search of new farmland and firewood.

As purchasing power rises in a country, so does pressure on the environment. While local pollution can often be addressed adequately after the fact, in our experience the contribution to the global environmental burden increases through emissions of greenhouse gases, loss of biodiversity and increasing amounts of waste. Hence the overriding challenge today is to develop models for society's development where decent human welfare can be reconciled with environmental sustainability.

Over and above the problems of over-exploitation of natural capital and climate change, we also face the looming risk of scarcity of certain finite resources such as 'peak oil', 'peak rare metals' and 'peak phosphorus'. Such risks are confirmed in various reports from the Association for the Study of Peak Oil, US Joint Forces Command, the European Commission and the Institute for Sustainable Futures. So it is worth repeating the question: Given what we know about the close relationship between economic growth and the demand for energy, natural resources and ecosystems, how would it be at all possible to achieve an economy twenty times greater? What would such a society look like? Where would the resources come from? How would resource flows be organized?

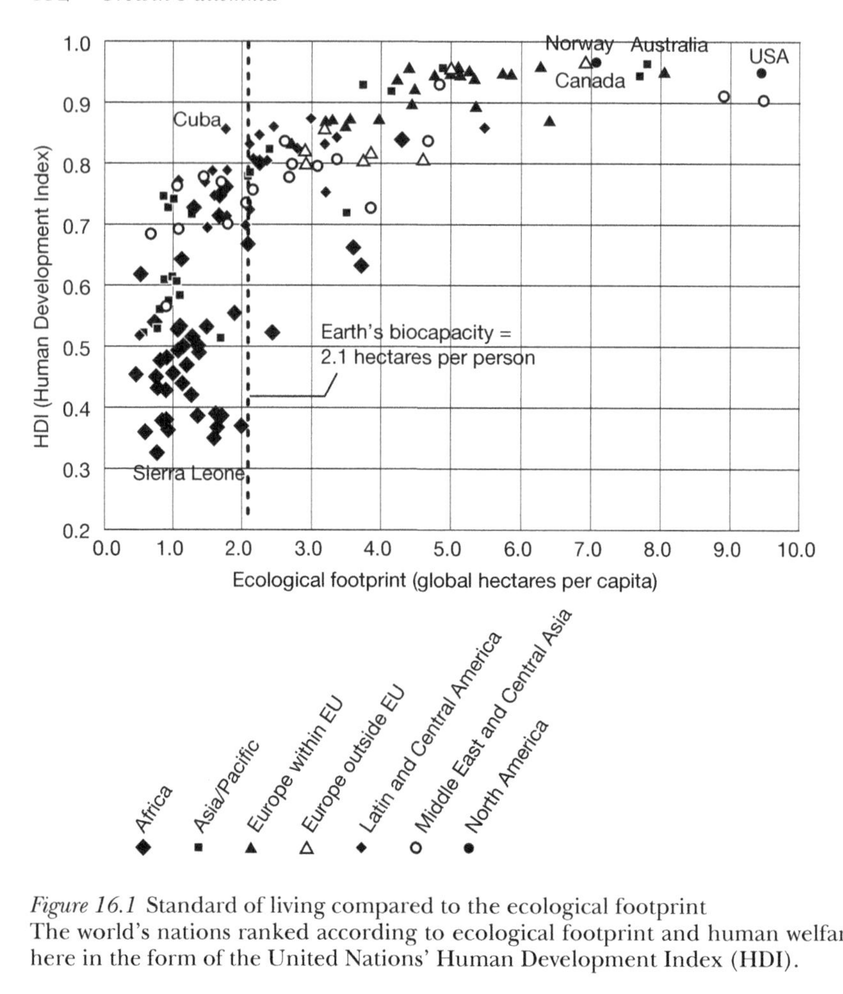

Figure 16.1 Standard of living compared to the ecological footprint
The world's nations ranked according to ecological footprint and human welfare, here in the form of the United Nations' Human Development Index (HDI).

Can we break the link between growth and resource consumption?

Ever since the Brundtland Report was presented in 1987, the discussions on sustainable development – or sustainable growth as many have chosen to call it – have been dominated by ideas of *decoupling*. This means that the link is broken between economic growth and the use of energy and materials. By decoupling, growth should turn 'green'. The results so far have been poor, for several reasons, of which the deregulation of financial markets, the advent of the WTO and far freer world trade, along with low oil prices throughout the 1990s, are the most important. In these circumstances it was not politically opportune to offer suggestions that could be perceived as barriers or constraints to the functioning of the free market.

Meanwhile, new research shows that the notion of 'decoupling' was overly optimistic, if not naive. The efficiency of energy use in the world has

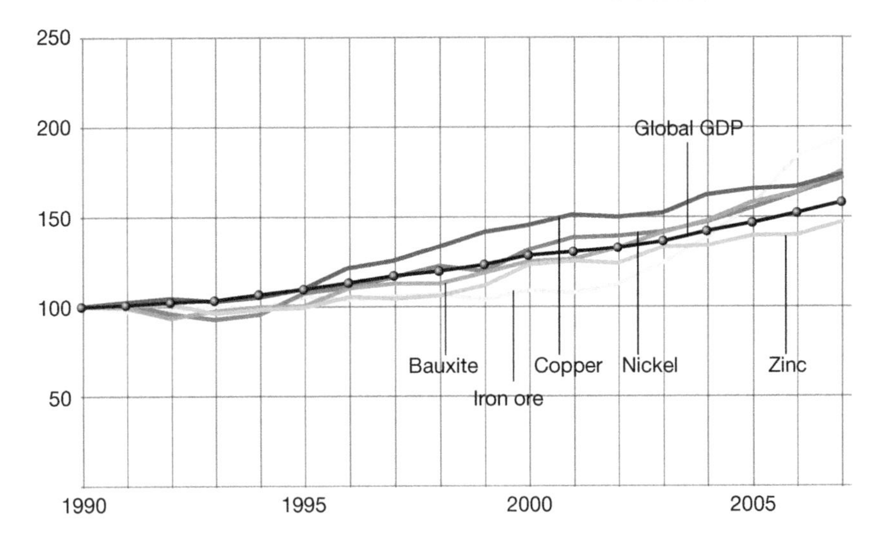

Figure 16.2 Demand for metal follows the growth of the economy
The demand for our most important metals in the past two decades. Only the growth in demand for zinc is somewhat slower than the growth in the world economy.

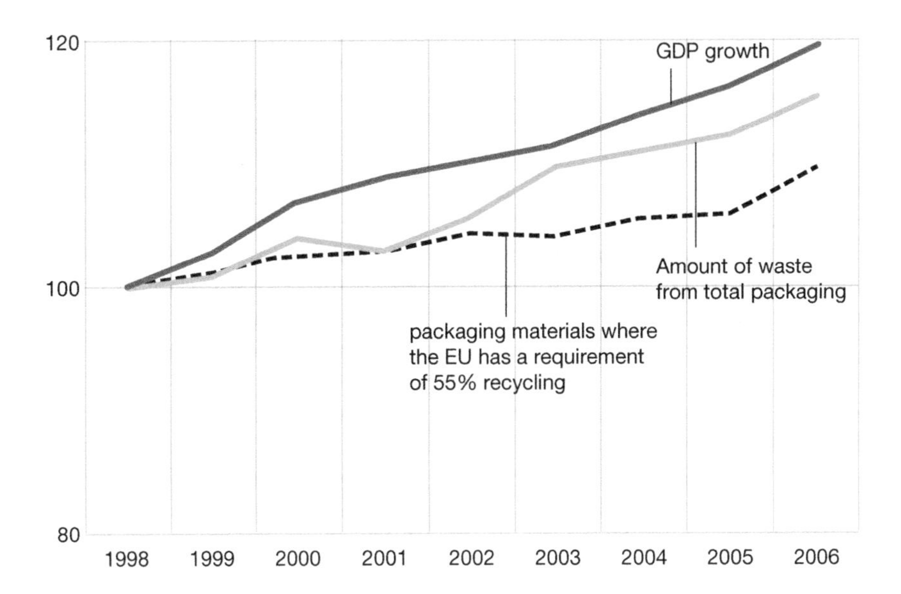

Figure 16.3 Waste continues to increase

increased over time, doubling in 56 years. But energy consumption has increased almost twice as rapidly, doubling in 37 years. Starting from 1980, the total use of commercial energy in the world increased by 60 per cent, from 9.48 terawatts to 15.8 terawatts (according to the US Energy Information Administration).

If we turn to climate change, studies show that the carbon intensity of the global economy has fallen from an average of one kilogram of CO_2 per dollar of production value in 1980 to 770 grams in 2008. But at the same time, total emissions of CO_2 increased rapidly, by 40 per cent from 1990 and 80 per cent from 1970. There is also a clear pattern emerging that GHG emissions tend to increase with income.

When we turn to commodities, the pattern is similar. Even in areas where legislation has been specifically introduced to promote recycling and re-use, it has proved difficult to break the link between growth and material use. Figure 16.3 shows the trend in the use of packaging materials in the European Union, where there is legislation requiring at least 55 per cent recycling rates for glass, metals, paper and plastics. Yet the use of these packaging materials increases over time as a consequence of economic growth, albeit at a slower pace than before.

The rebound effect: chasing one's own tail

The pattern that stands out is clear and unambiguous: efficiencies in energy and resource use have the same effect on the economy as increases in productivity in general: they increase growth. Economic gains from greater efficiency in energy or resource use are usually used by businesses to expand operations. The result is that demand for energy and resources will increase over time. For individual households, the result is often the same: savings are used to demand more energy elsewhere. One example is the car owner who buys an energy-efficient car. Experience shows that the lower cost of fuel normally means that the owner will drive even further.

This phenomenon is called the rebound effect and it means that efficiency, when seen from an environmental perspective, is double-edged. The rebound effect is like 'chasing one's own tail', as Professor Christer Sanne of the Swedish Royal Institute of Technology (KTH) put it in a report by the Swedish Environmental Protection Agency (Sanne 2006). The size of the rebound effect varies from area to area and is a combination of several things: an income effect, a substitution effect and the effects of a growing economy.

Dr Eva Alfredsson, currently attached to Tillväxtanalys (Growth Analysis), a Swedish government agency, has analysed the effects that a more environmentally friendly consumption among a group of households would have on energy and resource use. 'In my research,' says Alfredsson,

> I examined what the aggregate effect would be if we would change our consumption patterns, in line with the objectives that leading government

> agencies – like the Swedish Environmental Protection Agency – have advocated, to reduce climate impact. How big would the energy and carbon benefits be if people in general followed the guidelines?
>
> It proved somewhat surprising that a household's energy use and carbon emissions actually would increase if they chose to follow the climate diet developed by the Swedish Food Administration! The diet was indeed more carbon-efficient than a standard diet, but the money saving was even more, so when households used the savings for more consumption there was a net increase in energy use and carbon emissions. The result improved, however, when households had to follow the guidelines for climate-friendly transport and housing as well.
>
> Households that chose both a green diet, green travel and housing – which included both behavioural changes and investment in technology – could at best reduce their energy use by about 10 per cent and its carbon emissions by 20 per cent by 2020. The changes required by a household to achieve these levels were extensive. Assuming then that the household would have a normal income growth, then the reductions in energy and carbon emissions are swallowed up after just a few years. Given that the changes undertaken by households were quite significant, they would be difficult to replicate, meaning that changes in consumption patterns provide at best a temporary effect. (Alfredsson 2002)

Many will see this as a disappointing result, but this does not mean that we should focus less on choosing energy-efficient electronics and appliances, improving energy efficiency in our homes, eating less meat and buying fuel efficient cars. From a human welfare perspective, increased energy and carbon efficiency is always positive. We get more for our money and reduce waste. From a personal economic point of view this also means that giving priority to energy- and carbon- efficient technology, a well-insulated house and a fuel-efficient car would be a good insurance against a future drop in wealth due to recession and unemployment. An energy-efficient society is also much better prepared for recessions and higher energy and fuel prices. Given continued strong economic growth, however, the larger volume of the economy will eat up the savings over time, unless flanking measures such as gradually higher energy taxes are introduced to offset the increase in demand.

The lesson is thus that enhanced efficiency of energy and resource use alone is not a universal solution to problems of sustainability. There are clear limits to the opportunities to decouple growth from resource withdrawal. Much can be achieved in relative terms, but for the gains to last, other policies must be considered as well.

The rebound effect should not discourage societies from striving for maximum efficiency in both energy and material use. Policies to encourage resource efficiency are rational for many different reasons and, if nothing more, they buy time by deferring some of the environmental impact. Resource efficiency greatly improves the preconditions for economic growth in the world's poorest economies. When low-income countries simply skip an entire technology step, as when the rural poor move from no phone to mobile telephony, it means that they take a huge technology leap forward in a few short years and give local business communities strong injections.

Japan is an example of a country that has significantly brought down the energy demand by setting the right incentives in the economy. Japan uses only about half as much energy per unit as the EU average, and only one third compared to the US. The reason is that Japan is extremely dependent on energy imports and has therefore had to pay very high prices for energy ever since the first oil crisis in the early 1970s. The high price of energy was never a problem for competition. On the contrary, it stimulated the development of many new businesses – especially in IT – that require relatively little energy.

In the energy sector there are many good arguments for increasing efficiency; energy security is one. As oil at reasonable prices becomes more difficult to come by, countries that have improved their efficiency of energy use and become relatively less dependent on oil will reap great benefits. Regarding climate policy, a wide range of studies shows that at least half of the required reduction in CO_2 emissions must come from efficiency measures.

Green growth myths

In view of the UN Conference in Rio in June this year, many international institutions as well as governments were putting their hopes in the concept of 'green growth'. While there is no universally agreed definition of the concept, the main focus is on 'decoupling'. However, as we have already seen, decoupling alone is not likely to attain the goal of sustainability.

The UN Conference on Trade and Development (UNCTAD) has recently presented an interesting report analysing the potential for green growth. The report, written by researcher Ulrich Hoffman, makes the following comment:

> Growth, technological, population-expansion and governance constraints as well as some key systemic issues cast a very long shadow on the 'green growth' hopes. One should not deceive oneself into believing that such an evolutionary (and often reductionist) approach will be sufficient to cope with the complexities of climate change. It may rather give much false hope and excuses to do nothing really fundamental that can bring about a U-turn of global GHG emissions. The proponents of a resource efficiency revolution and a drastic change in the energy mix need to scrutinize the historical evidence, in particular the arithmetic of economic and population growth. Furthermore, they need to realize that the required transformation goes beyond innovation and structural changes to include democratization of the economy and cultural change. Climate

> change calls into question the global equality of opportunity for prosperity (i.e. ecological justice and development space) and is thus a huge developmental challenge for the South and a question of life and death for some developing countries (who increasingly resist the framing of climate protection versus equity). (Hoffman 2011)

Hoffman makes the point that to achieve the 2 degree target in climate policy by green growth policies would require carbon intensity reductions that seem to be totally beyond reach. Global carbon intensity of production fell from around 1kg/$ of economic activity to just 770g/$ (i.e. by 23 per cent) between 1980 and 2008 (a drop of about 0.7 per cent per annum). In a world of more than 9 billion people by 2050, however, and assuming an annual GDP growth of 2 per cent until then as well as an appropriate catching up of developing countries in terms of GDP per capita (to the EU average of 2007), carbon intensity would have to fall to just 6g/$ of production, almost 130 times lower than it is today and requiring an average annual fall in carbon intensity of 11 per cent, in order to limit global warming to 2 degrees. Even if recent trends of global population (at 0.7 per cent per annum) and income growth (at 1.4 per cent per year) were just extrapolated to 2050, carbon intensity would have to be reduced to 36gCO_2/$ – a 21-fold improvement on the current global average.

The UNCTAD study includes many more interesting analyses, all demonstrating the enormous difficulties encountered in obtaining the energy- and resource-efficiency gains needed for sustainability.

Growth's dilemma

The British economist Tim Jackson has written an important book on the problems of growth and sustainability. *Prosperity Without Growth: Economics for a Finite Planet* (2009) was written for the British Government's Sustainability Commission and is a most valuable contribution to the discussion on sustainable development. 'An economy predicated on the perpetual expansion of debt-driven, materialistic consumption is unsustainable ecologically, problematic socially, and unstable economically,' wrote Jackson.

The book identifies three main reasons why the current growth model is not possible to sustain. First, the current model assumes that material wealth is an adequate measure of prosperity. But a life worth living is much more complicated than that. Obsessed with rising GDP, we sacrifice community and wellbeing in the hope that just a little more will make everything all right. This is futile. The growth model is undermining our happiness and causing a 'social recession'. 'Our technologies, our economy and our social aspirations are all mis-aligned with any meaningful definition of prosperity,' in Jackson's words.

Second, growth is unevenly distributed, and so is not likely to ever succeed in providing a decent standard of living for everyone. Globally, the richest fifth of the world takes home 74 per cent of the income while the poorest fifth gets just 2 per cent. Since poverty is relative, growth will never fix it. It's a mathematical impossibility. 'You could grow the world economy for a million years and still not make poverty history.'

Third, we obviously can't continue to grow the economy much further. We've already gone into ecological overshoot. 'We simply don't have the ecological capacity,' says Jackson. 'By the end of the century, our children and grandchildren will face a hostile climate, depleted resources, the destruction of habitats, the decimation of species, food scarcities, mass migrations and almost inevitably war.' He concludes that from an environmental and climate perspective conventional growth is not sustainable. He also notes, however, that de-growth is no solution, for both economic and social reasons. 'Growth may be unsustainable, but de-growth is unstable.'

The challenge is that society is organized on the premise that the pie will continue to grow. Growth must increase in order to create jobs and fund social welfare. When growth goes down, everyone experiences problems. Merchandise sales decrease, companies cut back or close down, the number of jobs drops, and the same applies to wages and taxes. For all those who depend on large loans – whether we are talking about states, companies or individual consumers – low or negative growth is also a problem. Growth in the economy is absolutely needed to repay the loans, not least the interest on them.

Another dimension of growth is obviously the distribution policy. Even if income distribution is terribly skewed, it has been relatively easy to make the case for redistribution in a situation where incomes are rising all the time. When this is not the case, we can expect much sharper tensions between different groups in society.

Jackson has no ready solutions to the dilemmas of growth. He wrote his book primarily to raise awareness of the problems we face and stimulate discussion on possible alternative solutions. His book, no doubt, stimulated debate. But still today the discussion on the growth dilemma is on the margin, not in the mainstream. The authors of this book do not offer any ready solutions. But like Jackson we feel an almost desperate need for a broad discussion in society about the growth dilemmas. We also recognize opportunities for change and a number of possible ways forward, such as the following.

- Introducing mandatory targets for improving resource efficiency. Efficiency requirements in many areas should be set higher than the expected growth in the economy, preferably to 4 or 5 per cent. Only then can we break the steadily increasing throughput of both energy and raw materials.
- Implementing a tax reform, where taxes on labour are gradually lowered while the tax on fossil fuels and many crucial raw materials is raised. To handle the rebound effect, taxes must gradually increase in step with efficiencies in energy and resource usage – all with the aim of keeping relative prices at the same level.

- Identifying looming scarcity, such as fresh water in many regions, and developing smart market solutions to encourage more efficient use.
- Introducing strong incentives for companies to create long-lasting products that can be easily upgraded and repaired.
- Studying Nature's best ideas and imitating such designs and processes to solve human problems – a discipline known as biomemetics or biomimicry.
- Reviewing the balance between investment and consumption, as well as between private and public investment. The latter must focus on the renewal of energy and the creation of a far greener and sustainable infrastructure.
- Rethinking the framework of the financial system, with the particular aim of controlling the credit volume and obliging the banking sector to incorporate climate and environment risks in their operations.
- Introducing more flexible working hours. Many people, especially families with children, live under great time pressure and stress. Why not offer them the possibility of harnessing productivity gains through a reduction in working time?

In any case, a detailed discussion of growth's dilemmas is necessary. Burying our heads in the sand like today's political leaders and pretending that the problems do not exist is more than unduly irresponsible. We recognize that these problems are difficult to solve, especially as the whole organization of society is built on the premise of increased material expansion. But it must be possible to adapt society's development in such a way that key economic, social and environmental objectives are balanced against each other, instead of letting the economy erode the natural capital upon which society ultimately rests.

As already noted, the strategy to tackle the dilemmas of growth demands, that we use energy and natural resources much more efficiently. This we could achieve by, among other things, shifting taxation and/or imposing stringent productivity targets for the use of resources. How this would work in practice is not an easy question. Such a reform would ideally have to be made at international level, or at least at EU level.

This being said, achieving harmonized rules at international level has proved to be extremely difficult. We would therefore urge individual countries to spearhead a development in this direction. We need ad hoc solutions to both help raise awareness and also demonstrate that other ways of organizing the economy are both possible and beneficial. Against the backdrop of rising prices on energy and commodities, a development towards a radically more resource-efficient economy – in the form of a circular economy – should be both feasible and profitable.

17 Towards a circular economy

> Previous patterns of growth have brought increased prosperity, but through intensive and often inefficient use of resources. The role of biodiversity, ecosystems and their services is largely undervalued, the costs of waste are often not reflected in prices, current markets and public policies cannot fully deal with competing demands on strategic resources such as minerals, land, water and biomass. This calls for a coherent and integrated response over a wide range of policies in order to deal with expected resource constraints and to sustain our prosperity in the long run.
>
> (European Commission 2011)

Forty years ago, the Club of Rome presented the report *Limits to Growth* (1972). Its chief message was that a depletion of vital resources and increasing pressures from pollution of all kinds would create high risks for the global economy during the first half of the twenty-first century. Few reports have become so controversial and, in many circles, so criticized. It came at a time when optimism was blooming. Developed countries could look back on decades of high growth and rising living standards. Under such circumstances, pointing out that there should be limits to such growth was not popular.

The Club of Rome report became the target chiefly of many leading economists. The main criticism centred on the fact that the report was based on higher consumption trends, while not taking sufficient account of technological development and price correction mechanisms. Economists could simply refer to the price trends for most commodities, which obviously worked against the Club of Rome predictions. To bring the matter to a head, in 1980 one of the leading environmental critics, Paul Ehrlich, was challenged to a bet by the American economist Julian Simon. Simon argued that technological development would lead to continued falling prices for a number of important minerals. Ehrlich was able to choose the minerals he believed would be affected by scarcity. Simon won the bet. The metals Ehrlich selected were significantly cheaper a decade later.

The fact that Ehrlich would have won the bet if it had been made a decade after that was of little comfort to him in the 1990s. At the time, it simply reinforced the belief that the warnings of the Club of Rome were irrelevant. Many economists still treat the report with condescension. They simply do not accept that the combination of resource scarcity, overpopulation, and an increase in the amount of pollution and waste can lead to large and growing problems, or even a collapse of the world economy. But the debate is slowly sobering up. In time for the fortieth anniversary of *Limits to Growth*, a stack of international reports have emerged which essentially confirm the majority of the Club of Rome's conclusions (Dobbs *et al.* 2011; Ellen MacArthur Foundation 2012; WEF 2011; Pauli 2010; KPMG 2012; European Commission 2011; Blue Planet Prize Winners 2012; UN GSP Report 2012). The principals behind these reports, which essentially corroborate *Limits to Growth*, are various research institutions, the UN Secretary-General, the European Commission and OECD, but also organizations tied to the private sector. All of these reports issue strong warnings about the combination of an increasingly unstable climate and the over-exploitation of many important ecosystems and resources, renewable as well as finite. The criticism is tough on the economy's framework and the absence of incentives that can lead to a more positive direction of development, without increasing the risk of environmentally-driven shocks to the economy.

Recent scientific assessments show, moreover, that the predictions made by the Club of Rome are so far largely holding up (Randers 2012; Turner 2008; Meadows *et al.* 2004). The world is more or less following the development towards growing global resource constraints as predicted in the *Limits to Growth* report. This is remarkable, in relation both to the enormous critique the forecasts received (they were exaggerating risks and the forecasts would never materialize) and to the rudimentary data on global trends that were available at the time.

Among the reports referred to, the one by KPMG, *Expect the Unexpected: Building business value in a changing world* (2012), conveys a stark message:

> Population growth, exploitation of natural resources, climate change and other factors are putting the world on a development trajectory that is not sustainable. In other words, if we fail to alter our patterns of production and consumption, things will begin to go badly wrong.

Even stronger is the message conveyed by 'Environmental and development challenges: the imperative to act' (2012), a paper signed by all eighteen recipients of the Blue Planet Prize – among them Gro Harlem Bruntland, James Hansen, Amory Lovins, James Lovelock, Susan Solomon and Bob Watson:

> The human ability to do has vastly outstripped the ability to understand. As a result civilization is faced with a perfect storm of problems, driven by overpopulation, overconsumption by the rich, the use of environmentally malign technologies and gross inequalities. They include loss of the

> biodiversity that runs human life-support systems, climate disruption, global toxification, alteration of critical biogeochemical cycles, increasing probability of vast epidemics, and the specter of a civilization-destroying nuclear war. These biophysical problems are interacting tightly with human governance systems, institutions and civil societies that are now inadequate to deal with them. (Blue Planet Prize Winners 2012)

The statement continues:

> The rapidly deteriorating biophysical situation is more than bad enough, but it is barely recognized by a global society infected by the irrational belief that physical economies can grow forever and disregarding the facts that the rich in developed and developing countries get richer and the poor are left behind. And the perpetual growth myth is enthusiastically embraced by politicians and economists as an excuse to avoid tough decisions facing humanity. This myth promotes the impossible idea that indiscriminate economic growth is the cure for all the world's problems, while it is actually (as currently practiced) the disease that is at the root cause of our unsustainable global practices.

The magnitude of the challenges is exacerbated by the estimated increase both in population numbers and economic growth. Up to three billion new middle-class consumers are likely to emerge by 2030, compared with 1.8 billion today, driving up demand for a range of different resources. This soaring demand will arise just as finding new, reasonably priced and environmentally sound sources of supply becomes increasingly difficult. One obvious conclusion is that the expected increase in demand cannot be met, unless there is nothing less than a revolution in the way we use natural resources.

Efficiency alone won´t be enough

In Chapter 16 we explained the challenges so far of decoupling economic growth from the use of energy and materials. Simply increasing resource efficiency is not going to get us where we need to be. When economies continue to grow – indeed, are given a boost to grow by the productivity gains made – a large part of the savings will be eaten up over time. If the rebound effects are not taken into account, and acted upon, the gains will eventually be lost.

We are by no means questioning the objective of enhancing energy and resource efficiency. Essentially we have no choice. What has to be questioned, however, is the way production and consumption are being organized. The industrial economy of today is characterized by more or less linear flows of materials. The pattern is well described in a recent report by the Ellen McArthur Foundation, *Towards a Circular Economy* (2012):

> Throughout its evolution and diversification, our industrial economy has hardly moved beyond one fundamental characteristic established in the early days of industrialization: a linear model of resource consumption that follows a 'take-make-dispose' pattern. Companies harvest and extract materials, use them to manufacture a product, and sell the product to a consumer – who then discards it when it no longer serves its purpose. Indeed, this is more true now than ever – in terms of volume, some 65 billion tonnes of raw materials entered the economic system in 2010, and this figure is expected to grow to about 82 billion tonnes in 2020.

There are clear reasons behind the way the industrial economy evolved. Companies in most sectors have benefitted from falling commodity prices for long periods of time. Consequently, the focus in productivity was on labour and capital, not on resources. But times are changing. While the real price for most commodities, except crude oil, has declined over the last hundred years – on average by 70 per cent – that entire decline has been erased over the last ten years. The recent surge in prices is easily explained. One reason is the very rapid increase in demand from emerging economies. In 2010 China alone used almost half of the world´s cement, coal and iron ore and 40 per cent of its bauxite. Another reason is that the richest mineral ores have already been exploited. Further extraction means higher costs. Yet another important factor is that productivity increases in agriculture are lower today than in the 1970s and 80s, while demand for food is increasing. Even though modest efforts have been made in the past to enhance resource efficiency, the demand for both energy and resources continues to increase over time. Companies are beginning to realize, however, that the linear system of resource use exposes them to a number of risks, in particular higher prices and supply disruptions.

Recycling rates are ridiculously low

A first important step towards a more efficient use of resources – and a circular economy – would be to significantly increase recycling rates in society. According to a report released in 2011 by the United Nations Environment Programme (UNEP 2011c), recycling rates of metals are in many cases far lower than their potential for reuse. Less than one-third of some 60 metals studied had an end-of-life recycling rate above 50 per cent and 34 elements were below 1 per cent, yet according to the study many of them are crucial to clean technologies such as batteries for hybrid cars and the magnets in wind turbines. When launching the report, the executive director of UNEP, Mr. Achim Steiner, said:

> In theory, metals can be used over and over again, minimizing the need to mine and process virgin materials and thus saving substantial amounts of energy and water while minimizing environmental degradation. Raising levels of recycling worldwide can therefore contribute to a

transition to a low carbon, resource efficient Green Economy while assisting to generate 'green jobs'.

In spite of all this, recycling rates remain far from optimal for most metals. Data from the Bureau of International Recycling confirm the findings of the UNEP study:

- while CO_2 emissions are reduced by more than 90 per cent when aluminium scrap is used instead of bauxite, only one third of aluminium demand is supplied by secondary production;
- while CO_2 emissions are reduced by 65 per cent by using copper scrap, less than one third of copper production comes from copper scrap;
- while using secondary lead instead of ore reduces CO_2 emissions by 99 per cent, only 50 per cent of the world production originates from secondary lead;
- while the carbon footprint of nickel using primary production is 90 per cent higher than that of secondary smelting, the recycling rate is less than 25 per cent;
- while primary production of tin requires 99 per cent more energy than secondary production, the recycling rate is less than 15 per cent;
- while CO_2 emissions are reduced by 58 per cent through the use of ferrous scrap, only 40 per cent of world steel production comes from scrap.

When looking at the electronics sector the picture is particularly worrying. An estimated 50 million tonnes of e-waste is generated each year. The US Environment Protection Agency estimates that no more than 15 to 20 per cent of this is being recycled. The rest ends up in landfills or incinerators. Electrical waste is hazardous but also a potential source of valuable and scarce materials. One particular problem has to do with rare earth metals. These are crucial components of many new technologies. No one can say today how close we are to immediate shortages, not least because China controls most of the production. Many modern technologies will not be able to function if access becomes constrained.

From cradle to cradle

But enhanced rates of recycling would be just one of several necessary steps towards a circular economy. Decades ago the concept of 'cradle to cradle' was introduced, first in the early 1980s by Walter Stahel, secretary general of the Product-Life Institute and a leading advocate of using energy and materials in a more responsible way; and later by Michael Braungart and William McDonough in their landmark report *Cradle to Cradle; Remaking the way we make things* (2002). The main thrust of the concept is to create industrial systems that are not only efficient but essentially waste-free. The basis for this thinking is that the linear way in which the world economy currently operates fuels a culture of consumption and creates more waste than is sustainable in the long term. By contrast, the living world operates in a circular cycle where the waste of one species provides the food for another and resources flow. As Braungart and McDonough explain: 'In the cradle-to-cradle model, all materials used in industrial or commercial processes – such as metals, fibres, dyes – are seen to fall into one of two categories: "technical" or "biological" nutrients.

- *Technical nutrients* are strictly limited to non-toxic, non-harmful synthetic materials that have no negative effects on the natural environment; they can be used in continuous cycles, as the same product, without losing their integrity or quality. In this manner these materials can be used over and over again instead of being 'downcycled' into lesser products, ultimately becoming waste.
- *Biological nutrients* are organic materials once used, can be disposed of in any natural environment and decompose into the soil, providing food for small life forms without affecting the natural environment. This is dependent on the ecology of the region; for example, organic material from one country or landmass may be harmful to the ecology of another country or landmass.'

The main message was not to focus only on enhancing efficiency, but to increase effectiveness. 'If your system is wrong, increasing efficiency is not the solution.' What Stahel, Braungart and McDonough were advocating was to 'do things right'. The background, of course, was the realization that indefinite material growth on a planet with finite and often fragile natural resources cannot be sustainable.

The main principles behind 'cradle to cradle' – to extend wealth, minimize waste and go for maximum reuse and recycling of materials – is gradually gaining ground. The European Commission Flagship Program's report, Roadmap for a Resource-Efficient Europe, presented in September 2011, stressed that:

- improving the design of products can both decrease the demand for energy and raw materials and make those products more durable and easier to recycle;
- increasing recycling rates will reduce the pressure on demand for primary raw materials, help to reuse valuable materials which would otherwise be wasted, and reduce energy consumption and greenhouse gas emissions from extraction and processing.

The Ellen MacArthur Foundation report, *Towards a Circular Economy*, presented in early 2012 and backed up by a group of leading multinationals including B&Q, British Telecom, Cisco, National Grid and Renault, makes a strong pitch for a 'circular economy' and defines the objectives as follows:

> A circular economy is an industrial system that is restorative by intention and design. In a circular economy, products are designed for ease of reuse, disassembly and refurbishment – or recycling – with the understanding that it is the reuse of vast amounts of material reclaimed from end-of-life products, rather than the extraction of new resources, that is the foundation of economic growth. Moreover, the circular economy shifts towards the use of renewable energy, eliminates the use of toxic chemicals, which impair reuse, and aims for the elimination of waste through the superior design of materials, products, systems, and, within this, business models.

That such a radical definition for the future industrial system is supported by a group of multinationals is no small feat. It represents a fundamental shift in perspective as compared to the industrial system we have today.

Since his early interest in the 1980s, Walter Stahel has continued to give a lot of thought to the circular economy – and how to make it happen. In his seminal book *The Performance Economy* (2010) Stahel presents a convincing case for extending wealth and replacing material throughput with activities like recycling, reuse and reconditioning. The approach can be summarized as 'material as services'.

New business models

Today's business models are based on maximizing the volume of sales of various products. As an alternative, Stahel advocates instead a transition to offering services. Sales of products will be replaced by leases, coupled with exceptional service. Since responsibility for the material used in a product remains with the manufacturing company, strong incentives are created to fully exploit the material to earn money on what has already been produced for as long as possible. This is in great contrast to today's system, in which new models are constantly launched and consumers are encouraged to trade generally adequate products for the very latest thing. Products should instead be designed to both last longer and be easy to upgrade, reuse and recycle. A system like this would need to be adapted to the character of the product. Stahel shows in his book that there are already examples of this way of thinking and working, especially in relations between companies (Business2Business).

- Rolls Royce has replaced sales of jet engines to various airlines with leases.
- Michelin rents car tyres for heavy vehicles and is responsible for their maintainance, upgrading and recycling as waste product.
- Xerox offers copying services instead of selling photocopiers.
- Interface leases carpets and recirculates the material over time.

For these companies, the new way of working has meant that both energy and raw material consumption has been significantly reduced. The same applies to CO_2 emissions. And all the while profitability has improved. It becomes a win-win proposition.

An interesting option of the 'circular economy' is the 'reconditioning' of products that are going to be phased out. Stahel highlights the example of Deutsche Bahn and the choice faced when deciding on a new generation of trains: either recondition a total of 159 ICE train sets of type 1, or make an order for a brand new fleet of trains. The cost of a new train fleet was estimated at €25 million per unit. Reconditioning, which meant a significant upgrade from the current standard, was estimated at only €3 million per train. Deutsche Bahn chose the latter option, saving not only a considerable sum of money but also 80 per cent of the material required for a new train – a total of 16,500 tonnes of steel and 1,180 tonnes of copper. Not to mention avoiding CO_2 emissions in the order of 35,000 tonnes and 500,000 tonnes of mine waste.

The challenge for the future is to generate a strong breakthrough for the concept of 'service instead of products' for a wide array of consumer products, computers, cell phones, household appliances, cars, furniture and textiles. Even in the property market, the same principles apply. Construction modules and interiors that currently have a limited lifespan and are usually scrapped in connection with renovations can instead be rented out, enabling existing materials to be reused. In the energy sector work with these principles is already under way by offering energy services instead of selling energy in the form of kilowatt hours of electricity, or tonnes of oil.

The consequences of a model in which goods become services are unambiguously positive. Producers will be responsible for products and materials throughout their life cycle and disposal. It will become economically interesting to produce items that are easy to repair, upgrade, disassemble and recycle. The management of waste and residues are internalized and becomes the responsibility of the producer and not, as today, a cost for society to handle. Strong incentives are created to reuse and recondition and thereby increase the value – and revenue – for every pound of product or material that is used.

The model also leads to more new jobs being created locally in activities such as maintenance or servicing, recycling, recovery and reconditioning., while traditional jobs in manufacturing and minerals extraction will decrease. But the net effect on the number of jobs is definitely positive. The really significant benefit is the reduction of pressure on natural resources.

Improved resource efficiency leads to lower CO_2

One of the many advantages of the developmental model launched in *The Performance Economy* is the reduction of greenhouse gases. In a special study for the British government, the branch of the Stockholm Environment Institute (SEI) in York, under Professor John Barrett's leadership, analysed the impact on emissions of CO_2 from a more efficient use of resources (SEI 2012). The study included a number of sectors, which together accounted for about one-third of the British economy. The changes that were studied included measures to extend the life of various products, increased recycling, use of lighter materials, radically reduced household food waste and changing dietary habits. The results of this study show that CO_2 emissions will fall by almost 30 per cent by 2050 for the sectors studied. These reductions are expected to be added to those already identified in the context of climate change initiatives in the UK (which consist primarily of direct changes in energy use).

What incentives are needed to expand the circular economy?

The crucial question then is: How can we move society in the direction of a circular economy? It ought to be obvious to everyone that activities such as recycling and reuse and extending the longevity of products will contribute to reducing a company´s expenses both for materials and waste management. The question remains how these positive elements could compete with a production system that is being optimized for maximum throughput of energy and materials. How can the principle of 'earning more revenue by selling more stuff' be replaced by a business model in which revenue is primarily the result of quality of service?

The rapid price increase in recent years for many commodities, including energy, ought to encourage the business community to search for new ways to manage materials. However, to expect that price signals alone will be enough to initiate the necessary transition to a circular economy is probably naive. What will be needed, not least to counteract the economic forces that continue to benefit from today's production system, is policy action on many fronts. Any revolutionary change – and to move towards a circular economy is truly revolutionary – will imply both substantial dislocation and some 'losers'. Thus policy not only has to give the right signals in terms of incentives. It also has to manage change in the form of resistance and opposition.

Several policy instruments should be considered in the effort to implement a circular economy:

- *binding targets for resource efficiency*: setting such targets well above the expected growth rate in the economy industry would send the right signals to focus on the maximum reuse and recycling of materials;
- *sustainable innovation*: by giving priority to sustainable design and closed material loops, the research community would give maximum attention to the principles of a circular economy;
- *a tax reform:* by lowering taxes on labour and raising them on the use of virgin materials, similar incentives to those of binding resource efficiency targets would be at play.

Walter Stahel has written an interesting proposal on how to achieve a dematerialization of the economy through a shift in the tax system ('Sustainable taxation – Policy for Resource Taxation'; address given in Stockholm, April 2012). Taxing materials and energies will, according to Stahel,

> promote low-carbon and low-resource solutions and a move towards a 'circular' regional economy as opposed to the 'linear' global economy, requiring fuel-based transport for goods throughput. In addition to substantial improvements in material and energy efficiency, regional job creation and national GHG emission reductions, such a change will foster all activities based on 'caring', such as maintaining cultural heritage and natural wealth, health services, knowledge and know-how. (Stahel 2012)

We find his reasoning very convincing and hope that policy-makers in different parts of the world will consider the principles behind Stahel´s paper. The approach suggested is by its very nature more suited to the situation in OECD countries rather than that of many developing countries. But the general principle of providing incentives for extending wealth and maximum reuse of materials should be part of the policy mix in developing countries as well.

In conclusion, we find that ample evidence clearly points to a world development with serious threats to the modern economy, due to future resource constraints and the risk of transgressing safe planetary boundaries. The first warnings, forty years ago, that such a development path would experience increasing difficulties during the first half of the twenty-first century are by and large proving correct. Today we need to couple the advantages of an open and globalized market economy with regulations that enable consumers and producers worldwide not only to be more efficient in general in their use of natural resources but also effective – that is, to do the right things.

18 How much is enough?

There is enough for everyone's need but not for everyone's greed.
Mahatma Ghandi

A common thread throughout this book has been the realization that nature's cupboard is not infinite. We have shown that as the world economy is currently being organized, in terms of extraction of resources and waste, we are sawing off the branch we are sitting on. The combination of climate change, scarcity of energy and water and degraded ecosystems represents an enormous burden for communities worldwide. No part of the world will escape the consequences. From a short-term perspective, the rich countries are in far better condition than low-income countries to cope with price increases but also to adapt to climate change. But the prospects for generating human welfare during the next decade are already seriously undermined even for the rich countries.

The necessary societal transformation will be difficult and costly, measured in conventional terms. But it would also represent a truly positive development if today's rapid destruction of natural capital and the negative impact on the atmosphere were to be reversed. With the current way of measuring welfare, it would be difficult to estimate the change correctly. Even if broad investment to stabilize the climate and strengthen ecosystems – from the protection of tropical forests to better land management, the conservation of fresh water and the introduction of a sustainable fishery – represented a cost in the short term, it would help to strengthen the very capital resources that will ultimately determine living standards over time. Without a more appropriate management of natural capital, there isn't a chance in the long run of meeting the basic needs of today's population, much less an increasing population. Such a strategy would in addition generate many new jobs and new markets and gradually replace the kinds of production and jobs that are not sustainable over time.

To enable this transition, we will be forced to act in the short and long term simultaneously. In the short term, immediate measures are required in the current system to break the large negative environmental trends. We must act on a number of levels simultaneously, from individual households and companies to national governments and regional and global institutions. In the long term we need to develop radically new ideas and concepts on how society should be organized. This applies particularly to the economy and to international co-operation.

The look of the future

We are now approaching the end of this book and we will try to describe what the future might look like. The short-term proposals are intended to show that there are many concrete measures we can implement today. The aim is not to present a complete programme to meet the world's problems relating to the environment and natural resources, but rather to be pragmatic. By proposing steps in the right direction that can be taken now, we want to foster optimism. We have selected a number of areas that we see as top priorities during the coming decade.

In the long term other changes will be needed. Today's political vision, both of the right and left, is first and foremost about increasing people's material living standard. At the same time it is clear that the resource base is not sufficient for an ever-increasing material consumption. We also know that increased material consumption above a certain level does not automatically mean a better quality of life. Other values come into play, but these are difficult to assess correctly as long as GDP is the measure of development. When resources put a cap on growth, we must find ways to allocate them as fairly as possible between the current generation and, especially, future generations.

An important, perhaps even crucial, question is how we educate the younger generations that will have to take a lead in changing the world. Education and research are areas in great need of change. The design of the economic model is nevertheless the deciding factor. As discussed in previous chapters, a revision of the economic framework is necessary, with the primary aims of giving natural capital and ecosystem services their rightful place and making clear their value – and establishing smart markets in areas where the price mechanism does not function. In addition, besides a total revision of financial markets, the provision of decent jobs stands out as a top priority. Finally, international co-operation needs to be strengthened. Today's institutions were established for a different world. The challenges of tomorrow are poorly served by yesterday's institutions.

Climate Wars

The Canadian journalist Gwynne Dyer, in his book *Climate Wars* (2008), describes a variety of possible future scenarios as a consequence of climate change. His starting point is that governments will fail to get carbon emissions under control and that the warming will continue. Dyer has interviewed many experts in climate science and security. The picture he paints is distressing.

Our climate is getting warmer. Various feedback mechanisms, such as methane seeping from the tundra, reinforce the process. Among the consequences that Dyer highlights are the gradually elevated sea levels, increased frequency and intensity of extreme weather patterns, changes in rainfall patterns (too much rain in some places, too little rain in others) and worsening conditions for growing food increasing in different parts of the world. He emphasizes, as we have tried to do, that climate change takes place in a world already struggling with the growing problem of food supply.

Dyer paints a bleak picture of wars and civil wars over increasingly scarce resources and/or political systems that implode. Unless strong action against climate change is taken soon, there will be little chance, according to Dyer, to save the high-tech society that emerged after the Second World War, or even to do something about the climate problems. It is not that Dyer is over-confident about technological solutions, but he points out that a substantial number of promising areas of research, such as energy, water management and food production, all require a high level of education and research, stable institutions and a functioning market. All of this is threatened in a world where global warming is allowed to continue.

Another world is possible

This bleak future is not inevitable. Instead of increasing tension and conflict, we can see before us a world in which governments work in close co-operation and mutual trust in order to stabilize climate and conserve natural resources. The experience of the climate negotiations so far, however, demonstrates how difficult it is to bring about such co-operation.

Awareness is growing that the current institutions for global co-operation and governance are entirely inadequate. The UN and World Bank came into being in another time and to solve other problems. National sovereignty stood at the centre and along with it came the principle of decision by consensus, allowing individual countries to block decisions desired by the majority. Or a country could completely abstain, as the United States has done with respect to the Kyoto Protocol. Today it is Earth's 'sovereignty' that is threatened. But who defends it? Climate negotiations can appear more like trench warfare than a search for common solutions.

One critical issue has to be added to the list of problems that requires decision-making at the international level, namely geo-engineering. Several initiatives are under way in an effort to avoid runaway climate change. Some industrial interests already promote geo-engineering as an alternative to curbing emissions. Potential schemes include pumping sulphates into the stratosphere to simulate a volcanic eruption and so reduce incoming solar radiation, fertilizing the sea surface with iron to remove carbon dioxide from the atmosphere, and brightening clouds to reflect more sunlight back into space.

It is necessary to point out the need for legitimacy in any decision about geo-engineering. Some of the schemes suggested involve serious risks. The current situation is thoroughly unacceptable: no regulations exist, apart from a non-binding decision under the Convention on Biological Diversity, with its moratorium 'until there is an adequate scientific basis on which to justify such activities and appropriate consideration of the associated risks'. There is a risk that some countries will go ahead and initiate their own geo-engineering efforts without the assent of the rest of the world.

Changing global governance

The question is how to create the conditions for fundamental changes in global governance. The creation of the UN and World Bank was associated with great difficulties. Attempts were made before the Second World War but without success. It was only after the war, with its many tens of millions of deaths and enormous material destruction, that the United Nations came into being. Or take the example of co-operation within the European Union. Before the civil war in the Balkans in the 1990s, there was no EU foreign policy worthy of the name. Only when hostilities ended did the process of closer co-operation on foreign policy begin, because the Union does not want to risk being so constrained again when facing a crisis in the region.

The financial crisis in autumn 2008 led to the formation of the G20, a co-operation that appears to be permanent. Before the financial crisis, attempts to widen the circle of governments that meet regularly to discuss the economy and finances never got off the ground. It was only when the financial market in the United States teetered on the verge of collapse that the political will and interest to broaden the co-operation materialized.

Important changes in international co-operation only seem possible after large and serious crises – a disappointing conclusion. And yet we know that this 'wait and see' attitude is not an option with most of today's problems. Waiting to change course until a severe climate catastrophe occurs is unthinkable, especially since the consequences of such events could well be irreversible. It may take millennia to come back to a 'normal mode', even if at all possible.

Ad hoc solutions

So how can we implement reform of global governance? The situation did not become any easier after the mid-term elections in the US in early November 2010. On the contrary, a deal on climate change appears to be completely ruled out for the foreseeable future. Worse, the Republicans' general attitude towards international co-operation is, except for anti-terrorism, strongly negative.

The ideal would obviously be a strong and reformed United Nations, or a whole new world organization, whose task is to act in the interest of us all. Before this becomes a reality, 'ad hoc' solutions will be necessary in order to break the stalemate that now exists. President Bush launched the concept of a 'coalition of the willing' in connection with a war that has been seriously questioned. We would like to use this concept in a totally different context, one that involves peaceful co-operation to stabilize the climate, stop over-exploitation of our most important ecosystems, and strengthen efforts to combat poverty. A first step could consist of an agreement on close co-operation between the EU and Asia on a number of key global challenges. If and when such an agreement was made, it would be open to countries in other parts of the world to join. Such a course would mean that the US would be left aside, at least initially, though it would of course be welcome to join in if it so wished. But to be waiting for a country, year after year, that is not moving in the right direction is not reasonable.

How much is enough?

Almost 35 years ago, Swedish researchers Lars Ingelstam and Goran Bäckstrand wrote the acclaimed study of the future, 'How much is enough?', in *What Now,* the 1975 Dag Hammarskjöld Report on Development and International Cooperation (Ingelstam and Bäckstrand 1975). In their paper the authors took up many of the same issues as the Club of Rome had done a few years earlier in *Limits to Growth.* The starting point was that the small planet we live on would not be able to sustain the continued rapid increase of conventional growth. Problems and constraints would emerge in the long run, with regard to ecosystems, some finite resources such as crude oil, and pollution. In retrospect we can see that the Club of Rome and Ingelstam and Bäckstrand were all surprisingly accurate in their analyses.

'How much is enough?' went a step further than the Club of Rome. Part of the study included a number of concrete proposals to modify consumption trends in Sweden. Among them were proposals on a ceiling on meat consumption, a cap on oil use, more rational use of buildings, far more durable goods, and no privately owned cars. The study was controversial and led to an extremely lively debate. The proposals must of course be understood in the prevailing international circumstances. The first oil crisis had just hit the world and energy security emerged as one of society's Achilles heels. In the previous decade, many former colonies in Africa and Asia had received independence and there were broad discussions on a new and more equitable international economic order. An important part of that debate was the issue of resource allocation in the world and how consumer habits in rich countries affected the prerequisites for development and poverty reduction in developing countries.

Today, the debate situation is different. One reason is, of course, that the East–West conflict and the Cold War are behind us. There are few countries that currently support a socialist economy. Policy proposals for an extensive redistribution of resources have been put aside. But resource issues are more relevant than ever. What the Club of Rome and Ingelstam and Bäckstrand described as possible scenarios for development in the long run is now happening. Climate emissions, as well as other types of pollution, 'peak oil' and the over-exploitation of many important ecosystems are proof enough.

The idea of a 'moderate level' – in Swedish 'lagom'– in terms of material standards is beginning to be discussed again among both scientists and representatives of civil society. However, among political parties in general, there is still silence. We cannot see how the problems we face can be solved without a radically changed perspective on both the use and allocation of resources on Earth. A completely new kind of policy framework must gradually be developed. Even if we ignore a growing population and the rapid economic growth that is taking place in many developing countries, we know that the type of consumption economy developed in Western countries will not be sustainable over time.

Gaining support for this insight is not easy. Opposition to it is great. Large financial interests have invested in today's production and consumption economy. Many governments around the world are deeply in debt and need fast conventional growth to come back into balance. Hundreds of millions of consumers in developed countries are accustomed to equating increased material consumption with quality of life. Billions of people in developing countries are striving to achieve the lifestyles and consumer habits developed in the West.

What is needed is nothing less than a revolution, both in attitudes and in social and economic organization.

19 The road ahead

'Bankrupting Nature' might be considered a dramatic title. Businesses and individual households fall into bankruptcy. Occasionally, like Argentina more than a decade ago and possibly Greece now, individual countries are forced to suspend payments. But nature going bankrupt? Many people experience nature 'as the constant and stable foundation for economic activity', as R.V. O'Neill, and J.R Khan express it in their article 'Homo Economicus as a keystone species' (O'Neill and Khan 2001). Our hope is that this book will help explain the fallacy of such a belief. The consequences of climate change and overexploitation of many important ecosystems, the increasing depletion of biodiversity and subsequent risk of shortages of finite resources, such as crude oil, phosphorus and rare metals all point to the vulnerability of the planet.

We have but one Earth, and its natural assets are, by and large, finite. Thus depletion inevitably leads to resource constraints. Herman Daly has written persuasively about reaching a point of 'uneconomic growth' where the costs to society of an additional unit of growth (as conventionally measured) will be greater than the benefits (Daly 1999). In his writings, Daly covers a wide array of externalities such as pollution, depletion of natural capital, disruption of ecological life-support services, increases in unemployment and destruction of community in the interests of capital mobility. The discussion on 'uneconomic growth', however, is far from mainstream. Most decision-makers refuse to question the concept of conventional economic growth. They seem to believe that the problems we are facing can be effectively addressed through the conventional economic framework. We beg to differ.

One thing is clear: economic growth is not the same as economic wealth. While pointing out this fact, we do not advocate that de-growth is the solution. To quote Tim Jackson: 'While growth is unsustainable, de-growth is unstable' (Jackson 2009). The driving ambition behind this book is to initiate a debate in society about how we could move to a new economic paradigm.

We stand before a defining crossroad. Humanity has only a few years to break existing negative patterns. We are facing bankruptcy, not late payments.

Positive signs

The vast majority of environmental and climate trends point in the wrong direction. Still, there are many examples of positive efforts currently in the works, both in terms of policy decisions and promising technologies. In addition, individuals worldwide are increasingly questioning the conventional economic model. The so-called transition movement is growing rapidly.

Certain countries have introduced successful policies. Sweden enacted a CO_2 tax in 1991 which has resulted in the use of fossil fuels in the heating sector being almost totally phased out. Germany's system of fixed feed-in tariffs has triggered a remarkably rapid deployment of both solar and wind energy. The American government's support for research and development of alternative energy is equally impressive. The same must be said about the Chinese government's ambitions, both in terms of improved energy efficiency and the expansion of wind and solar energy. According to the latest plans, the solar energy base in China will grow by more than a factor of 10 by 2015, from 700 megawatts in 2010 to10,000 megawatts in 2015.

A multitude of research reports have shown that the world could eventually meet its total energy supply through a combination of energy efficiency and renewable energy. The expansion of both wind and solar energy has been extremely rapid in recent years: a more than 25 per cent increase per year in the last fifteen years for wind power and more than 50 per cent annually for photovoltaics during the last ten years (GEA 2012). The cost of both solar and wind has dropped precipitously with this expansion.

A Japanese study has estimated that solar cells installed on 4 per cent of the world's desert area could produce as much energy as the world produces today (Kurokawa 2007). Plans for DESERTEC, a project for large-scale power generation using solar energy in the Sahara desert, have become increasingly concrete. Once the supply of electricity in North Africa has been met – a region with chronic electricity shortages – the plan calls for the surplus to be exported to the EU through high voltage direct current cables under the Mediterranean Sea, with low losses of energy.

In the chapter on energy supply (Chapter 7) we referred to a number of important research studies, as well as technologies, that prove that the necessary energy transition is both possible and feasible: The studies by GEA and IEA, the Jacobson/Delucchi article 'A plan to power 100 percent of the planet with Renewables', as well as *Factor 5* by Weizsäcker and others and *Reinventing Fire* and *Winning the Oil Endgame* by Amory Lovins, all confirm that the challenges are not technological,but rather political in nature (GEA 2012; IEA 2012; Jacobson and Delucchi 2009; Weizsäcker *et al* 2010; Lovins 2004; Lovins 2012). We also referred to promising developments in the construction sector. The trend towards passive houses and zero net energy buildings has been rapid, and with renovations, major energy savings can be made that over time will have great significance. Many developing countries currently face a massive expansion of infrastructure. In China, the equivalent of two billion square metres of new living space will be built each year until 2020. Using conventional technology, the resulting CO_2 emissions would be devastating, but energy smart construction would radically reduce the burden on both climate and the environment.

Even with land use there are new methods being developed both for forest protection and in agricultural use. Through different agricultural practices, which include reduced tillage and transition to perennial crops, we could possibly turn agriculture into a carbon sink, reversing its carbon emissions.

The depletion of ecosystems and species is rapidly increasing. A step in the right direction was taken at the UN conference in Nagoya in October 2010, where consensus was reached among world governments to significantly increase the proportion of protected land and marine areas; 17 per cent of the land mass and 10 per cent of the oceans will be designated as nature reserves. This decision is a major success in the protection of ecosystems and species. But the devil will be in the implementation.

Depletion of fisheries in world's oceans is particularly serious. Research reports have determined that by the middle of this century the world oceans could be left completely empty. However, there is light in the tunnel: reduced fishing quotas in the Baltic Sea and a more resolute grip on illicit fishing have led to the recovery of cod stocks, and Iceland and New Zealand, both countries with large fishing industries, have shown that it is possible to create favourable conditions for sustainable fishing.

Designers of all kinds have long been fascinated by nature and the opportunities it offers as a model for different products. Gradually, a science has been evolving around the basis of 'biomemetics'. The American science journalist Janine Benyus, in her book *Biomimicry* (1997), presents a fascinating review of how natural ecosystems and species work. For close to four billion years of evolution, species and ecosystems gradually adapted to the conditions provided by the earth. By imitating nature, Benyus suggests, we can develop solutions to meet many of the challenges we face. Companies as varied as Airbus, Nike, Interface and several energy and construction companies are examples of businesses that have started using this approach. Airbus has initiated the development of an optimal fuselage design by studying different birds in flight. The petal configuration of the lotus flower has led to the development of building materials and colours that get dirty less easily. Elite swimmers are currently using swimsuits inspired by the design of a shark's skin. Increasing understanding of the role of friction has also led to more energy-efficient designs for boats, submarines and aircrafts. And these are but a few examples.

Another moving force in the field of 'learning from nature' is Gunter Pauli. Pauli was originally a businessman and entrepreneur, one of the founders of Ecover, the firm that produced the first commercial organic detergent. During the process of developing Ecover, Pauli experienced the serious lack of systems thinking in business. On leaving Ecover he started a research network, ZERI – zero emission research initiative. For nearly twenty years Paul worked with a primary focus: how to do more with the resources that come from nature and, more importantly, how to use residue materials in a more optimal way. Many years of co-operation with Janine Benyus led to the integration of biomemetics into Pauli´s work. His latest book, *The Blue Economy* (2010), contains a total of 100 examples of technologies inspired by nature, which together can form much of the basis for a sustainable society.

Solutions that work for nine billion people

While the many examples of positive change are encouraging, the transition needed will require much bolder steps, not least in the way the economy is organized. Incremental change will not do. We are compelled to think out of the box.

What the world truly needs is solutions that are basically transformative, particularly of the systems of production and consumption. Solutions that would be able to meet the needs and aspirations not only of today's global consumers but also of the billions of people who are currently deprived of their most basic needs, while staying within the carrying capacity of the planet. The world population may reach nine billion people by 2050 according to the most recent UN population projection. Hence the solutions we look for must be able to pass through a 'nine billion filter': they must be able to work for a population of nine billion people. Such solutions are not only an ethical imperative; they are also strongly motivated in terms of security. The only way to avoid rising tensions and, indeed, conflicts around access to increasingly scarce natural resources and environmental space will be through policies anchored in principles of equity and justice. The transformative solutions that will be needed after the application of a 'nine billion filter' represent a historic challenge both in terms of innovation and creativity.

What then are transformative solutions? There is, of course, no cut and dried definition, But together with the originator of the 'nine billion filter' principle, Dennis Pamlin (former WWF official and now an independent consultant advising, among others, the Chinese Academy of Social Sciences and the UN), we suggest the following criteria for transformative solutions:

- They should deliver services that result in gains in resource efficiency by a factor of five or more (this is the scope needed in most areas to ensure global sustainability).
- They should depend on infrastructure that is low-carbon and resource-efficient.
- They should go beyond resource efficiency by also aiming at effectiveness.
- They should be systems-oriented – focusing on the whole rather than on the parts.
- Some transformative solutions could even manage to turn problems into solutions, such as buildings that are net producers of renewable energy.

A good illustration of the difference between transformative and conventional solutions is the way climate impact from road transport is being assessed today. The focus so far has been mainly on the emissions from vehicles. But roughly 30 per cent of climate impact from the transport sector is linked to the supporting infrastructure. At present, three different categories of transformative solutions are emerging:

- New technologies that deliver the services we need with less demand for energy and resources, such as replacing physical meetings with video conferencing; teleworking instead of commuting to work – often by car; and accessing books, magazines and documents via the Internet instead of printed materials.
- New integrated systems that provide the services we need in superior ways, such as e-health, e-education and e-governance (using connectivity to keep costs down while improving quality).
- New systems solutions such as passive energy buildings that are net producers of renewable energy and electric vehicles that can also be used for backup power.

In addition to these three categories, an overarching principle emerges: a shift in focus from selling 'products' to providing 'services', such as leasing products instead of owning them. By turning business models upside down and offering 'materials as services', a new business logic will emerge that has already proved efficient for energy and materials as well as costs. In order to deliver transformative solutions, such a change in business models will be needed in many areas. Instead of earning revenue by constantly offering new versions of existing products – thus selling more cars, household appliances and electronic equipment – the focus would be on the functions these products offer. This would result in somewhat of a paradigm shift. Business models, which today are based primarily on volume, on selling more stuff, would be based on offering high-quality services. Prominent examples could be:

- car manufacturers turning into mobility/communication companies offering leasing contracts and car pools;
- household appliances and electronics companies offering leasing contracts or pay-per-use services, as well as the opportunity of updating existing models;
- energy companies, which today operate from the supply side maximizing the sales of kilowatt-hours or tonnes of oil, offering services instead, in the process giving maximum priority to efficiency measures.

Institutions also need to change

Technological improvements are only part of the solution. We must also review the organization of society's diverse institutions. Governments and governmental agencies are currently organized in separate vertical structures; major changes could address all those problems that cut across sectors. In order to speed up such change, or in many cases to make it possible in the first place, political reform is required.

A central part of the work for a more sustainable society needs to be a change in the organization of research and education in favour of more interdisciplinary scientific research and co-operation across disciplines. Scientists need to emerge from their ivory towers and work alongside major stakeholders, so that scientific inquiry can be more driven by solving problems in the real world. We do not question specialization in education, but we must create a system where the appreciation and understanding of the whole, of how things fit together and are interlinked, is radically improved. In no field is this more important than in economics.

The most difficult change will be the necessary redistribution of purchasing power and resources. Environmental and resource space is strained in several areas. Given continued widespread poverty and the great needs in low-income countries, access to that available space must be reserved first for their populations. This would put even greater demands on policy-making in developed countries. Only through a redistribution of income and a radical tightening of resource efficiency – in effect a cap on the increased use of resources in a number of areas – will conditions for development in the poorer parts of the world be improved.

A systems approach

We need to 'marry' efforts to eliminate poverty with measures to mitigate climate change and environmental impact. A more integrated approach to development, climate and environment is a prerequisite for making progress in terms of both climate change and the over-exploitation of many ecosystems.

Developing countries are by no means a homogeneous group. There is little that unites countries like China and Mozambique, or India and Nicaragua. But those outside the circle of industrialized countries have one thing in common: the modernization of their societies began much later and per capita income is low compared to that of industrialized nations. The modernization of the developed countries has already taken place. We were able to build our prosperity on cheap oil, but that option is no longer available for developing countries, partly because oil is many times more expensive today (and is expected to increase even more in price), and partly because of the climate threat. The only ethically defensible solution is that today's industrialized countries should radically rethink the extent of their consumption of energy and resources, in order to leave room for developing countries to grow.

Any solution to climate and environmental problems will require substantial transfers of financial resources from developed countries to developing countries. The decision at the Durban climate conference to establish a Green Fund, reaching $100 billion by 2020, is a positive step forward, but the support needed goes well beyond protection of the environment. Our proposal is a global agreement between developed and developing countries in which traditional work to eradicate poverty is 'wedded' to climate and environmental efforts.

The outlines for such an agreement are not new. The German Professor Franz Josef Radermacher launched the idea of a Global Marshall Plan more than a decade ago and it has gained widening circles of support. But the proposal has been met with international opposition. The traditional way of organizing international negotiations has been to approach it sector by sector; this proposal would require a holistic approach where traditional efforts to eradicate poverty are linked to the issues of climate, environment and ecosystems. As we see it, a global agreement of this kind is the only realistic way to improve the livelihood of poor people while stabilizing the climate and also protecting and regenerating important ecosystems.

The exact cost of such an agreement is difficult to estimate. Many attempts have been made to estimate the cost of measures to limit greenhouse gas emissions, protect tropical forests and adapt to a more stable climate. These total costs are conservatively estimated to be $150-200 billion per year. The cost of traditional development assistance would then have to be added. It may seem like a lot of money, and indeed it is a vast sum, but it is cheap insurance against the risks. Professor Radermacher's proposed financing would make use of, among other sources, a portion of the proceeds from future auctions of emission allowances within the UNFCCC framework and a global financial transaction tax of 0.01 per cent. Other possible sources of financing could be a levy on bunker fuel, aviation fuels or all trade in oil. A dollar surcharge on each barrel of oil would yield more than thirty billion dollars a year in revenue, just as one example.

One issue that merits special attention would be the overall implications of changing production and consumption patterns in industrialized countries for the economies of low-income countries. Income from trade is crucial to many poor countries, so climate and environment strategies should include efforts to ensure that shifts in such patterns as, for example, increased energy and resource efficiency, should bring benefits, not losses, to the exporters.

There's a growing awareness of the role of consumer choice in reducing greenhouse gas (GHG) emissions. As previously mentioned, a 2009 UK study showed that an ambitious effort to change consumption patterns – to buy fewer goods and more services, extend longevity, reduce waste, and eat less meat (while keeping overall spending levels the same) – could significantly reduce associated emissions (WRAP 2009).

For many of the goods made in lower-income countries, international trade can be a critical source of income. A new analysis by the Stockholm Environment Institute (SEI) shows that if all high-income countries were to shift spending to lower-GHG types of products and services, , the average GDP of lower-income countries could drop by more than 4 per cent, and the GDPs of Least Developed Countries (LDCs), by more than 5 per cent.

Elie Dawkins, a research associate in SEI's York Centre and co-author of the report, says:

> This may not seem like a lot, especially given the urgency of mitigating climate change, but people in these countries are already mired in poverty. Per capita incomes in LDCs are only one-tenth of those in the U.K. Clothing production in particular is a big source of revenue for several of them, so while the planet will thank you for buying fewer outfits, the people who sewed them may not be so happy. (SEI 2012)

Dawkins and her York colleagues, including co-author Anne Owen, have done extensive research on emissions associated with consumption, developing tools that help nations and communities gauge their carbon footprints and reaching out to consumers to show them how they can make a difference in the fight to prevent dangerous climate change.

Meanwhile the report's lead author , Peter Erickson, a senior scientist at SEI's US Centre, made the following comment in launching the report: 'If we want to keep temperatures from rising more than 2 °C above pre-industrial levels, shrinking our carbon footprint is a must. But we can try to find ways of lowering our footprint that do not disproportionally harm people in the process.'

The answer is *not*, the authors stress, to give up on efforts to reduce emissions from consumption, but rather to find ways to simultaneously promote sustainable development. One promising approach could be to focus on buying goods from countries with low-GHG production; by their preliminary calculations, the GHG intensity of clothing production, for example, can vary by a factor of four or more between countries. Preferentially sourcing clothes from lower-income, lower-GHG countries instead of from higher-income, higher-GHG countries could thus reduce emissions just as much as buying fewer clothes. High-income countries could also help the poorest countries lower the GHG intensity of their production, the authors say, through direct technology transfer, market-based mechanisms such as sectoral crediting, or climate finance.

A third strategy is to focus on importing higher-cost, higher-quality, value-added goods. This could have both GHG and development benefits if these goods both lasted longer and sold for higher prices, with a large share of the added value retained by the producing country. Further research is needed to determine how best to achieve this, but it could include technology transfer, technical assistance, and help in building local expertise and buying new equipment.

Reform the economic policy framework

We have discussed the economic policy framework at length in previous chapters. A reform seems urgent, not least to bring about the needed transformative solutions. The present economic model has serious shortcomings from a range of view points – economic, social, climate, environmental and resource availability. In previous chapters we have offered a large number of proposals for reform, such as replacing GDP as a target for development, recognizing the value of natural capital and ecosystem services, promoting a truly circular economy, establishing binding targets for energy and resource efficiency, reducing taxes on labour and increasing them on resource use, using public procurement proactively for environment- and climate-friendly solutions, scrapping quarterly reporting for corporations, rethinking compensation schemes in financial institutions and making it obligatory for banks and financial institutions to report their risk exposure in terms of high carbon investments.

The necessary transformation in society will only be possible if it is based on such policy measures. In addition, business models must be reconsidered. If companies can only earn more revenue by selling more stuff, then the equation is impossible. In many areas business models must be changed from selling products to offering services. Existing examples of such business practices – primarily in business to business (B2B) relations – confirm ample benefits. Energy and material throughput as well as carbon emissions are significantly reduced, jobs are increased and the same goes for revenues. Win-win strategies, without any doubt.

We need planetary solutions

We urgently need to reconnect our societies, and thereby our economy, to the biosphere. In the globalized phase of environmental change, where human societies in the Anthropocene are hitting the ceiling of Earth's biophysical, ecological and resource capacities, we need to recognize that future prosperity depends on our capacity to stay within the planetary boundaries.

Given the need to strengthen international co-operation and governance, dare we hope that people around the world – and their governments – will realize in time that we live in a new era where policies for *planetary* solutions are absolutely necessary? The lack of global governance to deal with a whole range of international problems is profoundly serious. There are many concrete and promising avenues by which to start a global transition towards sustainability through transformative solutions, technology leapfrogging, circular economy frameworks and new business models. However, such 'actions' alone will not be sufficient. In the Anthropocene we need to stimulate a myriad of sustainability strategies and practices on the ground, while at the same time developing the capacity to govern the Earth system collectively. We need to adopt strategies for planetary stewardship. This combination of strengthening bottom-up solutions in line with late Nobel Prize Laureate Elinor Ostrom's polycentric institutions, where communities successfully manage for sustainability, and top-down governance in line with the research by Frank Biermann, Victor Galaz and colleagues on strengthening Earth system governance (Biermann 2012; Galaz *et al.* 2012), is both the necessary, and also the only possible, pathway forward.

Currently we can see a number of promising signs of innovation and sustainable practice at the local and regional levels, from communities to businesses and nations. But at the planetary scale, we lack a functioning regime of governance. In simple terms, there is no Earth system governance that matches the challenges faced by humanity. The patchy signs of positive action on climate change by some governments and businesses fall far short of achieving the required reduction in emissions on a global scale. On the contrary, global emissions of greenhouse gases continue unabated, with clear signs that the pace is accelerating.

The world needs to stay within a fixed carbon budget, just as it needs to respect the boundary conditions for nitrogen, phosphorus, land and freshwater use etc. This is a challenge for all the nations of the world. We need a concerted effort by key countries to push for the strengthening of Earth governance.

The UN Earth Summit (Rio+20) was by many seen as an opportunity to move policies in the right direction. The outcome of the meeting, however, was a huge disappointment. The only positive decision made was to transform the UN Millennium Development Goals (MDGs) into Sustainable Development Goals (SDGs). It may seem as a small step. But if done in a comprehensive way, it could in fact pave the way for a planetary stewardship that is more integrative. It would allow all the nations to commit to targets for planetary sustainability within which the world can develop. It would also put pressure on the world's rich nations to provide space for development among the world's poorer nations. Such a proposition may sound totally unrealistic. But sooner, rather than later, it must come to pass. The challenges are formidable. The bankruptcy of nature is not only progressing, in some areas it may be imminent.

We started this book by quoting Chief Oren Lyons. His perspective – and the perspective of his Nation – is that today's actions should be for the good of future generations. We can see no better way of ending this book than by quoting Oren again. If all major decisions in society followed such principles we would finally manifest our responsibility as global citizens.

> We are looking ahead, as is one of the first mandates given us as chiefs, to make sure and to make every decision that we make relate to the welfare and wellbeing of the seventh generation to come.

References

This book is not written as a scientific paper, but it is nevertheless based on extensive research. Our aim has been to be as up-to-date as possible – a challenging task, given the rapid flow of new research reports. We have not done justice to all this research by specific reference in the book's content. Instead, we have chosen a format that indicates the most important sources.

Alfredsson, E. 2002. 'Green Consumption Energy Use and Carbon Emissions.' PhD thesis, Umeå University.

Allen, Myles R., David J. Frame, Chris Huntingford, Chris D. Jones, Jason A, Lowe, Malte Meinshausen and Nicolai Meinshausen 2009. 'Warming Caused by Cumulative Carbon Emissions Towards the Trillionth Tonne.' *Nature*, **458**, 1163–6.

Allwood, J. M. and Cullen, J. M. 2012. *Sustainable Materials With Both Eyes Open*. UIT Cambridge.

Anderegg, W, Prall, J. W., Harold, J., and Schneider, S. 2010. 'Expert Credibility in Climate Change.' *Proceedings of the National Academy of Sciences*, **107** (27), 12107–9.

Benyus, J. 1997. *Biomimicry*. HarperCollins.

Bergh van den, Jeroen 2009. 'The GDP Paradox.' *Journal of Economic Psychology*, **30**, 117–35.

Biermann, F. 2012. 'Planetary Boundaries and Earth System Governance: Exploring the Links.' *Ecological Economics*, **81C**, 4–9.

Blue Planet Prize Winners 2012. Gro Harlem Bruntland, James Hansen, Amory Lovins, James Lovelock, Susan Solomon, Bob Watson *et al.* 'Environmental and Development Challenges: the Imperative to Act.' Press release paper. United Nations Environment Programme, 17 February.

Braungart, M. and McDonough, W. 2002. *Cradle to Cradle: Remaking the Way We Make Things*. North Point Press.

Bruntland Report 1987. *Our Common Future*. UN Documents: Gathering a body of global agreements.

CA 2007. D. Molden (ed.). *Water for Food, Water for Life: A Comprehensive Assessment of Water Management in Agriculture*. Earthscan/International Water Management Institute.

Caillon, N., Severinghaus, J.P., Jouzel, J., Barnola, J-M., Kang, J., Lipenkov, V.Y. 2003. 'Timing of Atmospheric CO_2 and Antarctic Temperature Changes Across Termination III.' *Science*, **299**, 1728–31.

Canadell, J.G., Le Quéré, C., Raupach, M.R., Field, C.B., Buitenhuis, E.T., Ciais, P. *et al.* 2007. 'Contributions to Accelerating Atmospheric CO_2 Growth from Economic Activity, Carbon Intensity, and Efficiency of Natural Sinks.' *PNAS*, **104** (47), 18866–70

Carbon Tracker Initiative 2012. 'Unburnable Carbon: Are the World's Financial Markets Carrying a Carbon Bubble?' www.carbontracker.org

Carmack, E., McLaughlin, F., Whiteman, G., and Homer-Dixon, T., 2012. 'Detecting and Coping with Disruptive Shocks in Arctic Marine Systems: a Resilience Approach to Place and People.' *Ambio* **41**, 56–65.

Carpenter, S.R., and Bennett, E.M. 2011. 'Reconsideration of the Planetary Boundary for Phosphorus.' *Environ. Res. Lett.*, 6, doi: 10.1088/1748-9326/6/1/014009

Carson, Rachel 1964. *Silent Spring*. Fawcett Crest.

Clough, S.A. and Iacono, M.J. 1995. 'Line-by-line Calculation of Atmospheric Fluxes and Cooling Rates 2. Application to Carbon Dioxide, Ozone, Methane, Nitrous Oxide and the Halocarbons.' *Journal of Geophysical Research Atmospheres*, **100**, D8.

Club of Rome 1972. *Limits to Growth.*

Conway G. 1997. *The Doubly Green Revolution: Food For All in the Twenty-first Century.* Penguin Books.

Dahl-Jensen, D., Mosegaard, K., Gundestrup, N., Clow, D.G., Johnsen, S.J., Hansen, A.W. and Balling, N. 1998. 'Past Temperatures Directly from the Greenland Ice Sheet.' *Science*, **282**, 268–71.

Daly, Herman 1999. 'Uneconomic Growth in Theory, in Fact, in History and in Relation to Globalization', Clemens Lecture Series, No. 11 . Can be easily accessed on the internet.

Daly, Herman and John R. Cobb 1989. *For the Common Good.* Beacon Press.

Davis, S.J. and Caldeira, K. 2010. 'Consumption-based Accounting of CO_2 Emissions.' *PNAS*, **107**, 12, 5687–92.

Diamond, Jared 2005. *Collapse: How Societies Choose to Fail or Survive.* Allen Lane.

Dobbs, Richard, Jeremy Oppenheim, Fraser Thompson, Marcel Brinkman and Marc Zornes 2011. *Resource Revolution: Meeting the World's Energy, Materials, Food and Water Needs.* McKinsey Global Institute Report.

Domingues, C.M., Church, J.A., White, N.J., Gleckler, P.J., Wijffels, S.E., Barker P.M. and Dunn, J.R. 2008. 'Improved Estimates of Upper-ocean Warming and Multi-decadal Sea-level Rise.' *Nature*, **453**, 1090–94, doi:10.1038/nature07080.

Dyer, G. 2008. *Climate Wars.* Random House.

Ellen McArthur Foundation 2012. *Towards the Circular Economy.* www.ellenmacarthurfoundation.org

Ethical Markets 2012. *The Green Transition Scorecard.* Ethical Markets Media.

European Climate Foundation 2011. 'Roadmap 2050: Practical Guide to a Prosperous, Low-carbon Europe.' www.roadmap2050.eu

European Commission 2011. *Roadmap for a Resource-efficient Europe.*

Falkenmark, M. and Rockström, J. 2004. *Balancing Water for Humans and Nature: a New Approach to Eco-hydrology.* Earthscan.

Fan Gang, Nicholas Stern, Ottmar Edenhofer, Xu Shanda, Klas Eklund, Frank Ackerman *et al.* 2011. *The Economics of Climate Change in China: Towards a Low-Carbon Economy.* Earthscan/Routledge.

FAO 2011. *Save and Grow – a Policymaker's Guide to the Sustainable Intensification of Smallholder Crop Production.* UN Food and Agricultural Organization, p 102.

Feulner, G. and Rahmstorf, S. 2010. 'On the Effects of a New Grand Minimum of Solar Activity on the Future Climate on Earth.' *Geophysical Research Letters*, **37**, L05707.

Foley, Jonathan, Johan Rockström, Navin Ramankutty, Kate A. Brauman, Emily S. Cassidy, James S. Gerber *et al.* 2011. 'Solutions for a Cultivated Planet.' *Nature* **478**, 337–42.

Friends of the Earth 2010. *More Jobs, Less Waste: Potential for Job Creation Through Higher Rates of Recycling in the UK and EU.* Report.

Galaz, Victor, Frank Biermann, Beatrice Crona, Derk Loorbach, Carl Folke, Per Olsson *et al.* 2012. 'Planetary Boundaries – Exploring the Challenges for Global Environmental Governance.' *Current Opinion in Environmental Sustainability*, **4** (1), 80–87.

GEA 2012. *Global Energy Assessment.* Cambridge University Press.

Global Humanitarian Forum 2009. *The Anatomy of a Silent Crisis.* Human Impact Report, Climate Change.

Grantham, Jeremy 2011. 'Time to Wake Up: Days of Abundant Resources and Falling Prices Are Over Forever.' GMO quarterly letter, April.

Grufman, Björn 2011. Bureau of International Recycling presentation in Stockholm, November.

Hansen, J., Nazarenko, L., Ruedy, R., Sato, Mki., Willis, J., Del Genio, A. *et al.* 2005. 'Earth Energy Imbalance: Confirmation and Implications.' *Science*, **308**, 1431–5.

Hansen, J., Sato, Mki., Kharecha, P., Beerling, D., Berner, R., Masson-Delmotte, V. *et al*, 2008. 'Target Atmospheric CO_2: Where Should Humanity Aim?' *Open Atmospheric Science Journal* **2**, 217–31, doi:10.2174/1874282300802010217.

Harries, J.E., Brindley, H.E., Saggo, P.J. and Bantges, R.J. 2001. 'Increases in Greenhouse Forcing Inferred from the Outgoing Longwave Radiation Spectra of the Earth in 1970 and 1997.' *Nature*, **410**, 355–7.

Hirsch, Robert L. 2005. The Inevitable Peaking of World Oil Production. The Atlantic Council of the United States, **XVI** (3).

Hirsch, R.L., Bezdek, R.H, Wendling, R.M. 2005. *Peaking of World Oil Production. Impacts, Mitigation and Risk Management.* US Department of Energy and National Energy Technology Laboratory.

Hoffman, U. 2011. 'Some Reflections on Climate Change, Green Growth Illusions and Development Space.' UNCTAD Discussion Papers 205.

Hoggan, James 2009. *Climate Cover-up: the Crusade to Deny Global Warming.* Greystone Books.

Huffington, A. 2010. *Third World America.* Crown Publishers.

IAASTD 2009. Beverly McIntyre, Hans R. Herren, Judi Wakhungu and Robert T. Watson. *Agriculture at the Cross-roads.* Synthesis Report with executive summary. International Assessment of Agricultural Knowledge, Science and Technology for Development. Island Press.

Ingelstam, Lars and Goran Bäckstrand 1975. 'How Much is Enough?' in *What Now,* the 1975 Dag Hammarskjöld Report on Development. Dag Hammarskjöld Foundation.

International Energy Agency. *Energy Technology Perspectives.* Annual publication.

IPCC 2007a. Solomon, S., Qin, D., Manning, M., Chen, Z., Marquis, M.C., Avery, K. *et al.* (eds). *Climate Change 2007: The Physical Science Basis. Contribution of Working Group I to the Fourth Assessment Report of the Intergovernmental Panel on Climate Change.* United Nations/Cambridge University Press.

IPCC 2007b. Parry, M.L., Canziani, O.F., Palutikof, J.P., van der Linden, P.J. and Hanson, C.E. (eds). *Climate Change 2007: Impacts, Adaptation and Vulnerability. Contribution of Working Group II to the Fourth Assessment Report of the Intergovernmental Panel of Climate Change.* United Nations/Cambridge University Press.

IPCC, 2011: Field, C.B., Barros, V., Stocker, T.F., Qin, D., Dokken, D.J., Ebi, K.L. *et al.* (eds). *Managing the Risks of Extreme Events and Disasters to Advance Climate Change Adaptation. A Special Report of Working Groups I and II of the Intergovernmental Panel on Climate Change.* Cambridge University Press.

Jacobson, Mark Z. and Mark Delucchi 2009. 'A Plan to Power 100 percent of the Planet with Renewables. *Scientific American Magazine*, 26 October.

Jackson, T. 2009. *Prosperity Without Growth: Economics for a Finite Planet.* Earthscan.

Jacquet, P., Pachauri, R.K. and Tubiana, L. (eds) 2012. *Towards Agricultural Change?* TERI Press.

Jensen, E.J., Ackerman, A.S. and Smith, J.A. 2007. 'Can Overshooting Convection Dehydrate the Tropical Tropopause Layer?' *Journal of Geophysical Research.*, **112**, D11209, doi:10.1029/2006JD007943.

Kahan, Dan, Hank Jenkins-Smith and Donald Braman 2010. 'Cultural Cognition of Scientific Consensus.' Law working paper 205, Yale Law School.

Kiehl, J.T., Trenberth, K.E. 1997. 'Earth's Annual Global Mean Energy Budget.' *Bulletin of the American Meteorological Society*, **78**, 197–208.

KPMG 2012. *Expect the Unexpected: Building Business Value in a Changing World.* Report. KPMG.

Laszlo, E. 2001. *Macroshift: Navigating the Transformation to a Sustainable World.* UNESCO.

Lean, J., 2010. 'Cycles and Trends in Solar Irradiance and Climate.' *WIRE's Climate Change*, Vol 1.

Lenton, T.M., Held, H., Kriegler, E., Hall, J.W., Lucht, W., Rahmstorf, S. and Schellnhuber, H.J. 2008. 'Tipping Elements in the Earth's Climate System.' *PNAS*, **105** (6), 1786–93.

Lovins, A. 2004. *Winning the Oil Endgame : Innovation for Profits, Jobs and Security.* Rocky Mountain Institute, Snowmass, Colo.

Lovins A. and Rocky Mountain Institute 2012. *Reinventing Fire; Bold Business Solutions for the New Energy Era*, Chelsea Green Publishing.

Marchetti, C. 1977. 'Primary Energy Substitution Models: on the Interaction Between Energy and Society.' *Technological Forecasting and Social Change* **10**, 345–56.

Max Neef M., Elizalde, A. and Hopenhayn, M. 1991. *Human Scale Development.* The Apex Press.

Meadows, D, Meadows, D, and Randers, J. (2004) *The Limits to Growth – a 30-year Update*, Chelsea Green Publishing/Earthscan.

Meinshausen, M., Meinshausen, N., Hare, W., Raper, S.C.B., Frieler, K., Knutti, R. *et al.* 2009. 'Greenhouse-gas Emission Targets for Limiting Global Warming to 2°C.' *Nature*, **458**, 1158–62.

Millennium Ecosystem Assessment 2005. *Ecosystems and Human Well-being: Synthesis.* Island Press.

Morales, Alex 2011. Bloomberg New Energy Finance, 11 January.

Moran, K., Backman, J., Brinkhuis, H., Clemens, S.C., Cronin, T. *et al.* 2006. The Cenozoic palaeoenvironment of the Arctic Ocean. *Nature*, **441**, 601–5.

Murphy, D.M., Solomon, S., Portmann, R.W., Rosenlof, K.H., Forster, P.M., Wong, T. 2009. 'An Observationally Based Energy Balance for the Earth Since 1950.' *Journal of Geophysical Research*, **114**, D17107, doi:10.1029/2009JD012105.

Nobel Laureate Symposium on Global Sustainability 2011. *Memorandum.* Royal Swedish Academy of Sciences. Stockholm.

Nordic Council 2011. *Global Carbon Footprints.* Nordic Council.

OECD 2011. *Toward Green Growth.* Organisation for Economic Co-operation and Development.

OECD 2012a. *Environment Outlook to 2050.* Organisation for Economic Co-operation and Development.

OECD 2012b. *Promoting Inclusive Growth.* Organisation for Economic Co-operation and Development.

O'Neill, R. V. and Khan, J. R. 2001. 'Homo Economicus as a Keystone Species.' *Bioscience* **50**.

Oreskes, Naomi and Erik M. Conway 2010. *Merchants of Doubt.* Bloomsbury Press.

Pauli, G. 2010. *The Blue Economy*, Paradigm Publishers.

Petit, J.R., Jouzel, J., Raynaud, D., Barkov, N.I., Barnola, J.-M., Basileet I. et al. 1999. 'Climate and Atmospheric History of the Past 420,000 Years from the Vostok Ice Core, Antarctica.' *Nature,* **399**, 429-36.

Pooley, Eric 2010. *The Climate War: True Believers, Power Brokers and the Fight to Save the Earth.* Hyperion.

Radermacher, F. J. 2004. *Global Marshall Plan: a Planetary Contract for a Worldwide Eco-social Market Economy.* Global Marshall Plan Foundation.

Ramanathan, V. and Coakley, J.R. 1978. 'Climate Modelling Through Radiative-convective Models.' *Reviews of Geophysics and Space Physics,* **16** (4).

Randers, J. "2052", Chelsea&Green 2012.

Rockström, J., Steffen, W., Noone, K., Persson, Å., Chapin, F.S. III, Lambin, E.F. *et al.* 2009a. 'A Safe Operating Space for Humanity.' *Nature,* **461**, 472–5.

Rockström, J., Steffen, W., Noone, K., Persson, Å., Chapin, F.S. III, Lambin, E.F. *et al.* 2009b. 'Planetary Boundaries: Exploring the Safe Operating Space for Humanity.' *Ecology and Society,* **14** (2): 32. Online: www.ecologyandsociety.org/vol14/iss2/art32

Royal Swedish Academy of Agriculture and Forestry 2006. *After the Oil Peak.*

Sanne, C. 2006. *The Rebound Effect.* Report 5623, Swedish Natural Protection Agency.

Scharmer, Otto 2009. *The Blind Spot of Economic Thought.* MIT Press.

Schellnuber, H.J. 2009. 'Tipping Elements in the Earth System.' *PNAS,* **106** (49), 20561–3.

SEI 2002. Raskin, P., Banuri T., Gallopín, G., Gutman, P., Hammond, A., Kates, R., and Swart, R. *Great Transition: The Promise and Lure of the Times Ahead.* SEI PoleStar Series Report no. 10. Stockholm Environment Institute and Tellus Institute.

SEI 2009. Charles Heaps, Peter Erickson, Sivan Kartha and Eric Kemp-Benedict, *Europe's Share of the Climate Challenge.* Research Report. Stockholm Environment Institute.

SEI 2012. Peter Erikson, Anne Owen, Elie Dawkins, *Low Green-House-Gas Consumption Strategies and Impact on Developing Countries.* Policy brief. Stockholm Environment Institute.

Shakova, N., Semiletov, I., Salyuk, A., Yusupov, V., Kosmach, D. and Gustafsson, O. 2010. 'Extensive Methane Venting to the Atmosphere from Sediments of the East Siberian Arctic Shelf.' *Science,* **327**, 1246–50.

Singer, S. F. (ed.) 1970. *Global Effects of Environmental Pollution. A Symposium Organized by the American Association for the Advancement of Science.* Kluwer Academic Publishers.

Snow, C. P. 1959. *The Two Cultures.* The Rede Lecture 1959. Cambridge University Press.

Stahel, W. 2010. *The Performance Economy.* Palgrave-MacMillan.

Stahel, W. 2012. 'Sustainable Taxation – Policy for Resource Taxation.' Address given in Stockholm in April. www.slideshare.net/GlobalUtmaning/walter-stahel-stockholm-20120416

Stern, N. 2006. *The Economics of Climate Change: The Stern Review.* Cambridge University Press.

Stiglitz, J.E., Sen. A., Fitoussi, J-P. 2010. 'Report by the Commission on the Measurement of Economic Performance and Social Progress.' www.stiglitz-sen-fitoussi.fr

Svensmark, H., Bondo, T. and Svensmark, J. 2009. 'Cosmic Ray Decreases Affect Atmospheric Aerosols and Clouds.' *Geophysical Research Letters*, **36**, L15101 ff.

Swedish Environment Protection Agency 'Climate and consumption', report 6483, March 2012.

Swedish Government Task Force on Climate Change 2008. Report (in Swedish)..

TEEB 2010. Pushpam Kumar (ed.). *The Economics of Ecosystems and Biodiversity: Economic and Ecological Foundations.* TEEB 2009 report. Earthscan.

Trenberth, Kevin, John T. Fasullo,. and Jeffrey Kiehl 2008. Earth's global energy budget. *Bulletin of American Meteorological Society*, July.

Turner, G. M. 2008. A comparison of the *Limits to Growth* with 30 years' reality. CSIRO working paper series 2008-9.

UK Industry Taskforce on Peak Oil and Energy Security 2010. *The Oil Crunch: Securing the UK's energy future.* Report.

UNDESA 2006. Woodward, David, and Simms, Andrew 2006. *Growth is Failing the Poor.* Working Paper No. 20, UN Department of Economic and Social Affairs.

UNDESA 2011. *World Population Prospects, the 2010 Revision.* UN Department of Economic and Social Affairs.

UNDP 2010. *Human Development Report 2010: The Real Wealth of Nations: Pathways to Human Development.* 20th Anniversary Edition. UN Development Programme.

UNEP 2011a. *Principles for Responsible Investments*, UN Environment Programme.

UNEP 2011b. *Towards a Green Economy.* Report, UN Environment Programme.

UNEP 2011c. *Recycling Rates of Metals.* UN Environment Programme .

United Nations World Water Development Report 2009. *Water in a Changing World.* UNESCO/Earthscan.

UN Secretary-General's High-Level Panel on Global Sustainability 2012. *Resilient People, Resilient Planet: A Future Worth Choosing.* GSP Report. United Nations

US Joint Forces Command 2010. *Joint Operating Environment 2010.*

Wang, K., and Liang, S. 2009. Global atmospheric downward longwave radiation over land surface from 1973 to 2008. *Journal of Geophysical Research*, **14**.

WBGU 2011. *Solving the Climate Dilemma: the Budget Approach.* Special Report from the German Advisory Council on Global Change (WBGU), www.wbgu.de

Weizsacker, E. U. von, Hargroves, C., Smith, M.H., Desha, C. and Stasinopoulos, P. 2010. *Factor 5: Transforming the Global Economy through 80% Improvements in Resource Productivity.* Earthscan.

World Economic Forum 2010. *More Credit with Fewer Crises.*

World Economic Forum 2011. *The Global Risks Report.World Energy Outlook.* International Energy Agency, Paris, annual publication

WRAP 2009. *Meeting the UK Climate Change Challenge: The Contribution of Resource Efficiency.* Report prepared by Stockholm Environment Institute and University of Durham Business School. WRAP.

Yamamoto-Kawai, M., McLaughlin, F.A., Carmack, E., Nishino, S. and Shimada, K. 2009. 'Aragonite Under Saturation in the Arctic Ocean: Effects of Ocean Acidification and Sea Ice Melt.' *Science* **326**, 1098–1100.

Index